Contents

BALBRIGGAN BRANCH Ph. 8411128

ACKNOWLEDGEMENTS

First I would like to express my thanks to Dr Marilyn Glenville for making me aware of the nutritional needs of menopausal women, and for giving me the courage to quit HRT and explore the alternatives. Without her inspiration this book would not have been written.

The first draft of this book owed a great deal to my friends and family, especially Jo Baker, Vivienne Benson, Anita Townsend and Henrietta Usherwood and my sister-in-law, June Marriott, all of whom gave me recipes, encouragement, support and very useful feedback. I would like to thank my colleagues at the Institute for Optimum Nutrition for their invaluable help in testing the recipes and providing sound nutritional advice for the second draft, so that I really feel this was a joint effort rather than mine alone. The people to whom I am most indebted are Lynn Alford-Burow, Suzanne Bryson, Nina Coughlan, Linda Marais-Gilchrist, Jan Morris, Sharon Pitt, Carol Shaw, Coreen Tucker, Marion Turnbull and Hilary Wallace. I wish them all well in their careers as nutritionists. Marion Turnbull and Coreen Tucker kindly parted with their recipes; Wendy Buckley helped with recipe testing; Carol Champion gave professional advice; and Margaret Ritchie of the Department of Mollecular and Cellular Pathology at the University of Dundee gave me very useful information about phytoestrogens. To all of them I owe my sincere thanks.

Anne Dolamore at Grub Street deserves my unending gratitude for giving me the opportunity to turn my concept into a reality, and for her faith, patience and expert guidance.

Lastly, but definitely not least, my thanks go to my husband, John, for giving me the idea in the first place, and then for patiently enduring many months of experiments in the kitchen and failures at the dinner table. He has encouraged me throughout, and I could not have done without his support.

Introduction

I had an early menopause at the age of 38, and was prescribed HRT without hesitation by my doctor. The reason she gave was that, as I was comparatively young, I was at risk of developing osteoporosis from which HRT would protect me. I did not question this, and took the drug for ten years with, it has to be said, no discernible side-effects. Since in other ways I led a fairly healthy lifestyle, I became increasingly concerned at being obliged to take a drug every day of my life, apparently without an end in sight, for a condition which was, after all, a perfectly normal passage in life. The menopause is not an illness, and I do not think it should be treated as such. Having said that, I would like to stress that this book is not a polemic against HRT. There are some women who benefit greatly from taking it and I would be irresponsible if I tried to dissuade anyone from taking prescribed drugs. Therefore this book is aimed equally at those women who have elected to take HRT, those who have decided against it, and those who, for whatever reason, take it for a while and then abandon it. I fell into this third group. Some years ago my husband gave me for Christmas Marilyn Glenville's book *Natural Alternatives to HRT*. Until that point, I hadn't really considered that there was such a thing as a natural alternative. The seed fell on fertile ground, and I determined to give up the pills. I went to my doctor and informed her of my intention.

"You're on a slippery slope here", she said. "Of course you must do as you see fit, but I can't say I recommend it. Your hair and skin will dry out and you'll age much more quickly. The side effects of menopause, which have been masked by your taking HRT, will reassert themselves, and you'll probably have hot flushes, mood swings etcetera. In your case they probably won't be too bad, though. And you must watch your diet – lots of dairy products, and make sure you eat plenty of sardines – the bones are especially good for you – all that calcium. Plenty of exercise, too."

My doctor plays rugby and is a cross-country runner, so when she says exercise she means something pretty vigorous. I was up for that, and went home determined to run and swim, drink a pint of skimmed milk a day and eat a lot of sardine sandwiches, even though I had eaten a more or less vegetarian diet for some years.

But as I read around the subject of nutrition for the menopause, I began to realise that increasing my calcium intake by eating protein-rich foods like dairy products and lots of fish was not the only answer, or necessarily the right answer. The more I read and learned, the more I realised that if I was to do without HRT I was really going to have to take the subject of diet quite seriously, and thus the idea for this book was born.

What I did then is really not advisable – I simply stopped 'cold turkey'. That period when I first gave up the pills was not without its traumas – the hot flushes came back with a vengeance, and I endured many sleepless nights. If you are thinking of giving up HRT, I would advise that you follow the diet in this book for a few months first, then see your doctor to discuss the pros and cons. I now believe that you need to be weaned off slowly while at the same time giving your hormones every support with good nutrition.

I have always been an enthusiastic cook, starting from my days at university in Dublin in the late Sixties when to eke out my grant I cooked in a smart restaurant, to being a chef on the charter yacht circuit in the Caribbean and the Mediterranean in the late Seventies and early Eighties. I later spent some time running a directors' dining room in the City of London. In none of those roles did I have much of a care for good nutrition. My concern was to produce beautiful and tasty food for sometimes exacting clients. When I started to take an interest in good nutrition, I enrolled for the Cordon Vert diploma at the Vegetarian Society. While this greatly improved my cooking skills, it did not cover nutrition in as much depth as I felt I needed, and so I started studying to be a nutritional therapist. Thus this book is the synthesis of the two strands of my interest and experience with food. My aim is to create delicious dishes which cater for the nutritional needs of the menopausal woman without sacrificing either taste or time. All these recipes are easy and most of them (except the sourdough breads) are quick to prepare. An added bonus is that this is a way of eating which will benefit all the family, not just the menopausal woman.

The first draft of this book was entirely vegetarian, but during my studies at the Institute for

Optimum Nutrition I gradually became convinced that we do need oily fish, as they provide a good source of lean protein and essential fatty acids. From there it was a short step to deciding to include a little organic chicken and game – both excellent sources of lean protein. Chicken is very popular in this country, but eating it is potentially hazardous because there are so many stages in the production of chicken meat where it is vulnerable to contamination unless the strictest hygiene is observed. For that reason alone it is worth paying extra for organically produced chicken. Game is less of a concern because it is generally wild.

Milk is often touted as a good source of calcium, but actually the calcium in milk is not well-absorbed. Milk does not contain enough magnesium to balance the calcium. These two minerals are mutually dependent in the body, each requiring the other for absorption, so foods which are already calcium/magnesium balanced, such as seeds, nuts, dark green leafy vegetables and wholegrains, are preferable. Furthermore, casein, the protein in milk, is hard for some people to digest, while others lack the enzyme needed to break down the milk sugar, lactose. Ironically, semi-skimmed and skimmed milk, having had some of their fat removed, are more concentrated sources of casein and lactose than full-cream milk. I do not use milk itself, or cheese, in this book, because I firmly believe it is not good for your health, but I do use a little butter, which, being almost pure fat, contains little of the casein or lactose that seem to cause health problems in so many people. I do encourage the use of live yoghurt, too, because it contains 'good' bacteria, which have actually pre-digested the lactose before you eat the yoghurt. These bacteria, *Lactobacillus bulgaricus* and others, won't take up residence in your gut – they are only temporary visitors – but in passing through they crowd out any bad bacteria lurking there, so they tend to improve the environment in your digestive tract.

Personally I have found that the way of eating which suits me relies heavily on vegetables, fruit, soya products, pulses and some oily fish. This diet is ideal for the menopausal woman because it is relatively low in saturated fat and high in fibre, and contains plenty of natural plant hormones, which help to ease the whole process of menopause. There is a lot of evidence that women who follow a diet such as this are far less likely to have menopausal symptoms than those who carry on eating a more refined diet, high in sugar and saturated fats and low in fibre.

A diet that maintains balanced blood sugar levels is vital, because high sugar levels not only trigger emotional ups and downs, they also tend to erode calcium from our bones, far-fetched though this may sound. This means cutting out most of the sugar and empty carbohydrates (white bread, biscuits, cake, sweets, chocolate etc) and replacing them with whole foods – vegetables, fruit, wholegrains, beans and seeds.

Good, low-fat and vegetarian forms of protein, together with essential fatty acids (especially fish, nut and seed oils) are also important. These last, of which there are two families – Omega 6 and Omega 3 – play a large part in maintaining the body's normal hormone production as you go through the menopause. While your ovaries may be shutting down production of oestrogen, the adrenal glands continue to produce it. Oestrogen is made of essential fats, which are found in oily fish, nuts and seeds and are absolutely vital for your good health.

Organic food
I have not always specified organic ingredients in these recipes, but whenever you can afford them, I do advise you to use them. I have become thoroughly convinced that, for the sake of our health and for that of our environment, we should buy organic. For most of us the problem is that organic products still carry a premium price, but the more we demand them the more the price will come down. The price of eating non-organic produce may not be obvious in the short term, but it is much higher in terms of our health and general wellbeing. Non-organic food routinely contains pesticide and other chemical residues, which cannot be washed off as they are not water-soluble. Because they are fat-soluble, they collect in the fat cells of animals that eat the produce, including humans. They can disrupt our hormones, especially the oestrogens, which are also fat-soluble. However, if you cannot afford to go completely organic, choose organic fruit and vegetables as a first step. Think about the surface area of the fruit or vegetable, how much of it is exposed to the fungicides and pesticides that are sprayed repeatedly throughout the growing cycle (around 25,000 tonnes of

pesticides were applied to UK crops in 2000, the most recent year for which we have figures).[1] On that basis, for example, I would always choose organic lettuces, as they have a large surface area, and are one of the most heavily sprayed crops. Choose organic carrots, too. Not only do they have a much better flavour, but non-organic carrots have been found to contain a high level of pesticide residues, including Iprodione, a suspected hormone disrupter and carcinogen. A bonus with organic fruit and vegetables is that you do not have to peel them. Since most of the nutrients are in the skin or just below it, eating the skin will give you added nutritional value. If you cannot afford or cannot find organic produce, the next best thing is to wash non-organic produce in a weak solution of organic cider vinegar and water (about one cupful of vinegar to a sink full of water). This helps to remove some of the residues.

Nutritional supplements

While I have come to believe that in many cases supplements are a necessary adjunct to a healthy diet, diet must always come first. If you are considering taking supplements, I strongly urge you to consult a nutritional therapist (see Useful Addresses). It is easy to assume, for example, that if calcium is needed to prevent osteoporosis, a calcium supplement is sufficient, and that more is better. In fact, there are many forms of calcium, and some, such as calcium citrate, are better absorbed than others – calcium carbonate, or chalk, to give it its common name, is not a viable supplement, being only about 4% absorbable. Taking higher amounts of calcium isn't the answer, as it works in synergy with other minerals and vitamins, particularly magnesium, so that taking too much of one thing can disrupt the whole delicate balance. Excessive calcium supplementation, without the other bone-building nutrients, may actually contribute to the very problem you are trying to help. Furthermore, each person is biochemically different from everyone else, and we all require different levels of nutrients.

Herbs

Plant oestrogens, which are capable of causing a biological response in the body by binding to oestrogen receptors, are found in several herbs, such as dong quai, red clover, black cohosh and vitex agnus castus. These herbs can help diminish menopausal symptoms by their weak oestrogenic activity. Used together, they are even more powerful, but should be treated with respect. It is worth reflecting that herbs are medicines just as much as pharmaceutical drugs are. In fact in many cases drugs were developed from herbs traditionally used as medicines. If you wish to explore the use of herbs at menopause, consult a good herbalist who can help you decide which herbs are best for you (see Useful Addresses).

This is a cookery book rather than a self-help manual for the menopause, so here is not the place to discuss dietary supplements or herbs in detail. I believe that the recipes and menus in this book will go a long way towards providing adequate nutrients to prepare you for the menopause, to cope with it when it finally arrives and to set you on the path of eating healthily for the rest of your life. Don't forget the man in your life too – although men do not experience anything as sudden as the menopause, their levels of testosterone do drop off gradually with age, so they need the same hormone balancing diet as we do. They are also at risk in later life of the same degenerative diseases as women – heart disease, arthritis, even osteoporosis, so what's good for us is equally good for them.

Health risks associated with the menopause

As we enter the perimenopause, that transition phase between having regular periods and not having any periods at all, we begin to think about the particular health risks that women over the age of 50 are prone to. I have included a brief discussion of these health risks later on, and have borne them in mind when designing the recipes. If you wish to protect yourself from these diseases, I suggest you make the dietary changes advised in this book, and see a nutritional therapist who can recommend the correct supplements to support the diet and help you minimise the risks.

---

[1] 'The Truth About Food', Soil Association 2002.

Osteoporosis

Osteoporosis is the disease that has probably received the most attention in relation to the menopause. Osteoporosis is a reduction in bone tissue resulting in brittle and fragile bones prone to fracture, usually occurring in postmenopausal women.

Bones continue to become thicker and stronger in early adulthood, with peak bone mass occurring in the thirties. Thereafter it declines slowly until menopause, when it starts to accelerate rapidly. In the first 3-5 years after menopause, women lose 3-5% of their bone mass per year. After about 10 years, bone loss tapers off only to increase again after the age of 80. It appears that this has not always been the case. An article in *The Lancet* a few years ago[2] compared eighteenth century female skeletons dug up during the restoration of a London church with those of modern women, and found the rate of bone loss to have been much slower two hundred years ago. It also appears that osteoporosis is more prevalent in developed countries than in developing countries, so there must be environmental factors involved to account for the differences. We can only speculate at this stage what these factors might be. One observation is that the countries with the most osteoporosis are those where milk consumption is highest, but it is too early to tell whether there is a direct link. What we do know is that bone is a living thing, constantly undergoing breakdown and remodelling, and that a great many nutrients are needed to help with proper bone mineralisation. Along with calcium, the diet needs to provide adequate magnesium, silicon, manganese and vitamin C; vitamin K and boron to help the calcium get into the bones; vitamin D to help calcium be absorbed from the diet; and zinc and copper to help with bone repair.

There are various known risk factors for osteoporosis, such as family history of osteoporosis, smoking, premature menopause, childlessness, lack of exercise, eating disorders such as anorexia, or low body weight. If you fall into any of these categories, you may qualify for a bone-density scan on the National Health, so it is worth checking with your GP whether you qualify. Ideally you would have the test when you are still in your thirties or early forties, so that if there is a potential problem you can help to prevent it with diet and supplements. There is also a urine test which measures the daily turnover of bone. Together with the bone-density scan this would give you a true picture of the state of your bones.

Osteoarthritis

Like osteoporosis, osteoarthritis afflicts a high percentage of older people in developed countries, but it is rare in African and Asian countries[3]. If it is just 'wear and tear', why is it not more prevalent in countries where people lead a more active life than they do in the West? Although it primarily afflicts those joints that bear the most load, such as the hips and knees, why does it most often appear in the hands of elderly women who have not undertaken hard labour? There must be other explanations apart from wear and tear, and, as for osteoporosis, they must lie in our environment. One of the elements of our environment over which we have most control is our food.

There are several things you can do to relieve arthritis. The most obvious is to lose weight if you are overweight, as extra weight puts more strain on your joints. The next is to make sure your blood sugar is balanced, by avoiding sugar and stimulants such as tea, coffee and alcohol, and having a balance of protein and complex carbohydrates at every meal. A diet high in fruit and vegetables is also advisable. Not only do they provide lots of antioxidants, but also they are alkaline-forming. That is, when they are broken down in the digestive system they neutralise harmful acids. For example, an apple may appear acid when you eat it, but when it is metabolised in the body the alkaline minerals it contains, such as potassium, are released. Ideally the diet should be 80% alkaline-forming.

Food intolerances may also play a part in arthritis. In particular, gluten grains and dairy products have been implicated. The diet in this book would be beneficial for arthritics, as in general it favours vegetables and fruit, and there are plenty of gluten-free and dairy-free recipes. However, there is

[2] Lees B et al. Differences in proximal femur bone density over two centuries. *The Lancet* 341:673-675. 1993.
[3] Brighton SW, de la Harpe AL, Van Staden DA, The prevalence of osteoarthrosis in a rural African community, *Br J Rheumatol* 24:321, 1985.

some evidence that citrus fruits (oranges, grapefruit and lemons) and, interestingly, the nightshade family (potatoes, tomatoes, aubergines and peppers) are arthritis triggers for some people. If you have arthritis, do consider consulting a nutritional therapist who can design an elimination diet to help you identify which, if any, of these foods could be exacerbating your symptoms.

Heart disease

There are two possible theories as to why women's risk of heart disease, lower than men's in early adulthood, rises to the same level as men's after the menopause. One theory relates to homocysteine, which is a toxic amino acid produced in the body during normal metabolism of proteins. High levels of homocysteine have been found to be a good predictor of heart disease, and are found equally in men, menopausal women and postmenopausal women. Why this happens to some people and not to others is still not known, but a diet rich in the nutrients that normally clear homocysteine quickly from the body will certainly help. These nutrients are folic acid, vitamin B6 and vitamin B12, found in wholegrains, nuts, green leafy vegetables, mushrooms and seaweed among others.

The other theory is very controversial and relates to iron. Whilst lack of iron is the most common single-nutrient deficiency disease in the world, it is also known that iron accumulates in the body in the form of serum ferritin, a form of iron that is very hard to excrete and may be associated with a higher risk of cardiovascular disease.[4] Most studies have been conducted on men, who tend to have higher iron stores than women. During the reproductive years, women lose iron every month during menstruation, so that iron levels are kept balanced. But once menstruation has stopped, the theory is that serum ferritin becomes a problem for women too. This effect has been seen both in women who have experienced normal menopause and women who have had hysterectomies (which, if it includes removal of the ovaries, will put a woman into menopause overnight). By the age of 70, women have as high serum ferritin levels as men.[5] While this is still only a theory, it is a possible explanation for the increase in heart attack risk in women after menopause. Naturally occurring iron in a wholefood diet, such as that found in molasses and pulses, is poorly absorbed, so it could not contribute to iron overload, and indeed should be encouraged. However, it may be wise to limit processed foods fortified with iron and nutritional supplements containing iron.

The diet outlined in this book is naturally heart-healthy, being based on fruit, vegetables, nuts, seeds, oily fish and soya products and liberally laced with garlic, known to be an antioxidant and blood thinner. A note of caution, though: if you are on heart disease medication, and particularly if you are on Warfarin, daily aspirin or other blood thinners, please consult your GP before making huge changes to your diet, and certainly do so if you are thinking of taking any supplements such as garlic capsules, large doses of vitamin E or fish oil supplements, as these can increase the blood-thinning action of the drugs to unacceptable levels.

Hypothyroidism

The thyroid gland plays a vital role in regulating our metabolism, temperature control and our whole hormone system. Subclinical hypothyroidism, that is, an underactive thyroid not severe enough to be identified by a blood test, seems to affect women particularly as they approach their fifties. There is a huge variety of vague signs and symptoms, such as fatigue, weight gain, and a low body temperature, but these symptoms can vary from person to person, which is what makes it so difficult to identify. Diet has a part to play in supporting the thyroid gland. Your diet may be deficient in iodine (needed to make thyroid hormones), in which case consuming more fish and sea vegetables will help. On the other hand, there is a group of foods known as the goitregens that have a thyroid depressing effect. Unfortunately these are foods that are otherwise very good for you and indeed emphasised in this book, such as soy products and the cruciferous vegetables (cabbage and broccoli), so you should not limit these foods without being sure that you need to.

---

[4] Ramakrishnan U, Kuklina E, Stein A, Iron stores and cardiovascular disease risk factors in women of reproductive age in the United States. *American Journal Clinical Nutrition* December 2002 76, 1256-1260.
[5] Chazin S. Is Iron a Danger in your Diet? *Readers Digest* Dec 1995.

Rather than self-diagnose subclinical hypothyroidism, if you suspect that you may have an underactive thyroid, ask your GP for a blood test. This test measures the amount of the thyroid hormones T_4 and T_3 to assess how well your thyroid gland is working. However, be aware that the blood test does not necessarily register if your thyroid gland is underperforming just a little bit, or if the reference range of what is normal is too low for you as an individual. If you still feel that this may be playing a part in your symptoms, please consult a nutritional therapist (see Useful Addresses) or a naturopathic consultant.

For further information about subclinical hypothyroidism, do read Martin Budd's excellent book on the subject, *Why Am I So Tired?* (see Further Reading for details).

Breast cancer

The risk of breast cancer appears to rise with age. Like the other diseases discussed in this section, cancer appears to be multifactorial. My husband, who studies risk analysis, has impressed upon me the fact that disasters are always a matter of several factors conspiring together to produce a certain set of circumstances, and cancer appears to be no different. Some of the factors influencing whether or not a woman gets breast cancer are her genes (in about 10% of cases it appears to be hereditary), oestrogen dominance, particularly of the oestrogen-mimicking chemicals so prevalent in our environment today, eating too many of the wrong kinds of fat (saturated and hydrogenated fats) and not enough of the right kinds (essential fatty acids), obesity, alcohol consumption or emotional stress (it is well known that there is a link between bereavement and cancer, for example).

The most immediate tool you have at your disposal for the prevention of breast cancer is your diet, over which you have total control. The recipes in this book follow the general principles of a healthy diet, limiting saturated fats and avoiding processed foods and sugar, while encouraging the intake of antioxidants and fibre from fruit and vegetables; phytoestrogens from soya products, pulses and flax seed; and essential fats from oily fish, nuts and seeds. The lifestyle changes suggested below should also help to reduce your risk of breast cancer. For further information, I can do no better than guide you towards two excellent books devoted to the subject – Professor Jane Plant's *Your Life in Your Hands* and Suzannah Olivier's *The Breast Cancer Prevention and Recovery Diet*.

Lifestyle changes

Not only should we consider changing our diet at the menopause, we also need to take a long, hard look at other areas of our lives. Our hormones are all over the place at this time, and so we need to take steps to balance them as much as we can. Here are a few areas where we should make changes that could make a difference to our health:

Exercise more

Evidence is coming out all the time that exercise is helpful to the menopausal woman, and can help with the symptoms of hormone imbalance. And it doesn't have to be sweating it out at an aerobics class or in the gym. Just one 30-minute walk a day would suffice. Weight-bearing exercise (walking, for example) is absolutely vital for bone strength and the prevention of osteoporosis[6]. Tai Chi, a Chinese meditative form of exercise, has also recently been found to help retard bone loss and thus help prevent osteoporosis[7].

Reduce xenoestrogens

'Xeno' is the Greek word for foreign. Foreign oestrogens are the ones we don't want. These are chemicals that mimic the shape of the oestrogen molecule, so that our bodies can't tell the difference between the foreign intruders and the real thing. The xenoestrogens bind to oestrogen-

---

[6] Bonaiuti D et al. Exercise for preventing and treating osteoporosis in postmenopausal women. *Cochrane Database Syst Rev* 2002;(3):CD000333.
[7] Qin L et al. Regular Tai Chi Chuan exercise may retard bone loss in postmenopausal women: A case-control study. *Arch Phys Med Rehabil* 2002 Oct;83(10):1355-9.

binding sites in the body and can aggravate menopausal symptoms. What are xenoestrogens? Well, many of the chemicals in our environment, including pesticides and substances found in plastics, hair dyes, cosmetics, spermicides and the chemicals used in household cleaning materials are xenoestrogens. Although they are everywhere, we can reduce the load in our own homes by taking the following steps:

● Don't microwave food in plastic boxes, as xenoestrogens can leak from the plastic into the food as it cooks. When heating up a meal, transfer the food to a glass dish.
● Steer clear of products in plastic bottles, clingfilm and tins that are lined with a plastic coating. Avoid products with words like methyl-, ethyl-, propyl- and butylparaben which are xenoestrogens.
● Purchase cosmetics from a reputable company that does not use xenoestrogens such as dibutyl phthalate (DBP), used as a consistency enhancer to keep products blended and as an ingredient to help cosmetics penetrate the skin, or mineral oil, which includes the contaminant polycyclic aromatic hydrocarbons (PHAs). Good brands are Green People and Weleda.
● Purchase household products free from phenols from responsible companies that can demonstrate care for the environment (and for the health of consumers) such as Ecover, or make your own (for information see *Your Healthy House* – a What Doctors Don't Tell You publication.)

Plant oestrogens, also called phytoestrogens, may be able to protect us from the toxic xenoestrogens in our environment. They bind to the oestrogen receptors in the body in much the same way as the xenoestrogens do, but they differ markedly from xenoestrogens in that they are easily broken down, are not stored in tissue, and spend very little time in the body. So if you eat these compounds regularly, the xenoestrogens have nowhere to go and will be excreted harmlessly. Phytoestrogens are found in soya, flax seed, lentils and beans. Included at Appendix 2 is a list of the approximate concentration of phytoestrogens in the foods that we know about currently. Research in this area is still continuing.

Reduce aluminium exposure
Aluminium has been implicated in osteoporosis and in Alzheimer's Disease. We have no known nutritional requirement for aluminium, yet it is gradually building up in our bodies because it is everywhere in the environment. It is now known that aluminium can accumulate in the brain and in the bones, where it appears to accelerate bone loss. It would therefore be wise to limit your exposure to aluminium. Avoid drinks in aluminium cans, do not use aluminium pots and pans for cooking, and replace aluminium foil with greaseproof paper or baking parchment. Aluminium is used in many processed foods, such as sausages, processed cheese, white flour and table salt. Check labels for the following additives: E520, E521, E522, E523, E541, E554, E555, E556 and E559. All these contain aluminium. Finally, avoid stomach antacids containing aluminium hydroxide – use one based on calcium or magnesium instead.

Reduce stress
We need a healthy balance between stress hormones and sex hormones when we are approaching menopause. Unmanaged stress can lead to overworked adrenal glands which can heighten fatigue and mood swings. If you have a stressful life and have difficulty sleeping, take up stress-reducing techniques such as yoga, meditation or Tai Chi.

Nutrition and Ingredients
Many of the ingredients used in this book are familiar, everyday items. Some may be unfamiliar, and some, which you may have been used to buying only occasionally, are set to become staples in your larder. Below is a table showing the nutrients we are aiming to increase, why we need them, and which foods we can get them from.

Nutrient	Purpose	Available from
Phytoestrogens	Help to diminish hot flushes and other menopausal symptoms.	Soya beans and soya products are the best sources, followed by other pulses, sprouted beans, whole grains, fruit, all seeds, particularly flax seed (linseed), carrots, French beans, garlic, lentils, citrus fruit, plums, rhubarb, potato, broccoli, peanuts, mushrooms. Levels are hard to measure and vary according to when and where the food was grown (see Appendix 2). The best strategy is to eat a wide variety of these foods, with particular emphasis on soy products and flax seed.
Calcium	Needed for strong bones (see also magnesium, vitamin D and boron) to help prevent the onset of osteoporosis.	Plain low fat yoghurt, oats, tofu (made with calcium sulphate), tahini, sesame seeds, blackstrap molasses, green leafy vegetables (spinach, kale, parsley, watercress, broccoli), rhubarb, fortified soya milk and soya flour, swede, almonds, brazil nuts, figs.
Magnesium	Helps your body to absorb calcium. The calcium:magnesium ratio is very important. Too much calcium (particularly if taken in supplement form) adversely affects the ratio. Magnesium and zinc can be low in people with osteoporosis even if they have adequate calcium.	Green leafy vegetables, soya products, cashew nuts, brazil nuts, almonds, peanuts, broccoli, wholegrains, wheatgerm, wholemeal flour, bananas, prunes, oats, rye.
Potassium	Rather like the calcium:magnesium ratio described above, the potassium: sodium ratio is very important, as both these elements are used in the communication mechanisms between cells. Because the potassium in fruits and plants was freely available to our primeval ancestors, and sodium harder to get hold of, bodies are designed to hold on to sodium and excrete potassium. So we need to eat more potassium to redress the balance.	All fruits and vegetables, but especially sea vegetables (hijiki, dulse, wakame and kombu), dried apricots, figs, raisins and dates, soya beans, chickpeas, nuts, potatoes, green vegetables, avocadoes, blackcurrants and bananas.
Vitamin A and beta-carotene	Vitamin A is a fat-soluble vitamin needed to nourish your skin and the membranes covering all your internal organs. Also needed for thyroid health. Beta-carotene and the other carotenes are precursors of vitamin A, that is, the body can make vitamin A from them.	Vitamin A from fish and butter. Carotenes from sea vegetables (especially nori), carrots, green leafy vegetables such as kale, spinach and broccoli, sweet potatoes and dried apricots.
Vitamin D	Helps increase the amount of calcium retained by the kidneys, and increases the absorption of calcium from food in the intestinal tract.	Oily fish such as kippers, herring and mackerel, salmon and tuna; eggs; some foods fortified with D_2, such as vegan margarine and some soya milks; sunshine (Note: the ability to absorb vitamin D from sunshine decreases with age).

Nutrient	Purpose	Available from
B vitamins	All the B vitamins work together to help release energy from food. They also protect against heart disease and possibly also from cancer.	Wholegrains, walnuts, hazelnuts, bananas, avocado, green leafy vegetables, brewers yeast, marmite, peanuts, mushrooms, currants, soya flour, seaweed. Beneficial bacteria in the gut also make B vitamins, so eating live yoghurt is a good idea.
Vitamin B1 (Thiamine)	First discovered by a scientist who noted that chickens fed white rice developed deficiency symptoms and when they were fed the rice husks they were cured. Essential for energy production, carbohydrate metabolism and nerve cell function.	Brown rice, sunflower seeds, millet, wheatgerm, sesame seeds, soya beans, nuts – especially brazil nuts. Needs magnesium to activate it. Destroyed by coffee and tea.
Vitamin B2 (Riboflavin)	Needed for the production of energy, can help prevent migraines.	Brewers yeast, almonds, mushrooms, wheatgerm, pulses such as soya beans and lentils.
Vitamin B3 (Niacin)	Part of Glucose Tolerance Factor (GTF) which helps control blood sugar levels. Essential for energy production, antioxidant mechanisms and detoxification. Helps reduce cholesterol. Niacin is a vasodilator (widens blood vessels) so helps prevent headaches.	Brewers yeast, peanuts and peanut butter, fish such as salmon and tuna, sesame seeds, brown rice, wholewheat.
Vitamin B5 (Pantothenic acid)	Helps convert fats and carbohydrates into energy. Known as the 'antistress' vitamin because it is needed for the manufacture of adrenal hormones.	Egg yolks, broad beans, peanuts and peanut butter, pulses such as split peas and soya beans, eggs, buckwheat and mushrooms.
Vitamin B6 (Pyridoxine)	Important for many enzyme systems, the immune system, membranes and skin. Also plays a critical role in brain chemistry. Used as a supplement to treat PMS and depression. Low levels of B6 may be connected to osteoporosis risk.	Sunflower seeds, wheatgerm, soybeans, walnuts, lentils, buckwheat flour, brown rice, bananas.
Vitamin B12	Plays a critical role in energy metabolism, immune function and nerve function.	Rabbit, eggs, oily fish such as sardines, trout, salmon and anchovies. There is also B12 in tempeh and sea vegetables but some evidence indicates that it is not exactly the form that meets the body's requirements, so that form may be useless, and strict vegetarians and vegans are advised to supplement vitamin B12.
Folic Acid (Folate)	Together with vitamins B6 and B12, can detoxify homocysteine, increased levels of which have been demonstrated in postmenopausal women and may play a role in osteoporosis as well as heart disease.	Dried yeast, pulses such as blackeye beans and kidney beans, endive, chickpeas, soya beans, dark green leafy vegetables especially broccoli and spinach.

Nutrient	Purpose	Available from
Vitamin C	Helps regulate metabolism. Needed for the formation of collagen which makes up most of the bone matrix. Vital for immune function, an important antioxidant. A high dietary intake has been shown to significantly reduce risk of heart attack, strokes and cancer in numerous population studies.	Citrus fruits, green and leafy vegetables, cauliflower, berries, potatoes, sweet potatoes, cabbage, broccoli, peppers, parsley, oranges, blackcurrants, strawberries, kiwi fruit, apple juice, lychees. (Note: Vitamin C cannot be made in the body so must be obtained from the diet on a daily basis.)
Vitamin E	Possible relief from breast tenderness; can help relieve hot flushes and vaginal dryness.	Cold pressed vegetable oils, wheatgerm, tahini, nuts (especially hazelnuts, almonds, pine nuts, peanuts, brazil nuts), seeds, avocadoes, sweet potatoes.
Vitamin K	Needed to activate the proteins that build bone.	Dark green leafy vegetables, especially kale, spinach and broccoli, lettuce, cabbage, watercress and asparagus.
Zinc	Involved in many enzyme systems. Helps in the formation of strong bones by encouraging the absorption of calcium. Also helps control night sweats. Important for immune function, skin health and appetite control.	Seafood (especially oysters), pumpkin seeds, eggs, brazil nuts, peanuts, almonds, wholemeal flour.
Selenium	Maximises effectiveness of Vitamin E which helps reduce hot flushes.	Sea vegetables, brazil nuts, wholemeal flour, lentils, cabbage, molasses, eggs.
Boron	Decreases the amount of calcium being excreted; plays a part in the enzyme system that moves calcium into the bone matrix. May increase the body's ability to use available oestrogens.	Plums, prunes, strawberries, peaches, cabbage, apples, asparagus, celery, figs, kelp, leafy greens, alfalfa sprouts, nuts.
Fibre	Helps to balance blood sugar, helps digestion and removes toxins from the body.	Beans, pulses, wholegrains, nuts, oats, wheatgerm, unpeeled fruit and vegetables.
Bioflavonoids	Help to improve immunity; increase tone, elasticity and lubrication of tissues; reduce hot flushes; relieve muscle cramps.	Rutin in buckwheat, hesperidin in citrus fruits (especially in the pith). Also in rosehips, berries, broccoli, cherries, grapes, papaya, cantaloupe, plums, tomatoes and cucumbers.
Chromium	An essential part of Glucose Tolerance Factor (GTF) which helps control blood sugar, and therefore weight gain. Helps reduce cholesterol. May also help with night sweats, together with vitamin B3 and zinc.	Wholewheat, whole rye, potatoes, wheatgerm, green peppers, apples, parsnips, cornmeal, bananas, spinach, carrots. Eating refined white flour products, refined sugar and lack of exercise may deplete chromium levels.
Essential Fatty Acids (Omega-3 and Omega-6 families)	Help to maintain heart health, prevent arthritis, protect against cancer, control weight and control menopausal symptoms. Act as building blocks for making sex hormones.	Choose rich sources of Omega-3 over Omega-6 as Omega-6 is easy to obtain. Go for walnuts, flax seeds, flax oil and oily fish (salmon, trout, mackerel, herrings, sardines, tuna).

Foods to avoid or to eat in moderation

As well as increasing your intake of all the nutrients in the table above, there are some foods to avoid as they deplete the body's intake of minerals and especially calcium. These foods are:

- Red meat
- Dairy products (except for live yoghurt)
- Alcohol
- Caffeine
- Sugar
- Excessive salt
- Excessive phosphorus from processed foods and fizzy drinks.

Animal protein: Most research shows that meat eaters tend to have a lower bone density that non meat eaters, which makes sense because protein acts as an acid in the body, and the body's reserves of calcium (an alkaline mineral) are leached from the bones in order to correct the acid/alkali balance, whereupon the calcium is excreted through the urine. One particular study showed that eating more than 100g animal protein a day increased the risk of bone fractures[8], whereas a more recent study[9] – a very good one because it measured three different markers of bone density – showed exactly the opposite – that animal protein had a protective effect, particularly in the skeletal health of elderly women. Such diversity in research findings is very confusing for all of us. However, there are other risks associated with the consumption of red meat, such as an increased risk of bowel cancer. Also, along with the protein, meat is high in saturated fat and contains large amounts of phosphorus and sulphur, which are known to deplete the body's calcium resources. Toxic xenoestrogens (chemicals that mimic oestrogen) concentrate in meat fat, and synthetic oestrogens are given to cattle as growth promoters, so on balance it seems wise to reduce meat consumption, and if you do eat it, choose organic meat.

Dairy products are an animal protein food, too, and as mentioned above, protein may leach calcium from the bone. Not only that, but the calcium present in milk is not easily absorbed, nor does it contain sufficient magnesium to balance the calcium. On top of this, unless you use only organic dairy products, there are antibiotic and hormone residues in milk and milk products that may disrupt your own hormone balance. A case can be made for eating live yoghurt because of the beneficial bacteria it contains, but do make sure you choose organic.

Alcohol can inhibit calcium absorption, reduce the amount of vitamin D formed by the body, and increase the loss of calcium via the kidneys. It depletes the body of B vitamins (needed for energy) and is also thought to lower oestrogen levels.

Caffeine has been linked to calcium excretion in the urine as it has a diuretic effect. It is said that the body loses 11 grams of calcium with every cup of coffee drunk. Don't forget that tea, chocolate, Lucozade and colas contain caffeine too. Decaffeinated coffee is not a good choice, as it contains other stimulants – theobromine and theophylline. Healthy alternatives are dandelion root coffee (which is very good for your liver), rooibosch tea and other herbal teas.

Sugar may impede the uptake of essential nutrients and encourage water retention, as well as being full of 'empty' calories, i.e. calories without nutrients. Sugary snacks make your blood glucose rise sharply, giving you 'instant' energy, but all too often this is followed by a sharp dip in blood glucose, leaving you feeling tired and drained. Fresh fruit is a much better choice for sustained energy than anything containing sugar.

It is also wise to avoid all these stimulants (alcohol, caffeine and sugar) as the blood sugar swings they cause also increase the likelihood of hot flushes. This is particularly true of alcohol – many women can predict that a glass of wine is almost invariably followed by a hot flush.

Salt causes fluid retention and induces calcium loss via the urine. Too much salt is linked to high blood pressure. It is thought that if we reduce the amount of salt we eat while at the same time

8 Feskanich D et al, Protein Consumption and Bone Fractures in Women, *American Journal of Epidemiology* 1996, Mar 1;143(5):472-9.
9 Promislow J et al. Protein Consumption and Bone Mineral Density in the Elderly, *American Journal of Epidemiology* 155, 7: 636-644.

reducing the amount of protein, particularly animal protein, our calcium needs will in fact decrease. We should also consider our sodium/potassium balance. These two elements work together in our bodies, but we need far more potassium than we do sodium. Many thousands of years ago, when our ancestors were hunter-gatherers, potassium (widely available in plants) was easy to come by, but sodium was quite rare. So the human body evolved to hold on to sodium whenever it was available, and to excrete potassium. The modern diet is poor in potassium but rich in sodium, but our bodies haven't had the chance to catch up with this change in diet, so we have to help them along by consuming as many plant foods and as little sodium as possible. In this book I usually specify low sodium salt, which is a mixture of potassium chloride and sodium chloride. You can also try sea salt, which is very concentrated so you only need a pinch, or 'sel gris' (grey salt) which is from France and contains a lot of magnesium. Another option is seaweed flakes which, as well as being rich in minerals, are naturally salty (see Useful Addresses).

Phosphorus competes with calcium and magnesium for absorption in the intestines, and if we take in too much phosphorus, it increases resorption of calcium from the bones by raising parathyroid hormone levels. Avoid fizzy drinks and beer which contain a lot of phosphorus, and avoid also processed foods in which phosphates are used as stabilisers and thickeners. We do need some phosphorus though. Together with calcium, it forms calcium phosphate, a major component of bone. We should ideally be taking in similar levels of calcium and phosphorus, whereas the modern diet commonly provides two to four times as much phosphorus as calcium. Some researchers think the calcium:phosphorus ratio is more important for the prevention of osteoporosis than calcium alone. The other side of this coin is that, just as too much phosphorus can lead to osteoporosis, so can too little. It would be hard to take in too little, but the use of antacids containing aluminium hydroxide can prevent phosphorus from being absorbed from the intestines and lead to a deficiency.

The list above is short because I do not want to dwell on the negatives. My hope is that you will find this new way of eating so easy and pleasant that your body will gratefully adjust to it and you will reap the benefits.

Foods to Emphasise
This is a list of the ingredients which should be included in the shopping basket of every menopausal woman, and the reasons why they should.

Soya products
These include:

- Soya beans
- Tofu, both firm and silken
- Shoyu and tamari (naturally fermented soy sauces)
- Tempeh
- Miso
- Soya flour
- Soya milk, soya yoghurts and soya creams.

Soya has had a bad press recently, because of the use of genetic modification in its cultivation, particularly in the United States, where most of the world's soya crop is produced. If you are concerned about GM foods, it is highly advisable to check with the manufacturer as to whether the product you are buying is made from genetically modified soya beans. Many wholefood retailers have done the research for you, and will display a statement reassuring customers that they do not stock GM foods. Organic soya products, now quite widely available, are guaranteed to be made with non-genetically engineered soya beans.

Soya beans are sold as dried beans in this country. They need to be washed well and soaked overnight before cooking. They need longer cooking than most other beans – often up to three hours, although this time can be shortened if you have a pressure cooker. They can also be roasted: after soaking, drain well and place on an oiled baking sheet. Roast for about 20 minutes at

180°C/350°F/Gas Mark 4 or until golden. Sprinkle with sea salt or tamari (q.v.) and serve as a snack with drinks. Delicious!

Tofu is a nutritionally brilliant food. In a 140g serving you get about 15 grams of protein and only 140 calories. If it's made with calcium sulphate (a natural coagulant) it will give you 0.29 grams of calcium in a serving – that is over a quarter of the recommended daily calcium intake of menopausal women. As well as protein, it gives you iron, zinc and B vitamins.

Firm tofu, which is usually marinated to impart some flavour to an otherwise bland ingredient, can be used in casseroles and bakes; it can be grilled, fried or poached, puréed and used in cheesecakes, quiches and pâtés. Firm tofu is also available in ready-marinated and smoked forms. Silken tofu is very versatile and can be used in sauces and any dish requiring a creamy texture.

Okara is the residue left after you have made tofu, if you make your own. It is a fibrous, quite sweet tasting material, which adds bulk and nutrients to loaves, mueslis, baking etc. Just recently the Japanese have developed a tea made from okara.

Soya Milk is easy to get used to. I quickly learned actually to prefer it to cow's milk on cereal and porridge, and it can safely substitute for milk in sauces. The only thing it's not good for is putting into coffee, as it curdles if the coffee is too hot, but we shouldn't be drinking coffee anyway. Soya milk comes in unsweetened or sweetened form, the latter usually sweetened with fruit sugar and enriched with calcium. A word of warning, however: soya milk can increase mucus production in some people, much like dairy milk. Also, it is as well to be aware that soya milk is not a traditional food like tofu or tempeh. The cheaper, non-organic brands may be made by an industrial process from soya protein isolate, a white powder extracted from genetically modified soya beans. This kind of soya milk is made in aluminium tanks washed with acid – hardly a natural product. Do look for organic soya milk made from whole beans.

Soya flour, which is simply ground up dried soy beans, is a bit of a miracle ingredient.

It can take the place of about 20% of the flour in any baking recipe – it adds a smoothness and a glossy appearance to breads and cakes as well as adding extra nutrition. A tablespoon of soya flour mixed with water can replace a beaten egg in many recipes, too.

Soy sauces. There are two kinds of soy sauce: Shoyu is made from wheat and soy and is a lighter sauce. I tend to use it where the sauce is to be cooked. If the soy flavour is used as a condiment, without cooking, then I use tamari.

Tamari is a naturally fermented soy sauce made without wheat, aged in wooden vats for at least two years to develop a full bodied flavour. It has a more pronounced flavour than shoyu. There are plenty of inferior soy sauces on the market which are made with the addition of caramel, flavourings, salt and preservatives, so it is as well to avoid these.

Tempeh, which comes as a firm block, is made from fermented whole soybeans. It is the only soy food not to have originated in China or Japan, but comes from Indonesia. It is a wholefood, unlike tofu which has been processed, and contains therefore all of soy's nutrients and fibre. It has the advantage of freezing well, so if you do come across it in a health food shop, buy some to put in the freezer. Unfortunately it doesn't look very appealing, with grey or dark spores on it which look like dirty cotton wool. It is worth experimenting with, though, as you may like the taste, and it is very good for you. I have therefore included one or two recipes for the intrepid.

Miso is a very concentrated soya bean paste, full of protein and minerals. Cooked soya beans are mixed with grains or beans inoculated with a mould, fermented and aged until they form a dense, rich-flavoured, paste. There are basically two forms of miso. Sweet white miso, which ferments in a few weeks, is low in salt, high in simple sugars and lactic acid bacteria. Dark brown miso, marketed as Genmai miso if it is made with brown rice, and Mugi miso if it is made with barley, is fermented for up to three years and has a strong salty taste. There is another sort of dark miso, called Hatcho miso, which is concentrated pure soy beans, and therefore very high in plant oestrogens. Miso is very good in soups and sauces, and in many recipes can be used instead of salt.

There are two good reasons to increase your intake of these products. The first is to minimise the risk of osteoporosis. The plant oestrogens in soy (called isoflavones) have been found to have a modest positive effect on bone tissue in studies, in which women with the highest level of isoflavone consumption had greater bone density of the spine.[10, 11]

The second reason is that isoflavones have been found to reduce menopausal symptoms such as hot flushes. A recent meta-analysis – a review of other studies – found that foods that contain phytoestrogens, the richest source of which are soya products, show promise for the treatment of menopausal symptoms.[12] Several studies have reported reductions in hot flushes for menopausal women consuming soya products. One study found that there was up to a 45% reduction in women consuming 60 g of soy per day.[13]

Hot flushes are uncommon in women in countries where the consumption of soya products is high, such as Asian countries. Japan has the highest consumption of the isoflavones found in soy – up to 80 mg per day. It is interesting that, until recently, there was no precise Japanese word to describe a hot flush, although a newly coined term for hot flush, derived from English, has now started to appear in the Japanese media. Perhaps this is due to the fact that the Western diet contains so few soy isoflavones – 1-3 mg at most – and that the urban Japanese are starting to adopt such a diet. In one Japanese study, menopausal women who ate a large amount of fermented soy products, such as miso and tempeh, had fewer and less severe hot flushes than those eating unfermented soy, or little soy at all. The researchers concluded that the intake of fermented soy products alleviates the severity of hot flushes.[14]

An added bonus is that the phytoestrogens in soya may help to control your blood sugar and blood fats, thereby reducing the risk of cardiovascular disease.[15]

It is difficult to say how much soy we should consume each day. One study indicated that one serving of soy per day may reduce the risk of breast cancer; one to two servings may diminish menopausal symptoms; two to five servings may lower cholesterol; and three to eight servings per day may help prevent osteoporosis[16]. Admittedly this research was conducted by a consultant to the US Soybean Association, which may not be unbiased, so more independent research still needs to be done. Meanwhile, my advice is to aim for at least one portion a day – that is 2 oz/60 g tofu or 1 pint/570 ml of soya milk.

Dark Green Leafy Vegetables
These include:

● Cabbage
● Broccoli
● Brussels sprouts
● Spinach
● Spring greens
● Watercress.

In general, the darker the green, the more nutritious the vegetable, and the less you cook them, the better. There are several important nutrients in these vegetables: they contain:

● Essential fatty acids
● Bioflavonoids

---

[10] Kritz-Silverstein D, Goodman-Gruen DL. Usual dietary isoflavone intake, bone mineral density, and bone metabolism in postmenopausal women. *J Womens Health Gend Based Med* 2002 Jan-Feb;11(1):69-78.

[11] Mei J, Yeung SS, Kung AW. High dietary phytoestrogen intake is associated with higher bone mineral density in postmenopausal but not premenopausal women. *J Clin Endocrinol Metab* 2001 Nov;86(11):5217-21.

[12] Kronenberg F, Fugh-Berman A. Complementary and alternative medicine for menopausal symptoms: a review of randomized, controlled trials. *Ann Intern Med* 2002 Nov 19;137(10):805-13.

[13] Albertazzi P et al. The effect of dietary soy supplementation on hot flushes. *Obstet Gynecol* 1998 Jan;91(1):6-11.

[14] Nagata C et al. Hot flushes and other menopausal symptoms in relation to soy product intake in Japanese women. *Climacteric* 1999 Mar;2(1):6-12.

[15] Jayagopal V et al. Beneficial effects of soy phytoestrogen intake in postmenopausal women with type 2 diabetes. *Diabetes Care* 2002 Oct;25(10):1709-14.

[16] Messina M, Gardner C, Barnes S. Gaining insight into the health effects of soy but a long way still to go: commentary on the fourth International Symposium on the Role of Soy in Preventing and Treating Chronic Disease. *J Nutr* 2002 Mar;132(3):547S-551S.

- Sulphoraphanes which detoxify toxins
- Cancer-protective indoles
- Vitamin C
- Beta-carotene
- Calcium
- Potassium
- Vitamin K

Vitamin K is an important nutrient in the prevention of osteoporosis. There's no point taking in lots of calcium and magnesium if you don't have enough vitamin K to activate the proteins involved in building bone. Several recent studies have shown that post-menopausal women have low levels of vitamin K and therefore their bodies cannot activate the bone-building proteins[17]. The best source of vitamin K is broccoli. It's interesting that comfrey, which was traditionally known as 'knit-bone', contains a lot of vitamin K. We can't take comfrey (though it's good for your garden) as it contains an ingredient that damages the liver, but we can eat up our greens! You could also consider taking a vitamin K supplement – osteoporosis patients in Japan now regularly take 45 mg of vitamin K per day. However, a word of warning – do not take vitamin K or eat too many dark green leafy vegetables if you are on Warfarin or any other blood-thinning medication as it interferes with the effect.

All fruits and vegetables
Dark green leafy vegetables, along with almost all fruits and vegetables, contain good levels of vitamin C. The sodium/potassium theory also applies to vitamin C. Primates are one of only a handful of species that do not make vitamin C in their bodies (some of the others are guinea pigs and fruit bats). As mankind evolved in an environment in which plant foods were plentiful, there was no incentive for the body to develop a mechanism for making vitamin C. Unfortunately our bodies haven't yet cottoned on to the fact that we're shopping in supermarkets and living on nutritionally depleted foods rather than getting all the fruit and plant food we need from the forest around us. So we need daily supplies of vitamin C, as much as we can get. The menopausal woman particularly needs vitamin C because its main role is in the formation of collagen, which makes up most of the bone matrix. It is also vital for immune function and an important antioxidant. In addition, a high dietary intake has been shown to significantly reduce risk of heart attack, strokes, cancer and other degenerative diseases in numerous population studies. For example, a recent study by Cambridge University scientists showed that a high intake of fruit and green leafy vegetables may contribute to the prevention of diabetes.[18] Some nutritionists have estimated that we should consume 1 lb (450 g) of vegetables for every 50 lb (22.5 kg) of body weight. While that is an unrealistic goal for most of us, even 1 lb vegetables per day would provide the vitamin C necessary to help protect us against the risk of heart attack, strokes and cancer, as well as many of the beneficial phytochemicals for all our body systems.

Nuts and Seeds
I think of nuts and seeds, particularly seeds, as the Cinderellas of the food world. They are handy little packages full of nutrition, yet most of us only eat nuts bathed in oil and smothered in salt, and don't touch seeds at all. Think again! Nuts are a high protein food, full of vitamins A, B and particularly E, which menopausal women need. Although they are high in fat, it is a polyunsaturated fat, and they are filling, so you don't need to eat a lot of nuts at a sitting. Almonds are particularly valuable, because they contain a high concentration of calcium. Almond milk, for

[17] Hidaka T, Hasegawa T, Fujimura M, Sakai M, Saito S. Treatment for patients with postmenopausal osteoporosis who have been placed on HRT and show a decrease in bone mineral density: effects of concomitant administration of vitamin K(2). *J Bone Miner Metab* 2002;20(4):235-9.
[18] Sargeant LA, Khaw KT, Bingham S, Day NE, Luben RN, Oakes S, Welch A, Wareham NJ. Fruit and vegetable intake and population glycosylated haemoglobin levels: the EPIC-Norfolk Study. *Eur J Clin Nutr* 2001 May;55(5):342-8.

which you will find a recipe in the breakfast chapter, is a delicious substitute for milk in sauces, puddings and poured over cereals, and has a similar nutritional profile to human milk.

As for seeds, they are one of the building blocks of this way of eating. Along with sunflower seeds – rich in protein and minerals, pumpkin seeds – a good source of zinc, and poppy seeds – very high in calcium, there are two star performers in this category:

Sesame seed

You will find a lot of recipes containing sesame in this book. Not only is it one of the most concentrated plant sources of calcium, but also it tastes delicious. Many of my recipes recommend toasting (also called dry frying) the seeds, as this improves the flavour. To toast, simply heat the seeds in a small thick-bottomed pan, stirring frequently, until they start to turn golden and release a nutty aroma. Be careful not to over roast them or they turn dark brown and bitter, and the essential fatty acids they contain will be irretrievably damaged. As with nuts, the best way to access sesame's nutritional value is to grind the seeds, as otherwise they may go straight through your system. Tahini is a paste made of ground sesame seeds, therefore a very accessible source of calcium – it can be used as a spread on bread and toast and used in sauces. Gomasio is a Japanese condiment made of sesame seeds and salt which I sometimes use. To make it toast 120 g/4 oz sesame seeds as above, leave to cool, then grind in an electric grinder in several batches. Mix with a little sea salt (15 g/ ½ oz) and store in a dry place. Use as salt.

Flax seed (Linseed)

Flax seeds, the stars of the show, are dark brown or golden flat seeds, slightly bigger than sesame seeds. The golden sort is visually more appealing, but there is no difference in terms of nutritional value. Flax seeds contain about 18% protein. Three tablespoons of flax seed contain 76 mg of calcium and about 300 mg of potassium (weight for weight, that is seven times as much as a banana). They also contain iron and B vitamins and, most important of all for our purposes, they are a valuable source of plant oestrogens, called lignans. Alternative medicine has long used flax seed as a laxative because it is very high in soluble fibre. If you soak it in water overnight it combines with up to six times its own weight of water and turns into a gelatinous mass – the fibre actually begins to dissolve. The ability of flax seed to thicken in water makes it a very easy way to increase dietary fibre. You can replace an egg in baking recipes with a tablespoon of ground flax seed blended with 2 tablespoons of water.

Flax seed also contains essential fatty acids. Alpha linolenic acid (ALA, Omega-3) makes up the majority (46-64%) of the fatty acids in the seed. Flax seed is the highest known plant source of ALA and is the one to get more of in the diet to counterbalance the much more prevalent Omega-6. These Omega-3 fatty acids are very important in the prevention of cardiovascular diseases, kidney disorders, inflammatory and other disorders.

It is also possible that the lignans in flax seed may help protect women from breast cancer. Studies have shown that women with breast cancer have low lignan levels[19].

If you are not used to flax seed, it is advisable to get your body accustomed to it slowly as it can cause flatulence and bloating. Some people even experience allergic reactions to flax seed, so proceed with caution. The seeds contain a protective enzyme inhibitor that keeps them dormant until they meet optimal growing conditions. Apparently these inhibitors can sometimes be hard on digestive enzymes, resulting in gas and an upset stomach. Flax seed has the advantage, though, for those of us who want to lose weight, of being very filling as it absorbs so much liquid and fills up your stomach. Since I started using flax seed, mostly ground up and sprinkled on food or used in baking, I have effortlessly lost several pounds!

Purchase and storage of nuts and seeds

If possible, buy your nuts in the shell, although they are usually only available in the shell around Christmas time. The second-best option is to buy them from a reputable source that has a high

[19] Adlercreutz H. Phytoestrogens and cancer. *Lancet* Oncol 2002 Jun;3(6):364-73.

turnover, purchase in small quantities and keep them in the fridge. This also applies to seeds. This is important as the highly unsaturated oils in nuts and seeds are very fragile, and prone to damage from light and oxygen. For the same reason, do not grind seeds in advance of using them. Only remove from the fridge as you need and grind just the required amount for your recipe. I keep an old coffee-grinder for the purpose (since I don't need it for coffee any more!)

Sea vegetables
Sea vegetables, which are available from health food shops, are a fantastic source of minerals and iodine (needed by the thyroid gland to make thyroxin) and they make a refreshing change in your diet if you have not been used to them up to now. They contain large quantities of calcium and magnesium, both of which minerals we need during and after menopause in as large a quantity as we can get. Sea vegetables take a little getting used to, and research has shown that our bodies do not assimilate them very well at first, so introduce them into your diet slowly. Nori is a good variety to begin with as its delicate flavour is not as obviously 'seaweedy' as some of the others. It is wonderful lightly toasted and sprinkled as a garnish over rice dishes and salads. Sometimes it is sold ready toasted and seasoned with soy sauce. Arame is another good choice for the beginner. It is sold pre-cooked and finely shredded and looks like Chinese tea. It should be soaked for 10 minutes in tepid water before being drained and used in salads or stir-fries. It makes a delicious accompaniment to simply boiled rice. Later on, when your body has become accustomed to sea vegetables, you can introduce dulse, wakame, hijiki and kombu. Wakame, once rehydrated, miraculously resumes its fresh appearance of bright green wavy fronds. It is mostly used in clear soups and piquant salads. It is good combined with curly endive, cucumber and radish with a light mustard dressing. Kombu (kelp) is used to make stock, and is also a useful addition to the pot when you are boiling beans, as it makes legumes more digestible and less wind-inducing! You will find recipes for some of these sea vegetables in the chapter on salads and accompanying vegetables. Another option for increasing your intake of sea vegetables and the valuable minerals they contain is to use seaweed flakes as a condiment (see Useful Addresses).

Whole grains
Whole grains are those which have not been refined, and therefore still contain all the nutrients they started with. Whole grains, such as wholewheat bread and pasta, brown rice, millet, buckwheat and other more exotic grains such as quinoa and amaranth, are complex carbohydrates which fill you up and give you sustained energy. They will help to increase serotonin levels, which in turn will help to lift your spirits and iron out mood swings.

'Alkaline-forming' foods
This phrase is borrowed from the food-combining diet invented by Dr Hay in the 1930's, which is not food combining so much as food separation. One of Dr Hay's principles was that the diet should consist of 80% alkaline-forming foods, which means those foods which contain a high proportion of the elements which, when broken down in the digestive system, help to keep our blood slightly alkaline, as opposed to acid. This is beneficial for menopausal women as an alkaline environment helps us to hold on to the calcium in our diet. The alkaline-forming elements are calcium, potassium, magnesium and sodium. Fortunately it is easy to eat lots of foods containing these elements. For example, nearly all vegetables and fruit, most nuts, millet, beans and lentils are alkaline-forming.

A landmark study forty years ago showed that the minerals in bone serve as a buffer against all the acid foods we eat. After a lifetime of buffering the acid load from eating diets that are full of protein and grains, this leads to gradual loss of minerals in the bones. The researchers conducting the study concluded that "it might be worthwhile to consider decreasing the rate of bone attrition by the use of a diet favoring 'alkaline ash'", i.e. a diet high in fruit and vegetables.

Natural sweeteners
The sweeteners I most commonly use in place of sugar are: concentrated apple juice and blackstrap molasses, with occasional use of maple syrup, date syrup, brown rice syrup and honey. Sugar cane

in its natural state is fibrous and therefore balanced, but pure refined sugar is just empty calories with no fibre and no minerals. The suggested alternatives are unrefined and contain nutrients as well as providing sweetness, but they are still a form of sugar so should be consumed in moderation only. Molasses in particular is a brilliant source of minerals, although the taste is quite strong and doesn't appeal to everybody.

Fats and oils

Ideally we shouldn't heat fats at all, because over a certain temperature the fatty acids they contain get damaged and turn into 'trans' fats, which are very bad for us. However, you can't really cook without heating fats. I hope to minimise the damage by using only extra-virgin olive oil and, occasionally, organic butter. Being a monounsaturated fat, olive oil is quite stable, as long as it's not heated to too high a temperature. Butter is also relatively stable when heated because it is already a saturated fat. Why organic? Because organic standards demand that cows are fed a more natural diet consisting predominantly of grass or hay, and because the grass or hay they eat has not been treated with the fat-soluble pesticides and fungicides that may be concentrated in butter made from the milk of non-organic cows. And because routine use of antibiotics is prohibited under organic rules, so there is no danger of traces of antibiotics finding their way into organic butter.

I use extra-virgin olive oil because it has very low levels of acidity, and retains the fatty acids and antioxidants present in the whole olive. Refined or 'pure' olive oil has the same fatty acid composition as extra-virgin, but during processing it loses the antioxidants present in extra-virgin oil. In a recent study[20], researchers noted that when participants used extra-virgin oil, the levels of oxidized LDL ('bad') cholesterol in their blood were much lower. Oxidative damage of LDL cholesterol has been linked to the development of heart disease. The researchers credit the presence of antioxidants in extra-virgin olive oil with slowing the oxidation process of LDL cholesterol. Where only a little oil is required in a recipe, I use a stainless steel pump-action spray bottle for my olive oil, which covers the pan or the food in a fine mist of oil (available from good kitchen shops or from Lakeland Limited – see Useful Addresses). Do not use commercially produced sprays which have propellant added to them.

Cold-pressed oils are great to use on salads, adding different flavours, but should never be used for cooking, as they are so prone to heat damage. They all have different fatty acid profiles. The ones I use the most are walnut oil (high in Omega-3 fatty acids), pumpkin seed oil (a good source of Omega-6 fatty acids), and, most especially, flax oil. Flax seed and flax oil both have a very high Omega-3 content and an excellent balance of Omega-3 to Omega-6. A tablespoon of flax oil contains approximately 8 g of Omega-3 fatty acids, but only 2.2 g of Omega-6. No other oil comes close to this beneficial balance. This is why flax oil is sold in health food shops as a supplement – usually refrigerated in dark bottles to ensure freshness and prevent oxidation. One of the things that flax oil does best is to transport vitamin A (a fat soluble vitamin) to cells throughout the body, giving a boost to the immune system.

Water

Yes, water! You can't enter the nutrition world without being aware that water is the most important nutrient, yet it is often overlooked. Two-thirds of our bodies are made up of water, and we lose 1.5 litres a day through the skin and in urine in the elimination of wastes, so the advice to drink up to two litres of fresh pure water a day makes sense, but very few people do this. Instead, we drink coffee, tea, alcohol and fizzy drinks which rob our bodies of water. Sweet and salty foods, tobacco smoke, air conditioning, sitting in front of computer screens and television all further deplete the body of water. Not only this, but the effect of being slightly dehydrated, as most of us are, is to switch off the thirst mechanism, so that we may not even feel thirsty. The strategy that has worked best for me is to have 4 half-litre bottles filled at the beginning of the day from my water filter. I drink one before breakfast, one between breakfast and lunch, one in the afternoon and one in the evening, and that seems to work well without being a chore.

20 Ramirez-Tortosa MC et al. Extra-virgin olive oil increases the resistance of LDL to oxidation more than refined olive oil in free-living men with peripheral vascular disease. J Nutr 1999 Dec;129(12):2177-83.

Tap water, although the water companies assure us it is fit to drink, may contain traces of chemical fertilizers, fungicides, pesticides and other synthetic chemicals. Menopausal women should avoid tap water as these chemicals are oestrogen mimics – that is to say, they can bind to the oestrogen receptors in your body. The answer is to drink distilled, bottled or filtered water. A distillation system is probably the most efficient method for removing contaminents from tap water but it also removes all beneficial minerals such as calcium and magnesium, and is expensive to install and maintain. A reverse osmosis system totally removes chlorine, pesticides, fluorides and nitrates, but it also removes minerals and is expensive to install. Activated carbon filters, either under the sink or in a jug filter, are probably the best least-cost solution, although they only remove 85% of chlorine and 70% of pesticides, and may not remove all bacteria, so the filters must be changed frequently to prevent bacterial build-up. Bottled waters vary in quality. 'Spring' water could even legally be nothing more than filtered tap water, so look for 'natural mineral water' which is a guarantee of quality, but it doesn't come cheap.

The Recipes

All recipes serve four unless otherwise stated. All eggs are medium, not large. All tablespoon and teaspoon measures are level.

Each recipe is accompanied by a nutritional analysis detailing the amounts of protein, calories, fats, fibre, calcium and magnesium it contains. Additionally, if a recipe contains a significant amount of other important nutrients, this has been noted. But how do you know how much of each nutrient you need?

The current Government guidelines, published by the Department of Health in 1991, include up to four sets of figures – the estimated average requirement (EAR), the reference nutrient intake (RNI), which is the amount of a nutrient that is enough for almost every individual, even someone who has high needs for a nutrient, the lower reference nutrient intake (LRNI) and the safe intake. The four figures together are called the Dietary Reference Values (DRVs). The most relevant of the sets of figures is the RNI. The use of the word 'reference' indicates that people are not expected to use the figures as recommended or desirable intakes, but they are the best indication of average/desirable intake. So that you can check the amounts stated in the recipes against the RNI, the table below gives the RNI for women before and after the age of 50 (the only differences are in the amounts of calories and protein).

Nutrient	RNI per day up to age 49	RNI per day age 50 and over
Energy	1940 KCal	1900 KCal
Protein	45 g	46.5 g
Carbohydrates	60 g	60 g
Dietary Fibre	18-32 g	18-32 g
Fat – Total[21]	33-35% of total energy intake	33-35% of total energy intake
Saturated Fat	10% of total energy intake	10% of total energy intake
Polyunsatured Fat	At least 1.2% of total energy intake	At least 1.2% of total energy intake
Calcium	700 mg	700 mg
Magnesium	270 mg	270 mg

[21] The values for fat are Dietary Reference Values rather than RNI's. This is because, apart from the Essential Fatty Acids, there is no absolute need for fat or any fatty acid and, within overall energy needs, no well-defined signs or symptoms of deficiency or excess intake. Nevertheless, because of the relationship between fat and heart disease, an estimate was made of a desirable percentage of energy consumed as fat.

In addition, I have noted where a recipe contains a significant quantity of phytoestrogens. The principal phytoestrogens in food are the isoflavones, found in soya beans, lentils and chickpeas, the coumestans found in alfalfa sprouts and other sprouting legumes, and the lignans found in flax seed, most cereals, fruits and vegetables. However, it is very difficult to estimate the amount of phytoestrogens in any particular food, because until recently there has been a lack of suitable analytical methods and validation techniques. Not only this, but the phytoestrogen concentration of plants varies considerably according to when and where the crop was grown. See Appendix 2 for the approximate concentrations of phytoestrogens found in foods that have been measured so far.

So what quantity of phytoestrogens should a menopausal woman be eating? This question cannot be answered accurately because research is still continuing. However, it is interesting to note that the average Japanese person (where menopausal symptoms are almost unheard-of) consumes approximately 25-80 mg of isoflavones per day, whereas the average UK consumption is approximately 1 mg per day, with an average UK vegetarian eating up to 3 mg a day[22], so any increase in consumption should be beneficial.

---

[22] Source: The draft report of the COT Working Group of Phytoestrogens, 10 October 2002.

Breakfasts

Fruit and Vegetable Juices
Nutrient-Dense Fruit Juices
Vegetable Juices
Fruit Shakes and Smoothies
Nectarine and Berry Shake
Ginger and Pineapple Shake
Oat, Banana and Strawberry Smoothie
Fruits, Fresh and Dried
Bowl of Berries
Winter Fruit Salad
Whole Grain Hot Cereals
Quinoa Porridge with Dates
Millet Porridge with Raisins, Currants and Sunflower Seeds
Amaranth with Almonds and Apricots
Muesli for the Menopause
Super Seed Mix
Oat Pancakes
Blueberry Pancakes
Courgette Scramble
Potato and Mushroom Frittata
Nut and Seed Butters
Spreads
Ursula's Energy Spread
Molasses Syrup
Prune Whip Sauce
Tofu Whizz
Almond Milk

We are constantly being told that we must eat a healthy breakfast to see us through the morning. However, an informal survey of friends and acquaintances reveals that it is still the norm to grab a cup of coffee and a slice of toast with margarine or butter and marmalade, and/or a bowl of commercial cereal with milk and sugar – an inadequate breakfast in several respects:

● The coffee or tea prevents the absorption of minerals and artificially stimulates us, making it harder to keep blood sugar levels even throughout the day.
● Margarine should be avoided as it is a highly processed product, whether or not it is made with polyunsaturated oils.
● Butter, although a 'pure' food, is a saturated fat and should only be eaten in moderation.
● Marmalade and jam are full of refined white sugar, which is bad for us because it is an empty source of calories – it provides energy but no vitamins or minerals. Sugar without any fibre can cause swings in blood sugar levels and it also causes dental decay.
● Commercial cereals are full of added sugar and salt and contain very little of real nutritional value.

Instead of toast and cereal, try some of the recipes in this chapter.

I have based most of these recipes on fruit, soya and whole grains, with some suggestions for protein-packed egg breakfasts. Although fresh fruit contains simple sugar which theoretically we should avoid, it is combined with fibre, and fruit provides us with beta-carotene, B vitamins, vitamin C, and many of the minerals such as magnesium, calcium, sulphur and potassium. Dried fruits, particularly dried apricots, are very nutritious: they contain beta-carotene, iron, calcium, potassium, magnesium and vitamin B. You should avoid dried fruit preserved with sulphur dioxide, E220, however, which is used to retain the colour and plumpness of dried fruit and kill fly larvae, as it destroys B vitamins. Raisins and sultanas are treated with potassium carbonate and no-soak varieties of prunes are treated with potassium sorbate. Supermarket dried fruit is sprayed with mineral oil, and must be washed in hot water to remove the oil as it prevents the absorption of vitamins, calcium and phosphorus and encourages the excretion of oil-soluble vitamins such as vitamin E – all nutrients essential to the menopausal woman.

Since we are aiming at a moderate intake of soya, it makes sense to eat a portion of soya for breakfast once or twice a week. Try some of the fruit and soya shakes in this chapter, use Tofu Whizz on Pancakes and serve prorridge with soya milk.

We should eat more whole grains because they provide a good source of protein as well as magnesium (essential to help us access calcium from other sources), B vitamins, zinc and selenium. While researching this chapter I came to appreciate the variety of flaked cereals there are available and what interest they can add to the diet. Not only that, but a breakfast based on whole grains and fruit will keep you going all morning, without that familiar energy dip that comes around 11 am, when you might otherwise be tempted to grab a coffee and biscuit.

I have also included some ideas for breakfasts based on eggs. Eggs are a wonderful source of protein. They do contain cholesterol, but it is now generally accepted that eating foods rich in cholesterol is not a factor dictating cholesterol levels in the body, so eating an egg for breakfast once or twice a week will do no harm. As with everything else, moderation is the key.

FRUIT AND VEGETABLE JUICES

Generally, fruit should be eaten whole to preserve the natural balance of fibre and sugar. However, indulging in fresh home made juice once or twice a week is a real treat which gives

your body an injection of vitamins and minerals in a quickly and easily digested form, while at the same time being absolutely delicious. The pulp from juicing can be used as a filling for pancakes, so nothing need be wasted and you will still get your fibre. Since peeling fruit for juice is neither necessary nor desirable, as you want to preserve as many of the vitamins as you can, and they are to be found right under the skin, it is important to use organic fruit where possible for juicing. Washing will not remove the residues of systemic pesticides, widely used on conventionally grown fruit, because they are fat-soluble rather than water-soluble.
In addition, fruit and vegetables get their minerals from the soil. The soil on organic farms is less likely to be depleted of trace minerals by overuse of imbalanced fertilizers – another reason to go organic.

Vegetable juice for breakfast sounds a strange idea, but why not? We all need to eat more vegetables, and if we're aiming at five or six servings a day, we can't afford to let breakfast go by without featuring a portion of vegetables. And the most palatable way to get your veggies in the morning is with a shot of juice.

Juicers
You will, of course, need to purchase a centrifugal juicer if you are going to make juice regularly. There are lots of good juicers on the market these days, and some of them are quite inexpensive. Look for one of robust manufacture that will process the peel, core and seeds of fruits and vegetables, with as large a feed tube as you can find and as powerful a motor as your budget allows. It must also be easy to clean, as nothing is more offputting to the aspiring juice-maker than a machine that takes ages to clean.

To prepare fruit for juicing
Most fruit does not need to be peeled. Simply wash and cut into chunks small enough to fit into the juicer's feeding tube. Citrus fruit needs to be peeled, but you can leave the pith on – it contains bioflavonoids, thought to help combat hot flushes.

NUTRIENT-DENSE FRUIT JUICES

A nutrient-dense food is one that packs the maximum amount of nutrients in the minimum amount of space. The nutrients here are the carotenes (precursors of Vitamin A), potassium, calcium, magnesium (trace), Vitamin C and bioflavonoids. Vitamin C is never found on its own in nature – it's always accompanied by bioflavonoids, which are trace nutrients. The function of only a few of these is known, but those we do know of are valuable antioxidants.

These are the most nutrient-dense fruits, and can be combined in any quantity you like to make fresh juice:

Fresh apricots, bananas, blackcurrants, blueberries, cantaloupe, cherries, grapefruit, kiwi fruit, lemons, limes, mangoes, nectarines, pears, plums, raspberries, strawberries, tangerines and watermelon.

Make up your own combinations, or here are some ideas (all these combinations make one serving):

● A handful of blackcurrants and 1 grapefruit
● 3 fresh apricots, 1 orange and 1 banana
● 1 large orange and 1 nectarine
● 1 large orange, 1 banana and 6 strawberries or a handful of raspberries
● 2 kiwi fruit and 1½ apples (different varieties make very different juices – Coxes, for example, are great for juice)

- 6 strawberries and 1 grapefruit
- 2 kiwi fruit, 1 banana and 2 passion fruit
- 1 orange, 1 grapefruit and ½ lemon
- 2 thick slices of peeled pineapple and 1 orange
- 1½ apples, a handful of blackberries and ½ lemon
- 1 mango and 1 lime, diluted with water
- ½ large ripe papaya and 1 lime, diluted with water

Do not throw away the pulp from juicing, as it is a valuable source of fibre and can be used in all sorts of ways. However, it should be used soon after juicing in order to preserve the vitamin C. I suggest that you mix it with live yoghurt and eat it right away, or use it as a filling for breakfast pancakes.

I always add a dessertspoonful of ground seeds to my morning juice (see Super Seed Mix on page 13). These provide an easily assimilated source of Omega-3 fatty acids, which are anti-inflammatory and may help control hot flushes, besides being essential for nerve and brain cells.

VEGETABLE JUICES

Introduce yourself to vegetable juices gently, as some of them can turn out to have surprisingly strong flavours. On the other hand, there are so many nutritional benefits to be gained from vegetable juices.

The best vegetables for breakfast juicing are carrots, tomatoes and celery. Carrots contain beta-carotene, which is the precursor of vitamin A, and is needed for our eye and skin health, and also for our immune systems. Tomatoes also contain a carotene called lycopene (though it's more powerful in cooked tomatoes than in raw) and celery contains calcium and magnesium. 4-5 sticks of celery a day have been shown to be effective in helping to reduce blood pressure. So there you are – lots of reasons to introduce these less powerfully flavoured juices onto the breakfast menu. Start with carrot juice, mixing it half and half with apple juice – this makes a sweet, delicious combination. Tomato juice is easy to get used to, as well, and mixes well with either carrot or celery. Home-made tomato juice tastes so much better than the tomato juice you can buy, provided the tomatoes you use are really ripe and flavourful.

Here are some guideline quantities. All combinations serve one:

- 2 apples and 1 medium carrot
- 2 medium carrots, 1 apple and 1 kiwi fruit
- 2 ripe tomatoes, 2 carrots and 1 stick of celery – try adding a handful of basil for extra beta-carotene and a wonderful flavour
- 3 carrots and a handful of watercress – a good source of iron and vitamin C

For more adventurous ways with vegetable juices, see the chapter on starters.

FRUIT SHAKES AND SMOOTHIES

There is some confusion in my mind, and therefore perhaps in yours too, about the difference between smoothies and shakes. I have assumed that a shake is a combination of fruit and some sort of milk, and that a smoothie contains something a bit more substantial, such as yoghurt or tofu.

So here are a handful of shakes and smoothies, which make quick but nutritionally balanced breakfasts.

Try this with a peach, too. Depending on the size you may have to use more than one.

PER SERVING	
Energy Kcals	196.8
Protein g	6.7
Carbohydrates g	29.9
Dietary Fibre g	8.6
Fat – Total g	7.3
Saturated Fat g	0.7
Polyunsaturated Fat g	2.8
Calcium mg	58.4
Magnesium mg	47.8

Nectarine and Berry Shake

1 dstsp	mixed seeds, such as sesame, flax seed, hemp and sunflower seeds	1 dstsp
2	medium nectarines	2
3 oz	mixed berries (eg blueberries, blackberries, raspberries or strawberries)	90 g
4 fl oz	soya, nut or rice milk	120 ml

Grind the seeds in an electric grinder. Slice the nectarine but keep the peel on. Place all ingredients in a blender and blend until smooth. Serves 1.

You can successfully substitute other fruits, such as bananas, fresh apricots, kiwis or pears in this shake. Ginger is a natural anti-inflammatory and cleansing agent, and helps to overcome fatigue and weakness. It is also very good for your circulation, so should be eaten if you suffer from varicose veins. As for pineapple, it contains an enzyme called bromelain which aids digestion.

PER SERVING	
Energy Kcals	87.8
Protein g	3.9
Carbohydrates g	14.0
Dietary Fibre g	2.8
Fat – Total g	2.8
Saturated Fat g	0.3
Polyunsaturated Fat g	1.2
Calcium mg	12.4
Magnesium mg	38.9

Ginger and Pineapple Shake

This is quite heavy on the ginger, but I find ginger very refreshing in the morning, and it is one of the few 'hot' spices that don't encourage hot flushes.

$1^{1}/_{2}$ tbsp	fresh ginger root, peeled and chopped	$1^{1}/_{2}$ tbsp
1	large slice of pineapple, peeled and cored	1
5 fl oz	soya, oat, rice or nut milk	150 ml
$^{1}/_{4}$ tsp	pure vanilla extract	$^{1}/_{4}$ tsp

Put all the ingredients in the blender and blend until smooth. You may prefer to put this shake through a sieve if you find that the stringy bits of ginger and pineapple get stuck between your teeth. Serves 1.

Oats are one of the few readily available sources of chromium in our modern diet. We need chromium to help us metabolise the carbohydrate in our food. The orange provides 70 g vitamin C (nearly twice the RNI), whereas substituting strawberries would provide a little more.

PER SERVING	
Energy Kcals	281.8
Protein g	12.3
Carbohydrates g	52.0
Dietary Fibre g	7.0
Fat – Total g	4.8
Saturated Fat g	1.9
Polyunsaturated Fat g	1.0
Calcium mg	251.8
Magnesium mg	72.0

Oat, Banana and Strawberry Smoothie

This really is 'breakfast in a glass', and has the added bonus of being partially prepared the night before. In the summer I freeze the strawberries overnight for a really refreshing treat. It is also delicious made with the juice and grated rind of an orange instead of the strawberries.

$1/_2$ oz	rolled oats	15 g
2 tbsp	soya, oat, rice or nut milk	2 tbsp
1	small banana	1
4 oz	strawberries	110 g
$4^1/_2$ oz	live natural yoghurt or soya yoghurt	125 g
pinch	fresh nutmeg, grated	pinch

Soak the oats overnight in the soya, oat, rice or nut milk. In the morning put the soaked oats in the blender with the banana, strawberries and the yoghurt. Blend until smooth and serve with a topping of freshly grated nutmeg. Serves 1.

FRUITS, FRESH AND DRIED

I'm a bit of a fruitaholic myself – no meal for me is complete without fruit, and I eat it between meals as a snack, too. It is especially good at breakfast because it provides you with easily assimilated fruit sugars for instant energy and fibre to fill you up.

However, it's always wise to have your fruit with some protein and some complex carbohydrate at the same time, in order to keep your blood sugar levels even throughout the day. The fructose in fruit, while giving you an energy boost, would send your blood sugar up too high if eaten on its own. Get into the habit of starting a starchy breakfast with a piece of fruit, slice or grate fresh fruit on to your cereal, put sliced or mashed banana on your toast instead of jam, or try some of the ideas that follow.

Dried Fruit Salads

Since dried fruits, although delicious and packed with nutrition, are pretty high in calories, it is a good idea to soak and cook them to bulk them out. Wash them first, then soak in water, unsweetened fruit juice or herbal tea. The soaking liquid can then be used to cook them in.

When fruit is dried, the water-soluble vitamins, such as vitamin C, are inevitably depleted. However, some nutrients survive the drying process. For example the carotenes in prunes and dried apricots are intact, and they can add valuable antioxidants to the diet. All dried fruit, especially dried apricots and prunes, provide a good range of minerals, particularly potassium. Figs are a very good non-dairy source of calcium, and both figs and prunes provide fibre and act as gentle laxatives.

You can buy dried fruit salad in health food stores, or try some of the ideas below:

● Dried figs soaked in orange juice for 24 hrs then cooked for 15 minutes, served sprinkled with flaked almonds.
● Hunza apricots (whole, sun-dried apricots from Pakistan), soaked in mineral water or herbal tea, cooked in the soaking water until tender (about 20 minutes) and served with natural live yoghurt or soya yoghurt.
● Prunes, soaked and cooked in fruit tea with a slice of lemon and a cinnamon stick added.

Bowl of Berries

This isn't really a recipe, but just a reminder that berries are a wonderful food. Dark-coloured berries contain lots of phytonutrients, which help to strengthen collagen, the protein network that gives skin its structure. So a bowl of berries each morning just might help to delay the onset of wrinkles.

4 oz	strawberries	110 g
4 oz	raspberries or blackberries in season	110 g
4 oz	blueberries	110 g
4 tbsp	mixed seeds – flax seeds, sesame seeds, hemp seed	4 tbsp
4 tbsp	natural live yoghurt or soya yoghurt	4 tbsp

Wash and hull the strawberries, and slice them. Wash the other fruit and divide equally between four bowls. Grind the seeds in an electric grinder, then top the berries with the seeds and a spoonful of yoghurt. Serves 4.

This dish, for all its simplicity, provides carbohydrates, essential fats, protein, vitamins and minerals.

PER SERVING	
Energy Kcals	97.2
Protein g	3.2
Carbohydrates g	13.1
Dietary Fibre g	4.3
Fat – Total g	4.4
Saturated Fat g	0.5
Polyunsaturated Fat g	1.4
Calcium mg	74.1
Magnesium mg	25.2

The lemon juice here is not only to preserve the appearance of the apples and pears. Browning is an indication of oxidation, and the vitamin C in the lemon juice is an antioxidant, so in protecting the fruit from the oxygen in the air, it is preventing the formation of destructive free radicals.

PER SERVING	
Energy Kcals	218.7
Protein g	1.75
Carbohydrates g	55.6
Dietary Fibre g	7.2
Fat – Total g	1.2
Saturated Fat g	0.2
Polyunsaturated Fat g	0.3
Calcium mg	58.0
Magnesium mg	28.2

Right: Muesli for the Menopause (page 12) and Oat, Banana and Strawberry Smoothie (page 6)

Winter Fruit Salad

This is a delicious mixture of the fruits available in autumn and winter, for a quick fix of antioxidants.

3	ripe pears	3
1	large Cox's apple	1
1/2	lemon	1/2
1	large orange	1
1	banana	1
1	kiwi fruit	1
12 fl oz	pure unfiltered apple juice	340 ml
1	cinnamon stick	1
12	whole cloves	12

Dice the pears and apple, leaving the skin on. Sprinkle with lemon juice to keep from browning. Peel and slice the banana, orange and kiwi fruit, and toss with the other fruit.

Combine the apple juice, cinnamon stick and cloves in a small saucepan, bring to the boil and boil rapidly over high heat for about 10 minutes, or until the sauce is reduced by half.

Strain the sauce over the fruit and toss to coat. Cover, and leave to marinate overnight in a cool place. Serves 4.

WHOLE GRAIN HOT CEREALS

Cereal Flake Porridge

Hot porridge is delicious, easy to digest, quick to make and nutritious. It can be made with any cereal flakes, which are whole grains, flaked and lightly toasted. Try barley, rye, wheat, soya, millet, and rice flakes as well as the more usual oat flakes. These are all valuable sources of protein, complex carbohydrates, fibre, minerals and vitamins, particularly vitamins B and E.

Cook one part flakes with two to three parts water and simmer gently until cooked to the desired consistency. Millet flakes cook quickly; barley, rye and wheat are coarser and more chewy. Barley in particular never disintegrates like ordinary porridge, but keeps its shape no matter how long you cook it (See table on page 9). Alternatively, place the flakes and liquid in a non-metallic jug or bowl in the

microwave and cook on high for half the cooking time. Stir and cook for the rest of the cooking time or until the desired consistency is reached.

Flake	Cook on hob	Microwave
Barley	30 minutes	8 minutes
Millet	5 minutes	2 minutes
Rice	5 minutes	2 minutes
Rye	10 minutes	5 minutes
Soya	10 minutes	5 minutes
Wheat	15 minutes	6 minutes

Note: these timings are for guidance only.

If you don't have the time to cook your porridge in the morning, an alternative method is to place the cereal and the boiling water in a wide necked thermos flask the night before, close the thermos tightly and leave until the next morning, at which time the porridge will be ready to eat. In practice, I have found this method produces porridge too overcooked for my taste, but it is worth trying out, if only for the convenience factor.

Porridge does not have to be served with sugar, golden syrup or other 'baddies'. Instead, it may be served with soya milk and topped with fresh or dried fruit, or served with one of the sweet sauces later on in this chapter – or try it sprinkled with the Super Seed Mix on page 13.

Quinoa Porridge with Dates

Quinoa is a grain relatively new in Europe, though it has been used in South America for many generations.

3 oz	quinoa	90 g
8 fl oz	soya, nut or rice milk	225 ml
1 tsp	ground cinnamon	1 tsp
5	dates, stoned and chopped	5

Rinse the quinoa well to remove its soap-like outer coating. Put it in a saucepan together with 5 fl oz/150 ml water, bring to the boil and simmer for 15 minutes, or until all the liquid has evaporated.

Add the soya, nut or rice milk and cinammon and simmer for another 30 minutes until the porridge is creamy. Stir in the chopped dates before serving. Serves 2.

Quinoa is a whole grain high in protein, magnesium and iron, with plenty of B vitamins and other minerals. You could substitute bulgur wheat, which is wheat that has been boiled and cracked. It is therefore in one sense a refined grain and will not have as much nutritional value as quinoa.

PER SERVING	
Energy Kcals	263.7
Protein g	9.4
Carbohydrates g	48.8
Dietary Fibre g	6.4
Fat – Total g	4.9
Saturated Fat g	0.6
Polyunsaturated Fat g	2.0
Calcium mg	51.7
Magnesium mg	121.0

Left: Sardine Bruschetta (page 31) and Toasted Smoked Mackerel Sandwich (page 29) *Right:* Roasted Red Pepper, Hummus and Rocket Open Sandwiches (pages 26, 27), Grilled Tofu (page 24)

Millet is a grain that takes a long time to metabolise, due to its complex carbohydrate content, and so it provides a long, steady supply of energy that should last you through till lunch.

Millet Porridge with Raisins, Currants and Sunflower Seeds

Millet is not just for budgies! It is a very alkaline grain and contains complete protein. It is often tolerated by those who cannot eat other grains. It is also gluten-free.

6 fl oz	water	175 ml
3 oz	whole millet	90 g
2 oz	raisins	60 g
2 oz	currants	60 g
2 tbsp	sunflower seeds	2 tbsp

Bring the water to boil in a small saucepan. Add millet, cover and simmer for 15 minutes. Remove from the heat, add the raisins and currants and let stand, covered, for 10 minutes.

Serve the porridge with the sunflower seeds sprinkled over and with soya, nut or rice milk on the side. Serves 2.

PER SERVING	
Energy Kcals	265.4
Protein g	5.6
Carbohydrates g	55.0
Dietary Fibre g	4.5
Fat – Total g	4.4
Saturated Fat g	0.5
Polyunsaturated Fat g	0.3
Calcium mg	51.3
Magnesium mg	40.6

It is preferable to use unsulphured molasses and apricots (and other dried fruit) where possible. Sulphites are used to preserve foods and can cause nausea and diarrhoea in some people. Unsulphured dried fruit will not have the keeping quality of the sulphured variety, so buy in small quantities for a fast turnover.

Amaranth with Almonds and Apricots

This recipe started out with couscous, but blame my weakness for alliteration for the fact that I substituted a grain beginning with 'a'! Still, there are many good reasons for eating this ancient grain of the Aztecs. Like quinoa, it is high in protein, and is therefore a good way to start the day.
It also contains a useful amount of calcium and iron.
Amaranth is not easy to find in this country, but you should be able to source it in good health-food shops. It takes quite a long time to cook, but this is not a hardship since you can make this porridge the night before and gently re-heat in the morning.

This recipe includes blackstrap molasses as a sweetener. Molasses, the final product extracted from sugarcane during the refining process, is a really rich source of calcium, iron, potassium and B vitamins. It gives the dish a dark colour. If you find this aesthetically unpleasing, you can substitute honey, but you will lose the nutritional benefits of molasses.

2 oz	dried unsulphured apricots, chopped	60 g
4 oz	amaranth	110 g
$^1/_2$ oz	organic unsalted butter	15 g
2 oz	raw almonds, coarsely chopped	60 g
$1^1/_2$ tbsp	blackstrap molasses	$1^1/_2$ tbsp
$^1/_2$ tsp	cinnamon	$^1/_2$ tsp

Rinse the amaranth, and put it in a small saucepan, add water to cover, bring to the boil, then cover and simmer for 30 minutes. Then remove from the heat, add the chopped apricots, cover again and let stand for 5 minutes. Stir in butter with a fork and toss gently to blend. Up to this point recipe may be prepared the night before and left covered.

In the morning, add a little more water and reheat gently until piping hot.

Add the almonds, molasses and cinnamon and stir to combine. Serve hot with soya milk. Serves 4.

PER SERVING	
Energy Kcals	253.7
Protein g	7.4
Carbohydrates g	31.0
Dietary Fibre g	6.6
Fat – Total g	12.0
Saturated Fat g	2.9
Polyunsaturated Fat g	2.7
Calcium mg	155.8
Magnesium mg	138.4

MUESLI

After years of eating muesli straight from the packet, it was a surprise to me to discover that it was not originally intended to be consumed in this way. Dr Bircher-Benner, who originally formulated muesli as part of the treatment of the chronically sick in the first part of the twentieth century, always soaked it overnight and added substantial amounts of fresh fruit and yoghurt so that the cereal content was comparatively low. To get the full benefit of the nutrients muesli really needs to be soaked in soya or rice milk, water or fruit juice. This makes it not only more digestible, but also softer and therefore more palatable. The soaking process will cause it to swell tremendously and so you do not need very much at a sitting.

This muesli has a good balance of calcium and magnesium. If you are on a gluten-free diet, substitute the oat, rye, barley and wheat flakes with non-gluten grain flakes such as rice flakes, millet flakes or quinoa flakes.

Muesli for the Menopause

I have created this muesli to contain all of the nutrients that the menopausal woman should be eating – a great way to start the day.

1 lb	rolled oats	450 g
8 oz	barley flakes	225 g
4 oz	rye flakes	110 g
4 oz	whole wheat flakes	110 g
8 oz	raisins	225 g
8 oz	chopped dates	225 g
4 oz	chopped hazelnuts	110 g
4 oz	chopped brazil nuts	110 g
3 oz	flax seeds, ground	90 g
3 oz	sesame seed, ground	90 g

Mix all the ingredients together and store in an airtight container. To serve, soak about 2½ oz/75 g in a little water or apple juice overnight. Serve with soya, nut or rice milk and grated apple or other fresh fruit. Makes about 24 servings.

PER SERVING	
Energy Kcals	281.8
Protein g	8.7
Carbohydrates g	44.9
Dietary Fibre g	8.3
Fat – Total g	10.7
Saturated Fat g	1.5
Polyunsaturated Fat g	2.8
Calcium mg	75.4
Magnesium mg	80.4

The oils in seeds are relatively fragile, so it is not a good idea to grind large quantities in advance, as this would damage the oils. Keep in the fridge, and grind the seeds as you need them.

Super Seed Mix

This is possibly the most important recipe in the book. I eat this on everything from porridge to strawberries. It's also good in fruit and vegetable juices. You will find that it takes a bit of getting used to at first, but soon you won't be able to live without it. Seeds are very nutrient-dense – after all, they contain everything needed by the whole plant when it grows. They are especially high in Omega-3 fatty acids – the sort that we don't get enough of in the modern diet, and phytoestrogens. Flax seed is almost our only source of useful amounts of lignans, for example, while the other seeds contain some isoflavones. For a menopausal woman, taking a tablespoonful of seeds each day can really make a difference to symptoms such as hot flushes.

3 oz	flax seeds	90 g
3 oz	unhulled sesame seed	90 g
3 oz	hemp seed or sunflower seed	90 g

Simply mix all the seeds together and keep in an airtight container in the fridge. When you need them, take out a tablespoonful of seeds and grind in an electric grinder. Makes about 24 servings.

PER SERVING	
Energy Kcals	55.7
Protein g	2.1
Carbohydrates g	2.7
Dietary Fibre g	0.9
Fat – Total g	4.4
Saturated Fat g	0.4
Polyunsaturated Fat g	0.8
Calcium mg	48.1
Magnesium mg	12.4.8

PANCAKES

Living in America for some years made me very partial to pancakes for breakfast. The traditional way is with butter, maple syrup and bacon – a breakfast loaded with fat and sugar. Try some of these healthy alternatives, and check out the syrups and sauces on pages 19-20.

Oat Pancakes

These pancakes are very quick and easy to make, particularly as you make the batter the night before.
You could describe them as 'fried porridge', but that makes them sound horrible when actually they are very tasty.
I make them in a blender, which chops up the oats finely. However, if you prefer a chunky texture, just mix the batter in a bowl.

Try adding some dried or fresh fruit to the pancakes, such as raisins, chopped bananas, berries or grated apple.
You can serve them with poached eggs and grilled tomatoes for a healthy cooked breakfast, or serve them in place of toast, spread with fruit spread or nut butter.

4 oz	rolled oats	110 g
1	organic, free-range egg	1
	low-sodium salt to taste, a pinch	
1/2 pint	mixed water and soya milk	275 ml

Place oats, egg and salt in the blender goblet and blend for a few seconds. Gradually add the milk and water mixture and blend for a few seconds more. Let the batter stand for at least 10 minutes but preferably overnight to let the oats absorb the water. Blend briefly or stir well just before using. Pour large spoonfuls of the batter into a heavy, oiled frying pan and help it to spread out with the back of a spoon. Cook over moderate heat until the pancakes start to look dry, then turn over with a palette knife to cook the other side until golden. Do not hurry this operation or the pancakes will burn.
Serves 4, with 3 pancakes each.

PER SERVING	
Energy Kcals	141.9
Protein g	7.4
Carbohydrates g	19.6
Dietary Fibre g	3.5
Fat – Total g	4.0
Saturated Fat g	0.8
Polyunsaturated Fat g	1.2
Calcium mg	23.8
Magnesium mg	63.1

Blueberries contain more antioxidants than almost any other fruit or vegetable, owing to their dark colour. You could try these using blackcurrants or blackberries in season. Both are equally nutritious. These pancakes are also scrumptious with a grated apple stirred into the batter.

Blueberry Pancakes

These are American-style pancakes. They should be quite small and puffy. They are delicious with one of the pancake syrups on pages 19-20. This recipe makes quite a lot of pancakes, but could successfully be halved.

12 oz	wholewheat flour or gluten-free flour	340 g
1 tsp	bicarbonate of soda	1 tsp
1 tsp	salt-free baking powder	1 tsp
1	lemon, grated rind and juice	1
2 tbsp	concentrated apple juice	2 tbsp
1¼ pints	soya, nut or rice milk	725 ml
4 oz	fresh blueberries	110 g
1 tbsp	flour for dusting	1 tbsp
	olive oil spray or kitchen paper dipped in olive oil	

Stir together the flour, bicarbonate of soda, baking powder and grated lemon rind. In a separate bowl combine the lemon juice, concentrated apple juice and soya milk, then stir into the flour mixture until combined. Toss the blueberries in the remaining tablespoon of flour.

Heat a large, heavy frying pan, spray with olive oil or wipe round with kitchen paper dipped in olive oil, and ladle out tablespoonfuls of batter. Place a few blueberries on each pancake as the first side is cooking, then as soon as they are beginning to look dry, turn over and cook the other side until lightly browned. Makes about 24 pancakes – 6 servings.

PER SERVING	
Energy Kcals	276.5
Protein g	11.5
Carbohydrates g	49.2
Dietary Fibre g	9.1
Fat – Total g	5.8
Saturated Fat g	0.8
Polyunsaturated Fat g	1.7
Calcium mg	67.2
Magnesium mg	104.9

Eggs contain a phospholipid called lecithin. Although they contain cholesterol, this lecithin actually increases levels of HDL cholesterol (the 'good' sort) in your blood. They also contain carotenoids which give the yolks their yellow colour. The brighter yellow the yolk, the more carotenoids they contain. They are also a good source of sulphur-containing protein (good for detoxification), iron and selenium.

Courgette Scramble

This is a very easy and quick variation on scrambled eggs. If you find the prospect of garlic for breakfast too daunting, either leave it out altogether or substitute some finely chopped onion or chives.

4	small courgettes	4
4	organic, free-range eggs	4
2 tbsp	soya milk	2 tbsp
	low-sodium salt and freshly ground black pepper	
1 tbsp	extra virgin olive oil	1 tbsp
1	clove garlic, finely chopped	1
2 tbsp	fresh basil, torn into small shreds	2 tbsp
1 tbsp	flat-leaf parsley, chopped	1 tbsp

Wash the courgettes and grate coarsely, then squeeze with your hands to get rid of excess moisture. Beat the eggs with the soya milk and seasoning to taste, then set aside. Heat the oil in a wide frying pan and sauté the grated courgettes and chopped garlic, stirring frequently, until just beginning to colour. The pour in the beaten egg mixture, let it set for a minute, then stir with a wooden spoon, as for scrambled eggs. Add the chopped herbs at the last minute. Serve hot. Serves 2.

PER SERVING	
Energy Kcals	217.1
Protein g	13.2
Carbohydrates g	5.7
Dietary Fibre g	2.1
Fat – Total g	16.1
Saturated Fat g	3.7
Polyunsaturated Fat g	2.0
Calcium mg	71.7
Magnesium mg	46.0

There's a lot of good nutrition in this apparently simple dish. Mushrooms are a good source of boron, a very elusive mineral needed to help synthesise oestrogen, and the potatoes in this frittata provide nearly a quarter of your daily vitamin C requirement in one meal.

Potato and Mushroom Frittata

A frittata is an Italian omelette, closely akin to the Spanish tortilla. It's easy to make and doesn't take long. I make this when I have too many potatoes left over from the night before. For a change, try celery leaves, fresh lovage or other fresh herbs instead of the parsley.

1 lb	potatoes, cooked in their skins, cooled and sliced	1 lb
4 oz	button mushrooms, quartered if large	110 g
2 tbsp	extra virgin olive oil	2 tbsp
6	organic, free-range eggs	6
	low-sodium salt and freshly ground black pepper	
2 tbsp	flat-leaf parsley, chopped	2 tbsp

Heat the oil in a large frying pan and gently sauté the potatoes until lightly coloured, turning them once or twice. Add the mushrooms and cook for another 2-3 minutes. Beat the eggs with seasoning to taste, and add half the parsley. Pour the eggs into the pan and continue cooking over gentle heat until nearly set. If you like your frittata quite firm, preheat the grill while the frittata is cooking, then slip the frying pan under the grill for a minute or two, just to set the top. Serve hot or at room temperature, cut into wedges. Serves 4.

PER SERVING	
Energy Kcals	250.0
Protein g	10.9
Carbohydrates g	21.6
Dietary Fibre g	2.3
Fat – Total g	13.6
Saturated Fat g	3.0
Polyunsaturated Fat g	1.5
Calcium mg	41.2
Magnesium mg	31.6

SPREADS

The hardest thing to change in my diet has been my predilection for butter. There's nothing I used to like more than a piece of hot brown toast, liberally spread with butter and honey, and a cup of freshly brewed coffee. Although butter is not the 'demon' food it's sometimes made out to be, clearly I had to reduce my saturated fat intake. How was I going to replace it with a more healthy, unprocessed, unsaturated fat and still feel satisfied? Margarines are not the answer. All of them, though trumpeting the fact that they are made from polyunsaturated fat, are highly processed. During the processing, those polyunsaturated fats are turned from a liquid into a solid. How is this done? By hydrogenation, which means adding hydrogen atoms, thereby saturating the fat, and *voilà*, a fat that is no longer polyunsaturated, and is damaged (and damaging to anyone who eats it) into the bargain. There are one or two margarines on the market that are not made from hydrogenated fats (Granose is one of them), but they are few and far between.

I have experimented with mixtures of butter and olive oil, adding lecithin to emulsify the mixture, but I don't find them very successful. Olive oil will thicken almost to a spreading consistency in a very cold fridge, and this works quite well as long as your toast is not too hot. Failing that, use butter, but do choose organic butter if possible.

However, for spreading on your toast there is a better and more natural alternative: nut and seed butters. They are packed with nutrition, easy to digest, and a little goes a long way. There are plenty of nut butters to be found in health food shops, or you could make your own. One I particularly recommend is almond butter, as almonds are a fantastic source of calcium, and it is delicious as well. A new seed butter on the market, made by Omega Nutrition and distributed by Higher Nature, is pumpkin seed butter, which is a beautiful olive green colour, and a very good source of essential fatty acids (see Useful Addresses).

A word of caution about nuts, seeds and nut butters. Because of their highly unsaturated fat content, they are all prone to rancidity if not stored carefully. Always purchase in small quantities and keep them away from heat and light, preferably in the fridge. Nuts do also have high allergenic potential, and should of course be avoided by those who are allergic to them.

NUT AND SEED BUTTERS

Grind your chosen nuts or seeds in an electric grinder until a fine powder is formed. Turn out into a bowl and add a little cold pressed oil, if possible of a complementary flavour, eg almond oil for almonds, pumpkin seed oil for pumpkin seeds, walnut oil for walnuts and cashews etc. Stir until amalgamated. Add a little more oil if necessary, until the desired consistency is reached. Your home-made nut or seed butter will never be as smooth as those you can buy commercially, because a domestic blender cannot grind as finely. Also the oil will separate on standing, as you are not using emulsifiers. Just stir the oil back in before using. Keep your nut or seed butter refrigerated at all times.

Tahini is similar to a nut or seed butter, being made of ground sesame seeds. I have tried to make it myself but could never make the texture smooth enough. It is easy to find in health food shops, though. Look for the dark tahini which is made of whole unhulled sesame seeds, rather than the light variety, which has less fibre. Mix it with an equal proportion of honey for a delicious and nutritious spread for your toast.

Miso is a very concentrated fermented soya bean paste, full of protein and minerals, particularly selenium. There is some evidence that eating fermented soya products like miso is more beneficial for the control of hot flushes than unfermented soya in the form of soya milk or tofu[23].

Ursula's Energy Spread

This mixture, which isn't really a recipe, comes from Ursula Ferrigno, my tutor at the Vegetarian Society. It is quite a salty, savoury spread if you use brown rice miso and would be a good substitute if you like Marmite and butter on your toast. Sweet white miso would be the better choice if you prefer a sweet spread.

1 tbsp	miso	1 tbsp
1 tbsp	dark tahini	1 tbsp

Mix together and spread on toast or crackers. Serves 1.

PANCAKE SYRUPS AND SWEET SAUCES

Use these syrups and sauces on porridge and pancakes in place of sugar, golden syrup or honey.

Molasses Syrup

Molasses is a particularly rich source of iron. A serving of this syrup provides over half your daily requirement. Eating a vitamin-C rich food at the same meal, such as a glass of juice, will help your body to absorb the iron.

This syrup is very nutritious, having all the advantages of molasses with the phytoestrogens in soya as well.

8 oz	silken tofu	225 g
4 fl oz	soya, nut or rice milk	120 ml
5 fl oz	blackstrap molasses	150 ml

Blend all ingredients until smooth. Serves 6.

PER SERVING	
Energy Kcals	107.8
Protein g	2.4
Carbohydrates g	22.2
Dietary Fibre g	0.3
Fat – Total g	1.4
Saturated Fat g	0.2
Polyunsaturated Fat g	0.8
Calcium mg	306.4
Magnesium mg	88.3

23 Nagata C et al. Hot flushes and other menopausal symptoms in relation to soy product intake in Japanese women. *Climacteric* 1999 Mar;2(1):6-12.

Prunes are rich in fibre and known for their laxative properties. They are also full of minerals, particularly potassium and magnesium. This sauce has a good magnesium:calcium ratio, so eat it often.

PER SERVING	
Energy Kcals	75.0
Protein g	1.9
Carbohydrates g	14.4
Dietary Fibre g	3.2
Fat – Total g	1.6
Saturated Fat g	0.2
Polyunsaturated Fat g	0.9
Calcium mg	14.5
Magnesium mg	21.8

Prune Whip Sauce

This is an adaptation from a recipe in *Laurel's Kitchen*. Cook the prunes the night before so they are cold when you come to make the sauce.

4 oz	prunes, pitted	110 g
1½ tbsp	ground flax seeds	1½ tbsp
3½ fl oz	soya, nut or rice milk	100 ml

Cook the prunes in water to cover until soft (15-20 minutes). Drain and reserve 3 fl oz/90 ml of the juice. When the prunes are cold, put all ingredients into a blender and blend until smooth. Serve with pancakes. Serves 4.

You could use commercial orange or apple juice if you don't have time to make your own. The nutritional composition per serving is based on home-made apple juice.

PER SERVING	
Energy Kcals	94.5
Protein g	5.1
Carbohydrates g	13.6
Dietary Fibre g	1.7
Fat – Total g	2.7
Saturated Fat g	0.5
Polyunsaturated Fat g	0.8
Calcium mg	78.3
Magnesium mg	12.0

Tofu Whizz

I invented this as a way of introducing more tofu onto the breakfast menu.

8 oz	firm tofu (1 packet)	225 g
4 fl oz	home-made fruit juice (see pages 3-4)	120 ml
1	banana	1
1 tbsp	honey or rice syrup	1 tbsp

Put all the ingredients into the blender and blend until smooth. Use as a sauce on pancakes. Serves 6.

Nut Milks

Any nuts can be turned into milk, giving you an easily digestible way to assimilate the protein, monounsaturated fat and vitamin E to be found in nuts. The flavour makes a change from ordinary milk, too.

Almond Milk

Be sure to use pure almond essence and not almond flavouring, which isn't made from almonds at all.

6 oz	whole almonds	175 g
1¹/₄ pints	filtered or bottled water	725 ml
¹/₂ tsp	pure almond essence	¹/₂ tsp

Soak the almonds in water overnight. Drain well, discarding the soaking water, and grind in a blender until the almonds resemble breadcrumbs. Add ³/₄ pint/425 ml of the filtered or bottled water gradually as for mayonnaise. Let stand until the mixture begins to thicken.

Strain the resulting mixture through a wire sieve into a bowl. Lift the almond meal from the strainer with a spoon, but do not press on the mixture or grainy bits of ground almond will get pushed through the sieve into the milk.

Return the almond meal to the blender and add 150 ml/¹/₄ pint water, then put through the sieve again. Repeat with the last 150 ml/¹/₄ pint water. Discard almond meal, and add the almond essence to the almond milk. Use immediately or store for up to five days in the fridge.

This method can be used for any nuts or seeds, such as cashews, walnuts, pecans, sesame seeds or sunflower seeds (omit the almond essence, or substitute pure vanilla essence). Serves 4.

PER SERVING	
Energy Kcals	257.5
Protein g	8.8
Carbohydrates g	8.6
Dietary Fibre g	5.3
Fat – Total g	21.4
Saturated Fat g	1.5
Polyunsaturated Fat g	4.9
Calcium mg	3.7
Magnesium mg	1.9

Sandwiches, Light Meals and Snacks

In an ideal world, we would be eating our main meal in the middle of the day and eating more lightly at night. However, the world is not ideal, and whether we are working outside the home or not, lunch tends to be a quick snack and the main meal is saved for the evening. This chapter gives some ideas as to how to turn that hastily grabbed snack into a healthful, nutritious midday boost. Unusually, I have resorted to some tinned foods in this chapter in the interests of convenience – for example, tinned beans and tinned tomatoes. Choose a reliable wholefood brand such as Suma or Meridian, and choose products that are organic, not genetically modified, and that are packed without added sugar or salt. It is advisable not to rely too heavily on tinned foods, however, as the plastic lining of the tins can leach oestrogen-like chemicals into the food which, although in small quantities will probably do us no harm, are not desirable in large quantities. But we live in the real world, and not everybody has the time to soak and cook beans from scratch. If you do, so much the better. If you don't, limit tinned foods to once or twice a week.

We need to make sure that any meal taken in the middle of the day has some slow release carbohydrate to keep us going through the afternoon, some protein to help our bodies get on with the good work of maintenance and repair, some phytonutrients from fruit and vegetables, and some essential fatty acids to help us keep our hormones in balance. I have included some ideas for sandwich fillings, some light dishes that require cooking if you're at home, some quick snacks and ideas for foods to keep in your desk drawer or the glovebox of your car if you're driving around. Salads also make good lunches, as long as you choose a substantial one which contains both some protein and some starch to keep you going. Don't forget soup either – it is filling, nutritious and easy to carry in a thermos flask. See the soup chapter for ideas.

SANDWICHES

The sandwich is the quintessential working lunch. It is portable, quick to put together and can be nutritious if the filling is carefully chosen. At one time, I ran a small organic sandwich business and tried to encourage my customers to choose the more healthful fillings. But to no avail – invariably the most popular filling was cheese and coleslaw with lots of mayonnnaise – a fat-laden lunch even if it was all organic!

Use any of the breads in the Breads and Baking chapter, and try some of the fillings below, all of which can be made the night before. Other ideas can be found in the section on starters.

Grilled Tofu

Choose a brand of tofu that has been processed using calcium sulphate (for example Cauldron Foods), and you've instantly boosted your intake of calcium to help maintain bone density after menopause.

8½ oz	block tofu	250 g
2 tbsp	tamari sauce	2 tbsp
2 tbsp	cold-pressed sesame oil	2 tbsp
1	clove garlic, crushed	1
	piece of root ginger, peeled and grated (1 inch/2.5 cm piece)	
	miso, beansprouts, lettuce, tomato and cucumber to serve	

Drain and rinse the tofu, wrap in kitchen paper, and squeeze out as much of the moisture as you can. Alternatively, place a heavy weight on it for 10 minutes or so to get rid of all the moisture. Meanwhile, mix together the tamari, sesame oil, garlic and ginger.

Slice the tofu into thin slices, put into a shallow dish, pour over the tamari mixture, cover and refrigerate for about an hour or overnight.

Grill the marinated tofu slices under a hot grill for a few minutes, turning once. Cool and sandwich between two slices of bread spread with a thin smear of miso. Add beansprouts (see page 125), lettuce, tomato and cucumber to taste. Serves 2.

As well as being a good source of calcium, protein and isoflavones, tofu contains a good level of all the B vitamins, including folic acid, which are essential for the production of energy, so a grilled tofu sandwich should see you through the afternoon.

PER SERVING	
Energy Kcals	229.5
Protein g	18.5
Carbohydrates g	4.1
Dietary Fibre g	0.6
Fat – Total g	22.6
Saturated Fat g	3.8
Polyunsaturated Fat g	8.6
Calcium mg	255.3
Magnesium mg	40.2

Although this recipe is relatively high in calories, this pâté is nutritionally dense food, in which all the calories are working for you. The beans provide a significant amount of protein, fibre, iron and other minerals, while the apricots are a particularly rich source of potassium which helps to lower blood pressure.

Bean and Apricot Pâté

This is an unusual and tasty mixture, and goes well in a rye bread sandwich. If you don't have time to soak and cook dried beans, use a 14 oz/400 g can, drain the beans and rinse thoroughly before proceeding with the recipe.

3$\frac{1}{2}$ oz	dried white haricot beans	100 g
4 oz	dried unsulphured apricots, soaked	110 g
$\frac{1}{2}$ tsp	ground cumin	$\frac{1}{2}$ tsp
1 tbsp	extra virgin olive oil	1 tbsp
	low-sodium salt and freshly ground black pepper to taste	

Soak the beans overnight, then drain and refresh. Cover with cold water, bring to the boil, boil for 10 minutes, then lower the heat to a simmer and cook until tender. The time depends on the age of the beans, but is usually about 1 to 1$\frac{1}{2}$ hrs. When they are cooked, remove from the heat and drain, reserving a little of the liquid, then leave to cool.

Mash the beans with a potato masher or the end of a rolling pin. (Don't use a blender as this will make the consistency too smooth.) Chop the apricots finely and beat them into the beans with enough olive oil to make a stiff mixture. Add the cumin and season to taste. Serves 4.

PER SERVING	
Energy Kcals	378.2
Protein g	12.0
Carbohydrates g	65.6
Dietary Fibre g	10.4
Fat – Total g	7.9
Saturated Fat g	1.1
Polyunsaturated Fat g	0.9
Calcium mg	11.5
Magnesium mg	66.9

You could use yellow or orange peppers here, but red peppers are such a wonderful colour, aren't they? That colour is an indication of the nutrients they contain – each serving has over 2,500 mcg of beta-carotene and more than twice the RNI of vitamin C, though, being water-soluble, some of it is lost in cooking. That's why it's important to consume the pepper juice as it will contain a significant quantity of vitamin C.

Red Pepper and Tofu Pâté

Be careful not to make this mixture too wet. A sandwich filling must be firm and not soak into the bread, so hold back on the pepper juice as you may not need it. You can always add it to a salad dressing, as it's tasty and very nutritious.

2	large red peppers	2
2	garlic cloves, peeled	2
6 oz	tofu, drained, rinsed and dried (about 3/4 of a block)	170 g
2 tsp	balsamic vinegar	2 tsp
pinch	cayenne pepper	pinch

First grill the peppers under a hot grill until charred, turning once or twice. Leave to cool in a plastic bag, which makes the skin much easier to remove. When the peppers are cool enough to handle, slip off the skins, discarding the cores and seeds but retaining the juice. Chop roughly and transfer to a food processor together with the garlic, tofu and balsamic vinegar. Process until smooth, adding the pepper juice to achieve the right consistency. Serve as a sandwich filling with watercress or bean sprouts. Serves 4.

PER SERVING	
Energy Kcals	76.5
Protein g	6.3
Carbohydrates g	6.7
Dietary Fibre g	1.8
Fat – Total g	3.1
Saturated Fat g	0.6
Polyunsaturated Fat g	1.0
Calcium mg	96.0
Magnesium mg	20.2

Hummus is also particularly delicious, with or without the sun-dried tomatoes, as a sandwich filling with grated carrot. The smoothness of the hummus and the crunchiness of the carrots are very good together.

Hummus with Sun-Dried Tomatoes

Hummus is quite high in fat, but the home-made version is much less so than that which is offered in the supermarkets, and has a much more robust texture. It only takes a few minutes to make, and the addition of sun-dried tomatoes adds piquancy. If you don't have time to soak and cook dried chickpeas, use a 14 oz/400 g can, drain and rinse well, then proceed with the recipe. If you are using canned beans and need more liquid, use a little water.

3¹/₂ oz	dried chickpeas	100 g
3 tbsp	dark tahini (made from whole sesame seeds)	3 tbsp
1¹/₂	lemons, juiced	1¹/₂
2 tbsp	extra virgin olive oil	2 tbsp
3	garlic cloves, peeled and chopped roughly	3
2 tsp	ground cumin	2 tsp
	low-sodium salt and freshly ground black pepper	
6	sun-dried tomatoes, soaked in hot water for 20 minutes, then chopped	6
	handful of fresh basil, torn into small pieces	

Soak the chickpeas overnight, then drain and rinse. Cover with cold water, bring to the boil, boil for 10 minutes, then lower the heat to a simmer and cook until tender. The time depends on the age of the chickpeas. They can take anything from 1¹/₂ hrs to 2¹/₂ hrs, so check from time to time. When they are cooked, remove from the heat and drain, reserving a little of the liquid, then leave to cool.

Process the cooled chickpeas in a food processor, then add the tahini, lemon juice, olive oil, garlic, cumin, salt and pepper. Process until smooth, adding some of the reserved liquid to achieve the right consistency. (If the hummus is to be used as a sandwich filling, keep it quite stiff; if as a dip, add more liquid to make it really creamy.) Taste for seasoning and adjust the amount of lemon juice if necessary. Turn out into a bowl and stir in the chopped sun-dried tomatoes and basil. Serves 6.

PER SERVING	
Energy Kcals	187.1
Protein g	4.7
Carbohydrates g	12.1
Dietary Fibre g	2.9
Fat – Total g	14.0
Saturated Fat g	1.9
Polyunsaturated Fat g	2.9
Calcium mg	51.6
Magnesium mg	37.7

Other Sandwich Suggestions

Avocado sliced or mashed with a dash of lime juice, chopped coriander and toasted sunflower seeds, topped with lettuce; peanut butter and fresh bean sprouts; almond butter and chopped dried figs; mashed banana and chopped cashew nuts; grilled aubergine slices with basil and sliced tomatoes; chicken, lemon garlic mayonnaise and rocket; tuna with Menopause Mayonnaise and salad (add some flax oil to the tuna, as tinned tuna has had all its own valuable Omega-3 oil removed); tinned sardines, drained and mashed, with cucumber and lemon juice; smoked mackerel mixed with Menopause Mayonnaise and chopped chives.

Menopause Mayonnaise

The inspiration for this mayonnaise came from Adam Palmer's wonderful *Champneys Cookbook*, so the idea of using potato as a base is not mine. However, I hope that my treatment of it, adding flax seed, garlic and yoghurt, is original – it is certainly a lot more nutritious than traditional mayonnaise.

1	large baking potato (about 8 oz/225 g)	1
2	garlic cloves, left whole	2
2 tbsp	extra virgin olive oil	2 tbsp
$1/2$	lemon, juiced	$1/2$
	low-sodium salt and freshly ground black pepper	
2 tbsp	flax seed, ground	2 tbsp
1 tbsp	soya yoghurt or live natural yoghurt	1 tbsp

For speed, you could boil the potato instead of baking it, but it wouldn't have such a soft texture. A pretty and delicious variation is to subsitute a red pepper for the lemon and garlic. Roast the pepper for about 25 minutes, or until charred. Cool in a plastic bag, then deseed and chop.
Add to the food processor with the potato.

Preheat the oven to 200°C/400°F/Gas Mark 6.
   Prick the potato all over with a fork and bake until soft – about 1 hour.
   Next, boil the garlic cloves in a little water for 3-4 minutes (this is to mellow the flavour), then drain, peel and chop.
   When the potato has cooked, cut in half and leave to cool for a bit. Then scrape out the potato flesh into the food processor together with the chopped garlic, and process until smooth. Dribble in the olive oil, lemon juice and seasoning. Lastly, stir in the ground flax seed and yoghurt to make a creamy mixture. Use in sandwiches, on pasta, or with salads. Makes about 8 servings.

PER SERVING	
Energy Kcals	85.3
Protein g	1.4
Carbohydrates g	10.8
Dietary Fibre g	1.5
Fat – Total g	4.3
Saturated Fat g	0.6
Polyunsaturated Fat g	0.8
Calcium mg	12.5
Magnesium mg	17.8

LIGHT MEALS

What springs to mind when you think of a 'light meal'? Welsh Rarebit, perhaps – something really quick to put together, probably on toast. If you are to avoid the pitfalls of high fat junk food, keep a few healthy ingredients handy and you can whip up a healthful snack in no time. Most of the dishes that follow can be ready in under half an hour.

Watercress is a lot more than just a garnish. It contains iron together with vitamin C and beta carotene which help your body absorb the iron. Furthermore, it also contains isothiocyanates which may inhibit the formation of cancer cells.

Toasted Smoked Mackerel Sandwich

Mackerel is one of the oily fish that contain good levels of Omega-3 fatty acids. However, some nutritionists are concerned that smoked fish is carcinogenic. As always, I take a middle course, and would advise adding smoked mackerel to your diet once a week or so. They are cheap, readily available, and their nutritional advantages, to my mind, outweigh the disadvantages. Besides, they do taste good, especially in this little number. Choose smoked mackerel without artificial colouring.

1 oz	really quick hummus (see page 39)	30 g
4	small smoked mackerel fillets	4
2 tsp	horseradish sauce	2 tsp
	freshly ground black pepper and a squeeze of lemon juice	
8	slices calcium bread (see page 167)	8
2	bunches watercress	2

Skin and flake the mackerel and mix with the horseradish sauce. Season with black pepper and a squeeze of lemon juice to taste.

Wash the watercress well to remove any dirt, and tear into 'fork-friendly' pieces.

Preheat the grill. Toast the bread on one side only, then spread the untoasted side with the hummus. Spoon the mackerel on to four of the slices and grill for 2-3 minutes. Top with the remaining four slices of toast, press together firmly and cut each sandwich in half. Serve with the fresh, unadorned watercress. Serves 4.

PER SERVING	
Energy Kcals	368.8
Protein g	22.0
Carbohydrates g	38.4
Dietary Fibre g	4.9
Fat – Total g	14.3
Saturated Fat g	2.1
Polyunsaturated Fat g	2.8
Calcium mg	46.0
Magnesium mg	65.6

Home-made breads don't have the same 'shelf life' as bread bought in the supermarket, but that's because they don't contain preservatives. This means that they are particularly suited to using for crostini and toasted sandwiches a couple of days after baking.

Sourdough Rye Crostini with Aubergine Purée

Crostini are usually made with white French or Italian bread, but they are unusual and different made with sourdough rye. You can prepare the crostini in advance and keep them in an airtight tin, and if you have prepared the aubergine purée earlier, this is really quick to put together.

4	generous slices of Sourdough Rye with seeds (see page 165)	4
3 tbsp	extra virgin olive oil	3 tbsp
2	medium aubergines	2
1	clove garlic	1
1 tbsp	soya yoghurt or natural live yoghurt	1 tbsp
1/2	lemon, juiced	1/2
1 tbsp	chopped flat-leaf parsley	1 tbsp
	low-sodium salt and freshly ground black pepper	
4	sun-dried tomatoes	4
	fresh basil leaves	

Preheat the oven to 200°C/400°F/Gas Mark 6.

Brush both sides of the slices of bread using 1 tablespoon of the olive oil. Place the slices on a baking tray and bake for 10-12 minutes until brown. At the same time, prick the aubergines in one or two places, then place in a roasting tin and roast for 25-30 minutes until the skins are charred. Pricking the skins stops them from exploding, which is what happened to me once – there was a loud bang and aubergine purée all over the oven!

Take the toasted bread out of the oven and leave to cool while the aubergines finish cooking.

Scoop the flesh of the aubergines from their skins and put in the food processor with the garlic, yoghurt, lemon juice, salt and pepper. With the motor running, gradually add the remaining olive oil until a thick purée is formed.

Cut the sun-dried tomatoes into strips. To serve, spread the aubergine purée on the crostini, and decorate with sun-dried tomato strips and basil leaves. Serves 4.

PER SERVING	
Energy Kcals	215.8
Protein g	8.4
Carbohydrates g	37.4
Dietary Fibre g	9.5
Fat – Total g	5.8
Saturated Fat g	0.7
Polyunsaturated Fat g	1.0
Calcium mg	52.4
Magnesium mg	48.2

Three good reasons to eat sardines: canned sardines still contain their bones (don't buy filletted sardines, the bones will have been removed), which are a good source of calcium to help build and maintain our own bones. The Omega-3 fatty acids in sardines protect us against heart disease. Sardines also provide vitamin D, which helps to improve calcium absorption and decrease its excretion.

Sardine Bruschetta

Do not scorn the humble tinned sardine, as it is a very nutritious food. I usually buy the pretty retro tins of Portuguese sardines packed in olive oil. Here they've been transformed into rather a grand version of sardines on toast.

2	tins sardines in olive oil	2
4	generous slices of calcium bread (see page 167)	4
2	red peppers	2
2	red onions, peeled and thinly sliced	2
	freshly ground black pepper	
1 tbsp	chopped flat-leaf parsley	1 tbsp

Preheat the oven to 200°C/400°F/Gas Mark 6.

First, drain the olive oil from the sardines and set them aside, reserving the oil.

Brush both sides of the slices of bread with some of the oil from the sardines. Place the slices on a baking tray and bake for 10-12 minutes until brown.

Put the rest of the oil from the sardines into a small frying pan, heat gently and sauté the onion slices until soft but not browned.

Meanwhile, put the red peppers on a baking tray and roast them for 20 minutes until charred. Place in a plastic bag for a few minutes to cool, then peel, remove the core and seeds, and cut into strips.

To heat the sardines, put them on the baking tray when the peppers come out of the oven, and heat them in the oven for a few minutes while you are cooling and slicing the peppers. To serve, top each slice of toasted bread with the red pepper slices, the sautéed onions and the sardines. Season with black pepper and sprinkle with chopped parsley. Serves 4.

PER SERVING	
Energy Kcals	298.9
Protein g	18.7
Carbohydrates g	29.6
Dietary Fibre g	5.2
Fat – Total g	12.4
Saturated Fat g	2.1
Polyunsaturated Fat g	5.0
Calcium mg	240.0
Magnesium mg	81.4

This would be delicious made using the Sun-Dried Tomato Hummus on page 27.

Roasted Red Pepper, Hummus and Rocket Open Sandwiches

I adore rocket, and was often known to buy a packet and eat the entire contents then and there before I discovered how easy it is to grow, thereby saving quite a lot on the weekly food bill. I now grow it in odd corners of the garden.

It grows like a weed, and you can cut and come again, so you don't need to re-seed. You could grow it in a window box too.

1	red pepper	1
4 oz	really quick hummus (see page 39)	110 g
8 slices	pumpernickel	8 slices
	rocket, 2 handfuls, washed and dried	

Preheat the oven to 200°C/400°F/Gas Mark 6.

Put the pepper on a baking tray and roast for 20 minutes, turning once, until charred. Put in a plastic bag to cool, then peel off the skin. Slice the pepper into thin strips, discarding the core and seeds.

To assemble the sandwiches, spread the slices of pumpernickel with hummus, layer strips of red pepper over the hummus, and top with rocket. Serves 4, 2 slices per serving.

PER SERVING	
Energy Kcals	251.6
Protein g	11.4
Carbohydrates g	49.1
Dietary Fibre g	10.8
Fat – Total g	3.3
Saturated Fat g	0.4
Polyunsaturated Fat g	1.1
Calcium mg	81.7
Magnesium mg	95.7

Whenever you make polenta, always make too much, as it is so delicious grilled, or baked as in these pizzas. You can buy it ready made, but that's a poor substitute.

Polenta and Tofu Pizzas

For these, use cooked and cooled polenta (see page 76), about 1/2 inch/1 cm thick, and stamp out into rounds about 4 inch/10 cm in diameter.

4 oz	sun-dried tomatoes in oil	110 g
8	4 inch/10 cm rounds cooked polenta (about 1 1/2 inch/1 cm thick)	8
2 tsp	extra virgin olive oil	2 tsp
4 1/2 oz	firm tofu (half a block), drained and pressed, sliced into 8 thin slices	125 g
3	medium tomatoes, sliced	3
1	garlic clove, chopped	1
8	fresh basil leaves	8

Preheat the oven to 230°C/450°F/Gas Mark 8.

Process the sun-dried tomatoes with some of their oil in the food processor until puréed. Brush the polenta slices with extra virgin olive oil, top with the sun-dried tomato purée, then add the tofu slices and tomato slices. (You might want to trim the tofu slices into rounds, for the sake of neatness, but it's not necessary.) Divide the chopped garlic between the pizzas and sprinkle with more olive oil. Bake in the very hot oven for about 10-12 minutes, and serve garnished with fresh whole basil leaves. Serves 4.

PER SERVING	
Energy Kcals	289.1
Protein g	10.1
Carbohydrates g	45.6
Dietary Fibre g	6.6
Fat – Total g	8.7
Saturated Fat g	1.3
Polyunsaturated Fat g	1.6
Calcium mg	83.3
Magnesium mg	42.5

Onions are a very good source of chromium, an elusive mineral which we need in small quantities to help us balance our blood sugar, so include some onions somewhere in your lunch box, and maybe that will help you avoid the cakes and biscuits at tea-time.

Tofu and Almond Burgers

These are easy and quick to make, and are a good store cupboard standby for a weekday lunch.

1 tbsp	extra virgin olive oil	1 tbsp
1	large carrot, grated	1
1	large onion, grated	1
2 tsp	curry paste	2 tsp
8½ oz	packet tofu, rinsed and drained	250 g
1 oz	wholemeal breadcrumbs	30 g
1 oz	whole almonds, finely chopped	30 g
1 oz	flax seed, ground	30 g
	a handful of fresh coriander, chopped	
	low-sodium salt and freshly ground black pepper	
2 tbsp	wholemeal flour for coating	2 tbsp
2 tsp	extra virgin olive oil or use olive oil spray	2 tsp

Heat 1 tablespoonful of olive oil in a large frying pan. Add the carrot and onion and fry until softened, stirring frequently. Add the curry paste and continue frying for a further minute or two.

Meanwhile wrap the drained tofu in kitchen paper and squeeze or press it to get rid of the excess moisture. Mash with a fork or potato masher, then stir into the vegetables with the almonds, flax seed and coriander. Season to taste, then work the mixture until it holds together, adding a little water if necessary. Turn out the mixture onto a floured board and shape into eight burgers and dust with a little more flour.

Spray burgers with olive oil spray or drizzle with a little olive oil, and grill under a hot grill for about 4 minutes each side until golden. Serve with a cucumber and tomato salad or some fresh salsa (see page 53) and a green salad. Serves 4.

PER SERVING	
Energy Kcals	273.5
Protein g	13.0
Carbohydrates g	17.4
Dietary Fibre g	5.2
Fat – Total g	17.4
Saturated Fat g	2.3
Polyunsaturated Fat g	4.4
Calcium mg	153.0
Magnesium mg	49.6

You don't have to go to the trouble of making individual frittatas. If you're in a hurry, you could equally well make one large one and cut it into segments.

Little Vegetable Frittatas

These little frittatas are very pretty and quick to make – useful when you have some cooked vegetables left over from a previous meal. I sometimes deliberately steam more vegetables than I need so there will be some left over to make frittatas with.

7 oz	lightly cooked vegetables, such as leeks, carrots, peas, broccoli, cauliflower or courgettes	200 g
4 oz	baby spinach	110 g
6	organic, free-range eggs	6
4 tbsp	soya milk	4 tbsp
	freshly grated nutmeg, low-sodium salt and freshly grated black pepper to taste	
2 tsp	extra virgin olive oil, or use olive oil spray	2 tsp
3	tomatoes, skinned, deseeded and diced	3
	torn basil leaves, for garnish	

Slice or chop the vegetables to a suitable size to fit into 4 inch/10 cm egg poaching rings.

Pour boiling water over the spinach so that it wilts without cooking. Drain and press to extract as much liquid as possible and chop very roughly.

Whisk together the eggs, soya milk and seasoning. Stir in the sliced or chopped vegetables and spinach.

Spray a large non-stick frying pan and the insides of four egg poaching rings with olive oil spray, or use kitchen paper dipped in olive oil. Place the poaching rings in the pan and divide the egg mixture between the four rings. Fry over a gentle heat for 5 minutes until nearly set.

Meanwhile, preheat the grill, and slide the pan under the grill for a couple of minutes to cook the tops.

Remove the poaching rings, and serve the frittatas garnished with the chopped tomatoes and basil leaves. Serves 4.

PER SERVING	
Energy Kcals	151.4
Protein g	10.6
Carbohydrates g	11.1
Dietary Fibre g	2.2
Fat – Total g	7.5
Saturated Fat g	2.1
Polyunsaturated Fat g	1.1
Calcium mg	89.0
Magnesium mg	38.0

When choosing vegetables, go for freshness above all, because the vitamin content, at its peak when the vegetable is harvested, drops rapidly from then until the time you cook it. More is lost in cooking, too, so always cook for the minimum time possible.

Poached Eggs on Green Vegetable Purée

There is almost nothing as quick to cook as green vegetables, or as important in our diet, yet they are rarely seen in so-called 'quick' dishes. This recipe uses almost the same ingredients as for the little frittatas, yet with very different results. Use any green vegetables you have to hand, such as fresh spinach, broccoli, Swiss chard, courgettes, broad beans or fresh peas.

1¹/₂ lbs	mixed fresh green vegetables	675 g
	low-sodium salt and freshly ground black pepper	
4	free range eggs	4
2 tsp	sesame seed, toasted	2 tsp

Wash and roughly chop the vegetables. Put in a pan with 2 tablespoons of water, cover tightly and cook for about 7 minutes, until all vegetables are just tender. Meanwhile, poach the eggs. Take the vegetables off the heat, allow to cool slightly, then blend or process in the food processor until a rough purée is formed. Taste and adjust seasoning, and serve the eggs, one per person, on a bed of vegetable purée, with the toasted sesame seeds sprinkled on top. Serves 4.

PER SERVING	
Energy Kcals	151.6
Protein g	11.5
Carbohydrates g	13.1
Dietary Fibre g	5.5
Fat – Total g	6.7
Saturated Fat g	1.7
Polyunsaturated Fat g	1.6
Calcium mg	128.7
Magnesium mg	98.1

Huevos Rancheros

People eat this for breakfast in Mexico, and very delicious it is with corn tortillas to mop up the sauce. If you suffer badly from hot flushes, you might want to leave out the chilli, or replace it with a clove of garlic.

4	organic free-range eggs	4
2 tbsp	extra virgin olive oil	2 tbsp
1	onion, finely chopped	1
1	large tin chopped tomatoes	1
1 hpd tsp	ground coriander	1 hpd tsp
1	small, mild green chilli pepper, chopped and de-seeded	1
1	bunch of coriander leaves, washed and chopped	1
1	bunch of spring onions, including the green tops, chopped	1
	salt and pepper to taste	
1	avocado, roughly mashed with a little lime juice	1

Pre-heat the oven to 180°C/350°F/Gas Mark 4.

Heat the olive oil gently and sauté the onion lightly just until it begins to turn colour. Add the tinned tomatoes and their juice, the ground coriander and half the coriander leaves. Leave to simmer for at least 15 minutes to bring out all the flavours. Season to taste and transfer to a large, fairly shallow ovenproof dish. Make depressions in the salsa using the back of a large spoon, crack the eggs into them and place the dish uncovered in the oven. Cook for about 15 minutes, or until the eggs are set. Serve garnished with the spring onions, the rest of the fresh coriander leaves and a spoonful of mashed avocado.

Serves 4.

PER SERVING	
Energy Kcals	276.5
Protein g	11.5
Carbohydrates g	49.2
Dietary Fibre g	9.1
Fat – Total g	5.8
Saturated Fat g	0.8
Polyunsaturated Fat g	1.7
Calcium mg	67.2
Magnesium mg	104.9

You could use green or Puy lentils for this dish if you don't have brown ones.
The lycopene in the name of this dish is an antioxidant provided by the tinned tomatoes. It protects against cancer, particularly prostate cancer, so it is as good for men as it is for women.

Lycopene Lentils

Lentils cook very quickly, so you do not need to use tinned lentils, which don't taste right anyway, in my opinion. This is wonderful comfort food, and can be whipped up in no time from items that are usually in your store cupboard. I usually eat it straight away, but according to Carol Shaw who tested the recipe for me, it actually tastes better the next day when all the flavours have melded. I've never waited that long!

7 oz	brown lentils	200 g
2	bay leaves	2
2 tbsp	extra virgin olive oil	2 tbsp
1	onion, peeled and finely chopped	1
2	garlic cloves, peeled and chopped	2
2	large (14 oz/400 g) tins chopped Italian plum tomatoes	2
	low-sodium salt and freshly ground black pepper	
2 tbsp	fresh parsley, chopped	2 tbsp

Wash the lentils, then cover with cold water, add the bay leaves, and cook for 15-20 minutes or until tender. Drain.
   Meanwhile, sauté the onion and garlic gently in the olive oil until soft but not browned. Add the drained lentils and the tomatoes with their juice, and season to taste. Simmer for 10 minutes or so, until some of the liquid has evaporated. Serve sprinkled with chopped parsley. Serves 4.

PER SERVING	
Energy Kcals	309.5
Protein g	17.4
Carbohydrates g	44.4
Dietary Fibre g	15.8
Fat – Total g	7.4
Saturated Fat g	1.0
Polyunsaturated Fat g	0.9
Calcium mg	61.4
Magnesium mg	64.2

OFFICE DRAWER SNACKS

Finally, here are some ideas for snacks to take to the office or to keep in your car if you travel a lot. On the left are items you could keep in stock all the time, and on the right are items you would need to take to the office or the car each day, as they need to be fresh. The only other things you would need are a knife, a plate and some paper napkins. All these snacks provide some protein, some complex carbohydrate, some fibre and some essential fats, so they should help to keep your blood sugar on an even keel throughout the day.

KEEP IN THE DESK DRAWER OR GLOVE-BOX	BRING FRESH ON THE DAY
Corn cakes, tahini	Miso (spread on corn cakes together with some tahini)
Corn chips	Really quick guacamole*
Mixed pumpkin and sunflower seeds	Apple
Oatcakes	Really quick hummus*, celery sticks
Raw almonds	Apple
Raw unsalted cashew nuts	Banana
Rice cake, tahini	Hard-boiled egg. (Spread tahini on rice cake and top with sliced hard-boiled egg)
Rye cracker, nut butter (try hazelnut butter, or almond butter)	Apple. (Spread nut butter on rye cracker and eat with sliced apple)
Rye crackers	Really quick bean pâté*, cherry tomatoes

* – recipe below.

Really Quick Guacamole

REALLY QUICK GUACAMOLE	
PER SERVING	
Energy Kcals	141.5
Protein g	2.6
Carbohydrates g	8.5
Dietary Fibre g	7.6
Fat – Total g	12.5
Saturated Fat g	2.5
Polyunsaturated Fat g	0.0
Calcium mg	4.2
Magnesium mg	5.0

Whizz in the blender 1 avocado, 1 clove garlic, a very small handful of coriander leaves, a good squeeze of lime or lemon juice, salt/pepper/ground cumin to taste. Serves 2.

Really Quick Hummus

REALLY QUICK HUMMUS	
PER SERVING	
Energy Kcals	239.5
Protein g	8.9
Carbohydrates g	22.9
Dietary Fibre g	5.8
Fat – Total g	13.2
Saturated Fat g	1.7
Polyunsaturated Fat g	3.6
Calcium mg	119.3
Magnesium mg	68.1

Whizz in the blender 1 tin of chickpeas, drained and rinsed, 1 clove garlic, juice of 1 lemon, 2 tbsp dark tahini, salt/pepper/chilli powder to taste. Add olive oil if necessary to achieve desired consistency. Serves 2.

Really Quick Bean Pâté

REALLY QUICK BEAN PÂTÉ	
PER SERVING	
Energy Kcals	180.3
Protein g	9.2
Carbohydrates g	25.3
Dietary Fibre g	6.2
Fat – Total g	5.2
Saturated Fat g	0.8
Polyunsaturated Fat g	0.6
Calcium mg	61.0
Magnesium mg	59.2

Whizz in the blender 1 tin of any beans, drained and rinsed, 1 clove garlic, 1 tbsp tomato purée, 2 tbsp chopped parsley, salt/pepper to taste. Add olive oil as necessary to achieve desired consistency. Use a good brand of organic tinned beans, such as Suma or Meridian. Serves 2.

Soups and Starters

Vegetable Stock
Apricot, Carrot and Sesame Soup
Arame and Miso Soup
Asparagus and Fennel Soup
Black Bean Soup
Celery and Hazelnut Soup
Chilled Beetroot and Apple Soup
Nori Soup
Roasted Tomato and Garlic Soup
Split Pea Soup with Red Pepper Cream
Very Pumpkin Soup
Oriental Vegetable Juice
Watercress and Cucumber Juice
Amaranth, Sweet Potato and
Mushroom Croquettes with Avocado Salsa
Three Seed Pâté
Soya Bean Falafel
Tofu-Stuffed Peppers with Tomato and Mustard Dressing
Seared Salmon with Beansprout Salad and Tomato Vinaigrette
Smoked Trout Fillets with Beetroot Purée

Right: Black Bean Soup and
Spelt Rolls with Walnuts
(pages 45, 170)

SOUPS

The basis of all good soups is good stock. Here is my recipe for vegetable stock:

It is important to use organic vegetables wherever possible for stock making, as you are using the outer skin of the vegetables. Adding a thumb-sized piece of fresh root ginger gives the stock some zing and aids digestion.

Vegetable Stock

1	large onion	1
2	large carrots	2
3 sticks	celery	3 sticks
4	outside leaves of lettuce	4
	potato peelings	
	parsley stalks	
1	bay leaf	1
6	peppercorns	6
	low-sodium salt	
2½ pints	water	1½ litres

Simmer all the ingredients together for about half an hour. Drain and use as directed in soups and sauces. Makes about 1 litre/1¾ pints.

PER SERVING	
Energy Kcals	20.5
Protein g	0.7
Carbohydrates g	4.6
Dietary Fibre g	1.0
Fat – Total g	0.1
Saturated Fat g	0.0
Polyunsaturated Fat g	0.0
Calcium mg	16.4
Magnesium mg	13.4

Left: Soya Bean Falafel (page 55) with Millet Tabbouleh (page 129)

Dried apricots are a particularly rich source of potassium, which has been shown to lower blood pressure. Both the apricots and the carrots are good sources of beta-carotene – an antioxidant which helps protect our skin against loss of flexibility. Carrots also contain boron – an elusive mineral needed to help build strong bones.

Apricot, Carrot and Sesame Soup

This is an adaptation of a delicious sweet and sour soup from the Covent Garden Soup Company. It is supposed to be served cold, but my version is better hot. This is a good source of phytoestrogens.

8 oz	unsulphured apricots, soaked overnight in 2 pints/1.2 litres water	225 g
1	medium onion, finely chopped	1
3	medium carrots, sliced thinly	3
1 stick	cinnamon	1 stick
1	bay leaf	1
1¼ pints	vegetable stock (see page 41)	725 ml
	low-sodium salt and freshly ground black pepper	
¼ pint	soya milk	150 ml
1 oz	sesame seeds, toasted, to garnish	30 g
1 tbsp	cold-pressed sesame oil	1 tbsp

Drain the apricots from their soaking water, reserving 1 pint/570 ml of the juice. Place the apricots, juice, onion, carrots, cinnamon stick, bay leaf, stock and seasoning in a pan. Bring to the boil, cover and simmer gently for about 40 minutes, or until the vegetables and apricots are tender. Remove the cinnamon stick and bayleaf and discard. Cool a little, then purée in a liquidizer or food processor with the soya milk until smooth. Reheat, and serve with a drizzle of sesame oil and a sprinkling of toasted sesame seeds. Serves 4.

PER SERVING	
Energy Kcals	308.7
Protein g	6.1
Carbohydrates g	50.7
Dietary Fibre g	6.6
Fat – Total g	8.5
Saturated Fat g	0.6
Polyunsaturated Fat g	1.9
Calcium mg	70.9
Magnesium mg	19.3

Sea vegetables such as arame are a useful part of a weight loss diet, as they add physical bulk and fibre, yet are low in calories and fat.

Arame and Miso Soup

You'd be amazed at how much dried seaweed expands when it is soaked, so although 1/4 oz might seem a tiny amount, just weigh it, rinse it, then soak for 15 minutes, and you will see how much it swells in volume. Arame has been precooked and sliced finely, so it is an ideal seaweed with which to begin your exploration of sea vegetables.

1/4 oz	arame, a very small handful	7 g
1 tbsp	cold-pressed sesame oil	1 tbsp
1	medium onion, finely chopped	1
2	carrots, thinly sliced on the diagonal	2
1 1/2 pints	water	850 ml
2 tsp	miso	2 tsp
4	spring onions, chopped (green and white parts)	4

Soak the arame in tepid water to cover for 10 minutes, then drain well.

Sauté the onion over low heat in sesame oil a few minutes. Add arame and continue sautéeing for a few minutes. Add carrots and sauté for 1 minute. Add water and simmer for 15 minutes. Add a little of the soup to the miso in a cup, mix well, and return to the pan. Reheat gently, and serve very hot, garnished with chopped spring onions. Serves 4.

PER SERVING	
Energy Kcals	66.6
Protein g	1.4
Carbohydrates g	7.1
Dietary Fibre g	1.7
Fat – Total g	3.8
Saturated Fat g	0.6
Polyunsaturated Fat g	1.7
Calcium mg	30.8
Magnesium mg	15.0

Both fennel and asparagus are good sources of phytoestrogens, which have been shown to help reduce menopausal symptoms such as hot flushes, so they should be eaten freely by menopausal women. Fennel is also known for its diuretic effect, so it may help reduce water retention and bloating.

Asparagus and Fennel Soup

This is a pretty green colour, and I think the balance of flavours is just right. A good soup to serve at a dinner party, especially in May when the English asparagus is ready.

1 tbsp	extra virgin olive oil	1 tbsp
1	large onion, chopped	1
1	garlic clove, chopped	1
1 lb	asparagus	450 g
1 lb	fennel	450 g
1½ pints	vegetable stock (see page 41)	850 ml
4 tbsp	soya cream	4 tbsp
	low-sodium salt and freshly ground black pepper	

Heat the oil in a large saucepan and gently sauté the onions and garlic, without browning, until tender.

Trim the tough stalk ends of the asparagus, cut the tips off and set aside. Slice the rest into 1 inch/2.5 cm pieces. Slice the fennel thinly, reserving the leafy tops for the garnish.

When the onion and garlic are soft, stir in the sliced asparagus and fennel. Add the stock, bring to the boil, then cover and simmer gently for about 30 minutes until the vegetables are tender. Cool a little, then put into the blender and blend until smooth. If you want the soup to be smooth, pass through a sieve into a clean pan, reheat and season to taste. If you don't mind a few fibres from the fennel, then there is no need to sieve the soup.

Cook the reserved asparagus tips in boiling water for 3-4 minutes until tender, then drain and refresh in cold water to set the green colour. Add to the soup to warm through.

Chop the reserved fennel tops finely, then serve the soup garnished with a swirl of soya cream and a sprinkling of fennel tops. Serves 4.

PER SERVING	
Energy Kcals	190.9
Protein g	4.4
Carbohydrates g	25.8
Dietary Fibre g	5.1
Fat – Total g	8.7
Saturated Fat g	1.6
Polyunsaturated Fat g	0.6
Calcium mg	80.1
Magnesium mg	24.0

The kombu, here and in other bean soup recipes, is to prevent flatulence and to add minerals to the dish. It contains glutamic acid which tenderises pulses and enhances the flavour. Its own taste, after cooking for a while, is not really noticeable. If you like, you can remove it before blending. If you can't find kombu, a 1 inch/2.5 cm long piece of fresh root ginger has much the same effect. Black beans are a particularly rich source of iron – there are over 6mg in every bowlful of this soup. And just adding a little flax oil at the end gives you a really good dose of Omega-3 fatty acids, which are so hard to get from other sources.

Black Bean Soup

This is my husband's favourite soup, and mine too. It brings back instantly memories of the Caribbean, and is one of the few dishes I could live on if I was confined to one food. There are numerous recipes for this of course. My favourite is an adaptation of Alex D Hawkes, in his scholarly work *The Flavors of the Caribbean and Latin America*. He suggests serving it with accompaniments of finely chopped onion, wedges of lime and sliced avocado. Be sure to use the small black turtle beans, not black kidney beans which do not have the same flavour.

6 oz	dried black turtle beans, soaked overnight	170 g
2¼ pints	water	1.3 litres
1	large onion, coarsely chopped	1
4	spring onions, chopped	4
1	green pepper, coarsely chopped	1
1	garlic clove, chopped	1
1	bay leaf, crumbled	1
6 inch	strip of kombu	15 cm
	low-sodium salt and freshly ground black pepper	
¼ tsp	dried oregano	¼ tsp
few drops	hot sauce, eg tabasco, to taste	few drops
4 tsp	flax oil, to serve	4 tsp

Drain the beans of their soaking water, put in a pan and cover with fresh cold water. Bring to the boil and boil for 10 minutes, then reduce the heat and simmer, covered, for one hour. Add the onion, spring onions, green pepper, garlic, bay leaf, kombu, seasoning, oregano and hot sauce and continue to cook, covered, over low heat until the beans are tender – another hour or so. Cool slightly, then purée in the blender. Return to a clean pan and reheat. Serve very hot with a drizzle of flax oil in each bowl. Serves 4.

PER SERVING	
Energy Kcals	318.4
Protein g	17.6
Carbohydrates g	53.4
Dietary Fibre g	16.2
Fat – Total g	5.5
Saturated Fat g	0.5
Polyunsaturated Fat g	3.2
Calcium mg	130.2
Magnesium mg	13.7

Celery contains phytonutrients called phthalides which regulate the hormones that control blood pressure. Tests have shown that four sticks of celery a day can bring down the blood pressure by a few points. Celery is also a good source of phytoestrogens, which may help control menopausal symptoms.

Celery and Hazelnut Soup

This is a deceptively simple recipe for a quite delicious soup. The soup does require sieving, though, as celery strings can get between your teeth and quite spoil the experience of eating it. The hazelnuts are a good source of magnesium and zinc.

3 oz	hazelnuts	85 g
2 tbsp	extra virgin olive oil	2 tbsp
1 head	celery with leaves, chopped (reserve the leaves for garnish)	1 head
1	onion, chopped	1
1	garlic clove, chopped	1
1 tbsp	flax seeds, ground	1 tbsp
1¹/₂ pints	vegetable stock (see page 41)	850 ml
	low-sodium salt and freshly ground black pepper	

First toast the hazelnuts. Preheat the oven to 180°C/350°F/ Gas Mark 4. Spread the hazelnuts on a baking tray and toast in the oven for 8-10 minutes, turning frequently, until evenly golden but not brown. Cool the nuts, then rub the skins off. This is best done in a clean teatowel. Reserve a quarter of the nuts for the garnish, and grind the rest in an electric grinder.

Heat the oil in a large saucepan, and sauté the celery, onion and garlic for 10 minutes over a gentle heat. Add the stock and the ground hazelnuts. Simmer for about 20 minutes or so until the vegetables are tender. Cool a little, add the ground flax seeds, then purée in the blender. Pass the soup through a wire sieve into a clean saucepan. Reheat, check for seasoning, then serve garnished with the chopped celery leaves and reserved chopped hazelnuts. Serves 4.

PER SERVING	
Energy Kcals	259.9
Protein g	5.4
Carbohydrates g	15.4
Dietary Fibre g	5.7
Fat – Total g	21.1
Saturated Fat g	2.0
Polyunsaturated Fat g	2.3
Calcium mg	100.5
Magnesium mg	63.5

Beetroot has a high folate value, thus helping to decrease homocysteine in the blood, which, when raised, is a risk factor for heart disease and osteoporosis. Beetroot is also good for the liver, and the soluble fibre it contains may help to lower cholesterol levels. It is easy to cook beetroot in the oven (see page 58). However, if you do buy it cooked, make sure it's been packed without vinegar.

Chilled Beetroot and Apple Soup

This is a pretty pink soup to serve at a summer dinner party, and has the added benefit of being full of good nutrition.

9 oz	cooked beetroot, peeled and chopped	260 g
3	green dessert apples (eg Granny Smiths), peeled, cored and quartered	3
1¼ pints	vegetable stock (see page 41)	725 ml
1	lemon, juiced	1
2 tsp	grated ginger root	2 tsp
	low-sodium salt and freshly ground black pepper	
2 oz	cucumber, diced	60 g
2 tbsp	chopped fresh chives	2 tbsp

Put the beetroot and two of the apples in the blender with the stock and most of the lemon juice, and blend until smooth. You might have to do this in two or three batches. Squeeze the grated ginger with your hands to extract the juice so that it drips into the soup. Season to taste, then refrigerate for at least an hour.

Dice the remaining apple and toss with the reserved lemon juice.

To serve, pour into chilled bowls and garnish with the diced apple, diced cucumber and chopped chives. Serves 4.

PER SERVING	
Energy Kcals	101.4
Protein g	2.2
Carbohydrates g	23.2
Dietary Fibre g	4.3
Fat – Total g	0.8
Saturated Fat g	0.1
Polyunsaturated Fat g	0.1
Calcium mg	34.2
Magnesium mg	24.0

Nori is particularly rich in iron and potassium. It also has a high iodine content, even more iodine than fish. This is of benefit to perimenopausal women, as 5-10 days prior to menstruation there is a surge of oestrogen in the blood. Oestrogen is goitregenic, which means it tends to inhibit the thyroid gland. This particular soup may be helpful at this time of the menstrual cycle to boost the thyroid gland because of its iodine content. The egg provides zinc and selenium to help the iodine-based thyroid hormones do their work.

Nori Soup

This soup is terribly easy to make, light on the calories, but full of minerals from the nori. Buy your sea vegetables from a reputable company which harvests them from clean, unpolluted water (see Useful Addresses).

2	sheets nori	2
1¼ pints	vegetable stock (see page 41)	725 ml
3 tbsp	shoyu sauce	3 tbsp
2	organic free-range eggs, lightly beaten	2
4	spring onions, sliced on the diagonal	4
1 tsp	toasted sesame seeds	1 tsp

The nori sheets need to be toasted before they are ready to use. Hold a sheet directly over a gas burner, or under the grill, and move it back and forth until its colour turns from green to dark purple. When the nori is done, cool, then cut or tear into small pieces.

Bring the vegetable stock to the boil and then add the shoyu and slowly pour the eggs into the broth, stirring gently. Return to the boil and turn off the heat. Stir in the nori and spring onions. Sprinkle sesame seeds on top and serve very hot in small bowls. Serves 4.

PER SERVING	
Energy Kcals	72.8
Protein g	4.6
Carbohydrates g	6.5
Dietary Fibre g	1.3
Fat – Total g	3.0
Saturated Fat g	0.7
Polyunsaturated Fat g	0.3
Calcium mg	40.2
Magnesium mg	9.3

Besides lycopene and lots of beta-carotene, tomatoes provide useful amounts of both boron, needed to help you build strong bones, and chromium, necessary for the metabolism of glucose. This soup goes some way towards readjusting the calcium/magnesium balance, too, as it contains slightly more magnesium than calcium. Most of our diet favours calcium, and because of this many nutritionists consider that most of the population is actually lacking in magnesium, an important mineral for bone formation, the cardiovascular system and energy production.

Roasted Tomato and Garlic Soup

This soup is very simple, very healthy and good for your cardiovascular system because of the garlic and the lycopene in the tomatoes. Don't attempt to make it unless you can get flavourful sun-ripened tomatoes, preferably home-grown and/or organic. Using orange juice to sweeten the soup was suggested by Dr Nenita Shih-Coughlan, who helped to test the recipes in this chapter and provided invaluable nutritional advice.

2 lb	really ripe tomatoes	850 g
3	garlic cloves, whole	3
1¾ pints	vegetable stock (see page 41)	1 litre
1	large orange, juice only	1
	low-sodium salt and freshly ground black pepper	

Preheat the oven to 180°C/350°F/Gas Mark 4. Place the whole tomatoes and whole garlic in a roasting tin and roast for about an hour, until the tomatoes split.

Take out of the oven and leave to cool a little. Then pop the garlic cloves out of their skins and put in the blender with the tomatoes and enough of the stock to make a purée. Pass tomato purée through a fine sieve into a clean pan and add the rest of the stock. Add the orange juice and seasoning, and reheat to serve. Serves 4.

PER SERVING	
Energy Kcals	127.1
Protein g	4.6
Carbohydrates g	25.8
Dietary Fibre g	4.2
Fat – Total g	1.8
Saturated Fat g	0.2
Polyunsaturated Fat g	0.5
Calcium mg	48.6
Magnesium mg	50.7

Split peas are a good source of three different kinds of phytoestrogens: isoflavones, coumestrol and lignans. As part of an overall healthy diet, these may help to reduce your risk of breast cancer.

Split Pea Soup with Red Pepper Cream

This is a very pretty soup, as well as being nutritious, with the swirl of red pepper cream on a pale yellow background.

8 oz	yellow split peas, washed	225 g
1	bay leaf	1
1	onion, finely sliced	1
3	garlic cloves, crushed	3
1 tbsp	extra virgin olive oil	1 tbsp
2	carrots, peeled and chopped finely	2
1 stick	celery, finely sliced	1 stick
	low-sodium salt and freshly ground black pepper	
1 tbsp	chopped fresh marjoram	1 tbsp
Red pepper cream:		
1	large red pepper	1
2 tbsp	soya cream	2 tbsp
	low-sodium salt and freshly ground black pepper	

To make the red pepper cream: grill the pepper, turning frequently, until the skin is black and charred. Leave to cool, then skin the pepper, remove the seeds and chop roughly. Try to save the juice. Put the chopped pepper, any saved juice and the soya cream into the blender and blend until very smooth. Season to taste and reserve.

Put the split peas and the bay leaf in about 1.75 litres/ 2½ pints of water in a large pot. Bring to the boil, skim off any foam, reduce the heat and simmer, covered, for about 2 hours, or until very soft.

Meanwhile sauté the garlic and onion in the olive oil over medium heat until golden. Add the carrots and celery and continue cooking until tender. Add this mixture to the cooked split peas, season and serve garnished with the red pepper cream and a sprinkling of chopped marjoram. Serves 4.

PER SERVING	
Energy Kcals	284.0
Protein g	16.7
Carbohydrates g	47.9
Dietary Fibre g	2.3
Fat – Total g	3.7
Saturated Fat g	0.5
Polyunsaturated Fat g	0.4
Calcium mg	39.5
Magnesium mg	22,6

Pumpkin is a fantastic source of beta-carotene and lycopene, and the seeds are rich in iron and zinc, while the pumpkin seed oil provides valuable Omega-3 oil – and a delicious taste. Don't throw away the seeds from inside the pumpkin – they can be dried and eaten – and they'll be fresher than those you can buy in the shops.

Very Pumpkin Soup

This is an adaptation of a standard classic. I have garnished it with delicious smoky flavoured pumpkin seed oil and toasted pumpkin seeds for an additional dose of vitamin E and zinc.

2 tbsp	extra virgin olive oil	2 tbsp
1	red onion, peeled and finely chopped	1
1	garlic clove, finely chopped	1
2 lbs	pumpkin, peeled, seeded and cut into chunks	900 g
4 oz	new potatoes, peeled and cubed	110 g
1 tbsp	chopped fresh oregano	1 tbsp
	low-sodium salt and freshly ground black pepper	
1¼ pints	vegetable stock (see page 41)	725 ml
4 tsp	toasted pumpkin seed oil	4 tsp
2 tbsp	pumpkin seeds, toasted	2 tbsp

Gently sauté the onion and garlic in the olive oil until soft. Add the pumpkin, potatoes and oregano and cook for a few minutes. Add the stock and seasoning, bring to the boil, turn down the heat and simmer until the pumpkin is tender, about half an hour.

When the pumpkin is cooked, purée the mixture in a food processor and return to a clean pan to reheat. Check for seasoning and add more stock if necessary. The soup should be quite thick. Serve very hot garnished with a thin trickle of pumpkin oil and a scattering of toasted pumpkin seeds on top. Serves 4.

STARTERS

Apart from the recipes in this section, any of the snack recipes can be used as starters, or try any of the salads.

For a quick, nutritious and easy starter, serve freshly-made vegetable juices. Home-made juice must be drunk quickly in order for the vitamins not to be lost, so drink it while you're preparing the rest of the meal, or at any time of day as a pick-me-up. Below are some more robust mixtures than those in the breakfast chapter – strong tastes and high nutritional value. Give them a try!

PER SERVING	
Energy Kcals	208.8
Protein g	3.9
Carbohydrates g	22.5
Dietary Fibre g	4.2
Fat – Total g	12.3
Saturated Fat g	1.4
Polyunsaturated Fat g	3.0
Calcium mg	63.2
Magnesium mg	42.7

Chinese cabbage provides a lot of calcium for your bones, and the carrots provide beta-carotene for immunity and skin health, while between them they provide more than the RNI (reference nutrient intake) of vitamin C.

PER SERVING	
Energy Kcals	118.3
Protein g	5.1
Carbohydrates g	20.4
Dietary Fibre g	6.3
Fat – Total g	3.2
Saturated Fat g	0.5
Polyunsaturated Fat g	1.4
Calcium mg	183.2
Magnesium mg	69.9

Watercress is packed with antioxidants such as beta-carotene and vitamin C, and is one of the best vegetarian sources of calcium and iron. The vitamin C in the watercress helps your body to absorb the iron. Finally, apples contain phytoestrogens which may help with hot flushes and other menopausal symptoms.

PER SERVING	
Energy Kcals	107.1
Protein g	2.4
Carbohydrates g	27.9
Dietary Fibre g	5.2
Fat – Total g	0.3
Saturated Fat g	0.1
Polyunsaturated Fat g	0.1
Calcium mg	76.1
Magnesium mg	36.9

Oriental Vegetable Juice

This is an unusual take on juice, and could almost be described as a raw soup. It's a great way to start a Chinese meal, and just look at the nutritional value. You will need a juicer for this and the next juice recipe but they are well worth investing in.

1/5 oz	arame or hijiki (about a tablespoonful)	5 g
8	organic carrots, scrubbed and roughly chopped	8
4	celery sticks, roughly chopped	4
1 lb	Chinese cabbage, washed and roughly chopped	450 g
	fresh ginger root, peeled (2 inch/5 cm piece)	
1 tsp	tamari sauce	1 tsp
2 tbsp	sesame seeds, ground	2 tbsp

Soak the seaweed in tepid water to cover to soften it (10 minutes for arame, up to half an hour for hijiki). Drain well, then add to the juicer with all the other ingredients except the sesame seeds, which you should stir into the juice just before you serve it. Serves 4.

Watercress and Cucumber Juice

The watercress gives this juice quite a pronounced taste, but that is balanced by the mild sweetness of the cucumber and apples. Delicious.

2 bunches	watercress	2 bunches
2	cucumbers	2
4	green apples	4

Juice all ingredients (this will have to be done in batches) and serve immediately. Serves 4.

Amaranth, an ancient grain from South America, is rich in nutrients. It contains a very high level of all the B vitamins which we need for energy, lots of protein and plenty of iron. No wonder the Aztecs were able to climb the Andes with ease, fuelled on a diet of amaranth. They must have had very strong bones too – just look at the calcium and magnesium content of this dish.

Amaranth, Sweet Potato and Mushroom Croquettes with Avocado Salsa

You could serve these croquettes as a lunch dish or as a starter before a light meal, or even by themselves as a supper dish, as they are quite filling.

For the croquettes:

6 oz	amaranth	170 g
6 oz	sweet potato	170 g
3 oz	mushrooms, finely chopped	85 g
1	organic, free-range egg, beaten	1
4	spring onions	4
2 tbsp	fresh coriander, chopped	2 tbsp
2 tsp	extra virgin olive oil	2 tsp

For the salsa:

1/2	red onion, finely chopped	1/2
1	lime, grated rind and juice	1
1	garlic clove, finely chopped	1
1/2 tsp	ground cumin	1/2 tsp
	low-sodium salt to taste	
1	avocado, peeled and diced	1
1	tomato, peeled, deseeded and diced	1
2 tbsp	fresh coriander, chopped	2 tbsp

Preheat the oven to 200°C/400°F/Gas Mark 5.

Rinse the amaranth and put in a non-stick pan with 14 fl oz/570 ml water. Cover and simmer for 10 minutes. Meanwhile, peel and dice the sweet potato, then add to the pan of amaranth together with the chopped mushrooms. Do not stir, but replace the lid and continue cooking for another 10 minutes. There should be no liquid left.

When cooked, transfer to a bowl, cover and leave to cool. Stir in the beaten egg, spring onions and chopped coriander. The mixture should be quite firm. Divide into 16 croquettes or patties with floured hands. Place on an oiled baking tray and drizzle over a little olive oil, bake for 20 minutes or until

PER SERVING	
Energy Kcals	316.5
Protein g	10.4
Carbohydrates g	45.6
Dietary Fibre g	11.8
Fat – Total g	12.1
Saturated Fat g	2.4
Polyunsaturated Fat g	2.5
Calcium mg	105.0
Magnesium mg	151.8

browned, turning once. To make the salsa, combine all the ingredients in a bowl and stir gently to mix. Just before serving, stir in the chopped coriander. Serves 4.

This pâté is high fat, but I have included it as an example of a dish that can be made largely from seeds, and I feel their nutritional density makes up for the high fat content.

One serving of this pâté provides half the magnesium, iron, selenium and zinc that you need in a day. Selenium and zinc are both needed by the thyroid gland to help activate the thyroid hormones. Balance this pâté with a light main course, such as a salad.

Three Seed Pâté

On the principle that you can never have too much of a good thing, here is a pâté made largely of seeds.

2 tsp	extra virgin olive oil	2 tsp
1	onion, peeled and finely chopped	1
4 oz	mushrooms, sliced	110 g
1/2 oz	sun-dried tomatoes	15 g
	low-sodium salt and freshly ground black pepper	
4 tbsp	pumpkin seeds	4 tbsp
8 tbsp	sunflower seeds	8 tbsp
2 tbsp	sesame seeds, ground	2 tbsp
2 fl oz	water	60 ml
1 tbsp	chopped fresh basil	1 tbsp
1 tsp	chopped fresh thyme	1 tsp
1 tsp	chopped fresh marjoram	1 tsp
	toast and cherry tomatoes to serve	

Preheat the oven to 180°C/350°F/Gas Mark 4.

Heat the oil in a small pan, and gently sauté the onion until soft. Add mushrooms, sun-dried tomatoes and seasoning. Cover and cook over low heat for 5 minutes.

Meanwhile, toast the pumpkin seeds and sunflower seeds on a baking tray in the oven for 10 minutes or so, until browned. Leave to cool.

Stir the ground sesame seed and toasted pumpkin and sunflower seeds and water into the mushroom mixture. Cover and cook gently for 10 minutes. Turn off heat, stir in the fresh herbs, and leave to stand for 15 minutes. Purée in a food processor until not quite smooth, then tip into four individual ramekins. Refrigerate until needed. Serve with toast and garnished with cherry tomatoes. Serves 4.

PER SERVING	
Energy Kcals	305.6
Protein g	11.9
Carbohydrates g	18.6
Dietary Fibre g	5.3
Fat – Total g	22.4
Saturated Fat g	2.2
Polyunsaturated Fat g	10.8
Calcium mg	76.6
Magnesium mg	147.7
Selenium	20.4

Soya beans are a rich source of phytoestrogens, containing anything from 14 to 153 mg of isoflavones per 100 g of beans, as well as 2 g of lignans.
The isoflavones help to reduce menopausal symptoms such as hot flushes as well as having antioxidant effects. Lignans also have weak oestrogenic effects and may help to protect against heart disease.

Soya Bean Falafel

Falafel are customarily made with chickpeas, but, reluctant to let an opportunity to use soya pass me by, I have substituted soya beans. Traditional recipes use chickpeas that have been soaked but not actually cooked. However, it is essential to cook raw soybeans as they contain a trypsin inhibitor which must be killed off by boiling.

8 oz	soya beans, soaked overnight	225 g
1 tsp	ground cumin	1 tsp
1 tsp	ground coriander	1 tsp
1 tsp	cayenne pepper	1 tsp
1 tsp	low-sodium salt	1 tsp
1	large onion, chopped finely	1
1	garlic clove, crushed	1
2 tbsp	tahini	2 tbsp
3 tbsp	chopped fresh flat-leaf parsley	3 tbsp
2 tbsp	chickpea flour (gram flour)	2 tbsp
3 tbsp	extra virgin olive oil	3 tbsp
	plain live yoghurt or plain soya yoghurt, to serve	

Drain the soya beans from their soaking water, rinse, cover with cold water and cook until tender (about 2-3 hours) in a covered pan. Drain well. Alternatively, cook the beans in a pressure cooker – use $1^{1}/4$ pints/770 ml water, and add a spoonful of olive oil to prevent the foam from the cooking beans from clogging up the pressure cooker vent. The beans should be cooked at high pressure for 10-12 minutes.

When the beans are cooked and drained, put all the ingredients, except the gram flour and olive oil, in a food processor and process until the soya beans are finely chopped.

Turn the mixture into a large bowl and add enough water to make a kneadable dough. With floured hands, shape the mixture into about 20 small balls. Slightly flatten each ball. Heat the oil in a large frying pan and fry the falafel on both sides until golden. Serve with yoghurt. Serves 4.

PER SERVING	
Energy Kcals	263.4
Protein g	12.1
Carbohydrates g	13.0
Dietary Fibre g	4.9
Fat – Total g	19.7
Saturated Fat g	2.7
Polyunsaturated Fat g	5.5
Calcium mg	91.7
Magnesium mg	80.4

You could use this tofu stuffing for other vegetables, such as courgettes. It's a good way of sneaking tofu (phytoestrogens and a low-fat form of protein) onto the family menu.

Tofu-Stuffed Peppers with Tomato and Mustard Dressing

These stuffed peppers are a little bit fiddly to make, but the result is very attractive, and they make a nutritious start to a meal, or they can be served for lunch with a salad.

2	red peppers	2
2	yellow peppers	2
2	packets firm tofu	2
2	garlic cloves, chopped finely	2
1 tsp	chopped fresh thyme	1 tsp
1 tsp	chopped fresh rosemary	1 tsp
2	organic free-range eggs, beaten	2
	salt and freshly ground black pepper	
Sauce:		
1	tomato, peeled and chopped	1
1 tsp	Dijon mustard	1 tsp
1 tsp	balsamic vinegar	1 tsp
1 tsp	fresh lemon juice	1 tsp
3 tbsp	extra virgin olive oil	3 tbsp
	a handful of fresh basil leaves, torn (reserve a few whole ones for garnish)	

Preheat the oven to 200°C/400°F/Gas Mark 6.

Roast the peppers whole for 20 minutes or so, until starting to char. Remove from the oven, cool in a plastic bag, then peel. Remove the pepper stems and seeds but try to keep the peppers whole.

Reduce the oven heat to 170°C/325°F/Gas Mark 3.

Process the tofu, garlic, herbs, eggs and seasoning in the food processor, then stuff this mixture into the whole peppers. Place the stuffed peppers on a baking sheet and bake in the oven for 20 minutes. Leave to cool.

To make the sauce, whizz the ingredients in the blender.

When ready to serve, slice the peppers across into thick rings and serve, 2 or 3 per portion with the sauce drizzled over. Garnish with whole basil leaves. Serves 6.

PER SERVING	
Energy Kcals	219.3
Protein g	13.9
Carbohydrates g	9.4
Dietary Fibre g	1.9
Fat – Total g	14.5
Saturated Fat g	2.6
Polyunsaturated Fat g	52.7
Calcium mg	193.5
Magnesium mg	41.3

The salmon is a rich source of selenium, and, together with the flax oil, provides 3 g of Omega-3 fatty acids. Use flax oil whenever you can as long as it's not going to be cooked. It has a delicious, nutty taste and can be used wherever you would use extra-virgin olive oil.

Seared Salmon with Beansprout Salad and Tomato Vinaigrette

This is an elegant and economical way to serve wild or organic salmon. If you can, make your own sprouts as then you can eat them at the peak of their freshness. See page 126 for details of how to grow your own sprouts. The best alternative is to get your sprouts direct from Aconbury Sprouts (see Useful Addresses) where you can be sure of their freshness.

12 oz	tail-end piece of wild or organic salmon, skinned	340 g
4 tsp	toasted sesame seeds	4 tsp
	beansprouts, a handful	
	watercress, a handful	

For the tomato vinaigrette:

1 tbsp	extra virgin olive oil	1 tbsp
2 tsp	flax oil	2 tsp
1 tsp	red wine vinegar	1 tsp
1/2 tsp	concentrated apple juice	1/2 tsp
	low-sodium salt and freshly ground black pepper	
1	tomato, peeled, seeded and finely diced	1

First, make the tomato vinaigrette by whisking together the olive oil, flax oil, wine vinegar, concentrated apple juice and seasoning. Then add the diced tomato and stir to mix.

Slice the salmon into four small escalopes. Heat a ridged pan and spray with olive oil spray or wipe round with a piece of kitchen paper dipped in olive oil. Sear the salmon on both sides for a minute or two until lightly cooked.

To assemble, place a salmon escalope in the middle of each of 4 individual plates and top with beansprouts and watercress. Garnish with toasted sesame seeds. Whisk the vinaigrette again, then dribble round the perimeter of each plate. Serves 4.

PER SERVING	
Energy Kcals	238.0
Protein g	21.9
Carbohydrates g	6.7
Dietary Fibre g	1.2
Fat – Total g	13.5
Saturated Fat g	1.7
Polyunsaturated Fat g	4.4
Calcium mg	28.3
Magnesium mg	42.4

Trout is an excellent source of protein without containing much fat. In fact, of the oily fish, trout has the least fat. However, it makes up for this by having a high level of potassium, as does the beetroot, so eating this dish could help control your blood pressure. Even the chopped parsley provides much-needed nutrition – it's one of the richest sources of vitamin K, folic acid and magnesium.

Smoked Trout Fillets with Beetroot Purée

This is an attractive starter, with the light pink of the trout fillets and deeper pink of the beetroot. It's quite filling, and could easily be eaten as a light meal on its own with slices of pumpernickel bread.

4	smoked trout fillets	4
2	whole raw beetroot	2
1 tbsp	extra virgin olive oil	1 tbsp
1	medium onion, peeled and chopped	1
1	garlic clove, peeled and crushed	1
2	tomatoes, skinned, seeded and diced	2
2 tbsp	red wine vinegar	2 tbsp
	low-sodium salt and freshly ground black pepper	
3½ fl oz	vegetable stock (see page 41)	100 ml
1 tbsp	soya cream	1 tbsp
1 tbsp	fresh parsley, chopped	1 tbsp
	lemon wedges, to serve	

Preheat the oven to 180°C/350°F/Gas Mark 4.

Wash the beetroot but do not peel. Bake in the oven for about an hour. Leave to cool slightly, then slip them out of their skins and chop them roughly.

Sauté the onions and garlic in the olive oil over gentle heat until softened but not browned. Add the tomatoes, beetroot, vinegar and seasoning. Cover and simmer for half an hour, stirring from time to time.

Cool slightly, then put in the blender with the stock and blend until smooth. Put into a clean pan, add the soya cream and reheat gently. Check the seasoning.

Put the trout fillets on four plates, spoon the purée beside them, sprinkle with chopped parsley and serve with a wedge of lemon. Serves 4.

PER SERVING	
Energy Kcals	311.5
Protein g	33.9
Carbohydrates g	14.8
Dietary Fibre g	3.0
Fat – Total g	13.1
Saturated Fat g	3.1
Polyunsaturated Fat g	3.2
Calcium mg	33.0
Magnesium mg	66.5

Main Dishes – Vegetarian

Tofu with Shiitake Mushrooms and Kale
Szechuan Braised Tofu and Vegetables
Tandoori Tofu
Sweet and Sour Tempeh
Tempeh with Coconut Milk
Tempeh in Creamy Curry Sauce
Spicy Pumpkin Casserole with Ground Almonds
Vegetable Biriyani
Roast West Indian Vegetables
Butternut Squash with Millet Stuffing
Potato Pizza with Walnut Pesto
Pumpkin Risotto with Sage
Wakame and Lemon Barley Risotto
Grilled Polenta with Roasted Pepper Ragoût
Wholemeal Tortillas with Beans, Avocados and Alfalfa Sprouts
Quinoa Pilaff with Roasted Beetroot and Onions
Brazil Nut and Lentil Roast
Sunflower Seed Loaf with Fennel and Red Pepper Sauce
Pasta Primavera
Soba Noodles with Puy Lentils and Pumpkin Seeds

TOFU AND TEMPEH DISHES

As I mentioned in the introduction, soya foods are the mainstay of this way of eating, because they contain a good level of isoflavones. If menopausal women in the West ate tofu as frequently as Japanese women do, they would suffer less from hot flushes, night sweats, mood swings, and all the other unpleasant symptoms associated with the menopause. So eat and enjoy.

Why is it that there are so few recipes for tofu out there? If you look in most vegetarian cookbooks you will find tofu kebabs and that's about all. Try the following recipes, but also try to think of how you can use tofu just as you would chicken or pork. Look particularly at recipes for chicken breast and adapt them to tofu. This is quite easy, as tofu takes no time to cook really – it only needs to be heated up or browned. So think of it as a sort of cooked chicken breast and adapt recipes accordingly.

If there is an Oriental shop near you, the tofu they sell is superior to that available in the supermarket. Ask your local Chinese restaurant where they buy their beancurd, and they may be able to point you in the right direction.

Before using firm tofu in any of the following recipes, take it out of its packet or the water in which it is stored, rinse, and squeeze as dry as possible. If you have some time to spare, wrap the block of tofu in 4-6 layers of kitchen paper, and weight down with a heavy weight (a couple of tins of baked beans would be about the right weight) for half an hour or so. This gives a firmer texture and ensures that all liquid is squeezed out. It is not necessary to do this rinsing and draining with smoked tofu.

A note on quantities: I am quite capable of eating an entire 250 g/8$\frac{1}{2}$ oz block of tofu at a sitting, and I find recipes claiming that one block will feed 4 people incredibly mean. Therefore I am taking the middle way and allowing one block for 2 people. Remember that 120 g/4 oz tofu gives you about 15 g of protein and about 29 mg of calcium.

Shiitake mushrooms may lower cholesterol levels and blood pressure, and may even increase survival time of cancer patients. You can buy them dried in health food shops – Clearspring sell them in 50 g packets (See Useful Addresses). They are also increasingly available fresh in the supermarkets. If using fresh shiitake, there is no need to soak them.

Tofu with Shiitake Mushrooms and Kale

This is a nutritionally brilliant dish. Kale is one of the best possible vegetable sources of calcium, shiitake mushrooms are a well-known Japanese heart-disease preventative, and I don't need to sing the praises of tofu any more, do I?

2 oz	dried shiitake mushrooms	60 g
1 tbsp	cold-pressed sesame oil	1 tbsp
2	garlic cloves, chopped	2
	fresh ginger root, peeled and grated (piece 1 inch/2.5 cm)	
2 tbsp	shoyu sauce	2 tbsp
1 tbsp	cornflour dissolved in 2 tbsp water	1 tbsp
1lb 2 oz	firm tofu, rinsed and drained (2 packets), cut into 1 inch/2.5 cm cubes	500 g
1 lb	kale, tough ribs removed, and sliced into ribbons about 1/2 inch/1 cm wide	450 g

Pour boiling water over the shiitake mushrooms and leave to soak for half an hour to rehydrate. Drain and squeeze dry, reserving the soaking water. Heat the sesame oil in a medium pan and sauté the garlic and ginger until fragrant. Add 1/2 pint/300 ml of the soaking water from the mushrooms. Add the shoyu and slaked cornflour. Stir while the mixture thickens. Add the tofu and the soaked shiitake mushrooms (chopped if you prefer but can be left whole) and reduce heat to a simmer.

Meanwhile, steam the kale over boiling water until tender, about 6 minutes. Add to the tofu mixture. Serve with brown rice or buckwheat noodles. Serves 4.

PER SERVING	
Energy Kcals	265.0
Protein g	20.6
Carbohydrates g	21.1
Dietary Fibre g	4.3
Fat – Total g	12.5
Saturated Fat g	2.3
Polyunsaturated Fat g	4.3
Calcium mg	335.2
Magnesium mg	77.0

Szechuan Braised Tofu and Vegetables

This is one of those Chinese dishes where you should get everything prepared before you start. Then it's very quick and easy to make.

2 tbsp	extra virgin olive oil	2 tbsp
1 lb 2 oz	tofu, rinsed and drained, cut into 2 inch/5 cm x 1/2 inch/1 cm strips (2 packs)	500 g
1	small aubergine (about 12 oz/ 340 g), peeled and cut into 2 inch/5 cm x 1/2 inch/1 cm strips	1
1	garlic clove, chopped finely	1
8 oz	mushrooms, sliced	225 g
8 oz	green beans, sliced into 2 inch/ 5 cm lengths	225 g
5 tbsp	water	5 tbsp
1 tsp	cornflour	1 tsp
2 tbsp	tamari sauce	2 tbsp
4 tbsp	dry sherry	4 tbsp

Heat 1 tablespoon of the oil in a wok over medium to high heat. When it is hot but not smoking, add half the tofu strips and stir-fry until golden. Remove and repeat with the remaining tofu.

Add the rest of the oil to the pan and heat again. Then add the aubergine strips and stir-fry for about 3 minutes. The aubergine will absorb all the oil but do not add any more – just stir vigorously.

Add the garlic, mushrooms and green beans and stir-fry for another 2-3 minutes. Add a little more oil if you absolutely have to.

Next, add 4 tablespoons of water, cover the wok and turn down the heat. Cook for 4 minutes or until the water is all gone and the beans are tender. While this is cooking, blend together in a small bowl the cornflour and 1 tablespoon of water, then add the tamari and sherry.

Now return the tofu to the pan and toss well to mix. Then add the cornflour mixture and toss until well coated. Stir-fry for another couple of minutes, until the sauce is slightly thickened. Serve immediately with brown rice. Serves 4.

PER SERVING	
Energy Kcals	282.4
Protein g	20.3
Carbohydrates g	15.3
Dietary Fibre g	5.4
Fat – Total g	15.8
Saturated Fat g	2.8
Polyunsaturated Fat g	3.4
Calcium mg	289.2
Magnesium mg	71.1

This goes well served with brown basmati rice and a tomato, cucumber and onion salad with fresh coriander.

Tandoori Tofu

Drained tofu has much the same consistency as poached chicken breast, but takes almost no time to cook. It does, however, take very well to marinating, so tandoori is an obvious way to prepare it.

1 lb 2 oz	firm tofu, drained and rinsed (2 packets) cut into 1 inch/2.5 cm cubes	500 g
2	garlic cloves, crushed	2
	fresh ginger root, peeled and grated (1 inch/2.5 cm piece)	
1 tsp	ground coriander	1 tsp
1 tsp	ground cumin	1 tsp
1/2 tsp	ground turmeric	1/2 tsp
1/4 tsp	ground cloves	1/4 tsp
1/2 tsp	ground cardamon	1/2 tsp
1/2 tsp	cayenne pepper	1/2 tsp
1/4 tsp	ground black pepper	1/4 tsp
1 1/2 tsp	paprika	1 1/2 tsp
1 tsp	low-sodium salt	1 tsp
1	lemon, juice only	1
4 tbsp	natural live yoghurt or plain soya yoghurt	4 tbsp
2 tbsp	extra virgin olive oil	2 tbsp

For the garnish:

1	large onion, sliced thinly	1
1	lemon, quartered	1

Make tiny slits in the tofu cubes to help the marinade to penetrate. In a bowl, mix together all the other ingredients except the olive oil and garnish. Add the cubed tofu and mix gently to coat the tofu pieces with the marinade. Cover and refrigerate for a few hours or overnight.

When ready to cook, drizzle oil over the tofu pieces, and grill under a hot grill until golden, about 5 minutes per side. Garnish with the onion slices and quartered lemon. Serves 4.

PER SERVING	
Energy Kcals	241.9
Protein g	17.7
Carbohydrates g	7.8
Dietary Fibre g	1.6
Fat – Total g	15.9
Saturated Fat g	2.9
Polyunsaturated Fat g	3.2
Calcium mg	293.6
Magnesium mg	56.2

Tempeh is good for menopausal women to eat as it has all the oestrogenic properties of soya. Because it is a fermented food, it contains white spores that look a bit like cotton wool. They are perfectly safe to eat, and show that the beneficial bacteria are doing their work and making the tempeh more digestible. Although tempeh contains vitamin B12, which is impossible to get from other vegetarian sources (except for sea vegetables), unfortunately there is some evidence that it is not exactly the form that meets the body's requirements.

Sweet and Sour Tempeh

This recipe, together with the one following, is adapted from Madhur Jaffrey's book *Eastern Vegetarian Cooking*. Tempeh is a food that originated in Java and is the only soya product not to have originated in China or Japan. Unlike tofu, it has not been processed, so it contains all the soya bean's nutrients and fibre.

2	medium onions, peeled and finely chopped	2
3	cloves garlic, peeled and roughly chopped	3
3	fresh red chillies, seeded and roughly chopped	3
	fresh ginger root, peeled (1 inch/2.5 cm piece)	
12 oz	tempeh	340 g
2 tbsp	extra virgin olive oil	2 tbsp
1 tbsp	tamari sauce	1 tbsp
1 tbsp	concentrated apple juice	1 tbsp

Put the onions, garlic, chillies and ginger in a blender together with 3 tablespoons of water and blend until smooth. Cut the tempeh into matchsticks about 1¼ inch/3cm long.

Heat the oil in a large frying pan or wok and stir-fry the tempeh pieces in two batches until they become golden and crisp (about 5 minutes). Remove from the pan, drain on kitchen paper and keep warm. Add the paste from the blender to the pan (careful, it may spit) and stir-fry on medium heat for about 5 minutes until it starts to dry up. Add the tamari sauce and concentrated apple juice, stir to mix, then return the fried tempeh to the pan. Cook for a minute or two longer to heat through, and serve immediately with brown rice. Serves 4.

PER SERVING	
Energy Kcals	272.2
Protein g	17.6
Carbohydrates g	19.0
Dietary Fibre g	5.7
Fat – Total g	16.1
Saturated Fat g	2.8
Polyunsaturated Fat g	3.9
Calcium mg	115.1
Magnesium mg	85.6

Tempeh contains manganese, which assists your body in making hormones. Like all soya products, it also contains significant levels of isoflavones called genistein and diadzein, which may help to inhibit the growth of breast cancer cells, as well as damp down menopausal symptoms.

Tempeh with Coconut Milk

If you like the sweet taste of coconut, this is a very good introduction to tempeh, which itself has quite a strong, almost meaty taste.

14 oz	tempeh	400 g
2 tbsp	extra virgin olive oil	2 tbsp
2	medium onions, finely sliced	2
2	garlic cloves, finely chopped	2
	fresh ginger root, peeled and grated ($\frac{1}{2}$ inch/1 cm piece)	
1	fresh hot green chilli, seeded and cut into thin rings (optional)	1
2	green peppers, seeded and sliced into rings	2
15 fl oz	coconut milk	425 ml
2 tsp	tamari sauce	2 tsp

Cut the tempeh into $\frac{1}{2}$ inch/1 cm cubes. Heat the oil in a large frying pan or wok over medium heat and fry the onion, garlic, ginger and chilli (if using) for two minutes. Add the green pepper rings and stir-fry for another two minutes. Now add the coconut milk and tempeh pieces, bring to the boil, turn down the heat, cover and simmer for 10 minutes. Add the tamari sauce just before serving, and serve over brown rice. Serves 4.

PER SERVING	
Energy Kcals	307.0
Protein g	20.5
Carbohydrates g	21.1
Dietary Fibre g	7.3
Fat – Total g	18.2
Saturated Fat g	3.2
Polyunsaturated Fat g	4.5
Calcium mg	161.0
Magnesium mg	130.0

You could substitute tofu or even chicken breast for the tempeh.

Tempeh in Creamy Curry Sauce

If you're still not sure about tempeh, try this dish. I assure you, you will be won over.

14 oz	tempeh	400 g
1/2	lemon, juice only	1/2
2 tbsp	cold-pressed sesame oil	2 tbsp
For the sauce:		
2 tbsp	extra virgin olive oil	2 tbsp
	piece of fresh ginger root, peeled and grated (1 inch/2.5 cm piece)	
3	cloves garlic, finely chopped	3
1	large onion, finely chopped	1
1	small green chilli, seeded and diced	1
1/2 tsp	ground turmeric	1/2 tsp
5	tomatoes, peeled and diced	5
1/4 tsp	freshly ground black pepper	1/4 tsp
2 tsp	ground cumin	2 tsp
2 tsp	ground coriander	2 tsp
1/4 tsp	cayenne pepper	1/4 tsp
1/4 tsp	ground cloves	1/4 tsp
1/4 tsp	ground cinnamon	1/4 tsp
8 fl oz	soya milk	225 ml
	low-sodium salt to taste	
To serve:		
	a handful of fresh coriander, chopped	

PER SERVING	
Energy Kcals	411.0
Protein g	233.1
Carbohydrates g	27.2
Dietary Fibre g	9.6
Fat – Total g	26.7
Saturated Fat g	4.3
Polyunsaturated Fat g	8.0
Calcium mg	157.2
Magnesium mg	123.6

Cut the tempeh into strips about 2 inches/5 cm long, sprinkle with the lemon juice and leave to marinate while the sauce is cooking.

Meanwhile, heat the olive oil in a large pan and sauté the ginger and garlic for two minutes. Add the onion, chilli and turmeric and continue sautéeing until browned. Add the rest of the spices and continue cooking over medium heat for another couple of minutes. Add the tomatoes and chilli, reduce the heat and simmer until the tomatoes are soft, about 15-20 minutes. Take off the heat, cool for a minute or two, then put in a blender with 4 fl oz/120 ml water. Blend until smooth. Return to a clean pan, stir in the soya milk and bring gently up to the boil. Taste for seasoning and add salt if necessary.

Heat the sesame oil in a frying pan and saute the tempeh over medium high heat until golden brown and crisp on each side, about 5 minutes per side.

To serve, put the tempeh on a bed of brown rice, pour over the curry sauce, and garnish with chopped coriander. Serves 4.

Spicy Pumpkin Casserole with Ground Almonds

This is a lovely autumnal casserole. The amount of pumpkin looks a lot, but by the time you've peeled it and removed the seeds, you should be left with about half that weight in pumpkin flesh.

Pumpkin is an extremely good source of fibre as well as containing a lot of beta-carotene. Don't forget to save and dry the seeds for a highly nutritious snack. You could experiment with substituting other kinds of squash for the pumpkin if you prefer.

2 tsp	cumin seeds	2 tsp
1½ oz	sesame seeds	45 g
1 oz	ground almonds	30 g
2 tsp	paprika	2 tsp
2 tsp	dried oregano	2 tsp
2 tbsp	extra virgin olive oil	2 tbsp
2	onions, roughly chopped	2
2	cloves garlic, finely chopped	2
2 lbs	pumpkin, peeled and chopped into 1 inch/2.5 cm cubes	900 g
1¼ pints	vegetable stock (see page 41)	725 ml
2 lbs	fresh tomatoes, peeled, seeded and finely chopped	900 g
2 tbsp	chopped fresh coriander	2 tbsp
	live natural yoghurt or soya yoghurt to serve	

PER SERVING	
Energy Kcals	324.8
Protein g	9.7
Carbohydrates g	37.9
Dietary Fibre g	8.9
Fat – Total g	17.5
Saturated Fat g	2.3
Polyunsaturated Fat g	4.2
Calcium mg	150.9
Magnesium mg	117.3

First, lightly toast the cumin seeds and sesame seeds in a dry pan, until the aroma of the cumin seeds is released.

Grind the cumin and sesame seeds in an electric grinder, then stir into the ground almonds together with the paprika and dried oregano. Heat the oil in a large saucepan, add the onions and sauté over medium heat until softened. Add garlic, pumpkin and stock. Bring to the boil, then lower the heat, cover and simmer until the pumpkin is soft, about 20 minutes.

Add the ground almond mixture and peeled, chopped tomatoes. Season to taste and cook for a further 5 minutes or so until the mixture is well heated through. Stir in the chopped coriander and serve in deep warmed bowls, topped with a tablespoon of yoghurt each. Serves 4.

Vegetable Biriyani

This recipe is an adaptation of a Gujarati dish. Gujarati cuisine is noted for its subtle, sophisticated flavours.
Don't be put off by the long list of ingredients – the dish is really quite simple to make. The biriyani can be served on its own with raita (yoghurt and grated cucumber) and a salad, or with dhal (see page 117) and poppadoms.

4 oz	potato, diced but not peeled	110 g
4 oz	carrots, diced	110 g
4 oz	courgettes, diced	110 g
4 oz	green beans, cut into 1/2 inch/ 1 cm lengths	110 g
4 oz	cauliflower, cut into small florets	110 g
4 oz	fresh or frozen peas	110 g
1 hpd tsp	cumin seeds	1 hpd tsp
1 hpd tsp	coriander seeds	1 hpd tsp
8 oz	brown basmati rice	225 g
1/4 tsp	saffron threads soaked in 1 tbsp hot water	1/4 tsp
1	large onion, finely chopped	1
2	cloves garlic	2
1 tsp	poppy seeds	1 tsp
1 tsp	fennel seeds	1 tsp
	fresh ginger root, peeled and grated (1 inch/2.5cm piece)	

The vegetables in this dish provide plenty of beta-carotene, vitamin C and biotin, the brown rice provides protein and the cashews provide essential fatty acids and minerals, so this is a very nutritionally balanced dish.

1 tsp	chilli powder	1 tsp
1 tsp	garam masala	1 tsp
2 tbsp	extra virgin olive oil	2 tbsp
2	large onions, sliced	2
2 oz	cashew nuts	60 g
4 tbsp	live natural yoghurt or soya yoghurt	4 tbsp
1/2 tsp	low-sodium salt	1/2 tsp
2 tbsp	chopped fresh coriander	2 tbsp

First, steam the vegetables lightly over boiling water for no more than 5 minutes. Plunge into cold water, leave until quite cold, then drain and set aside. This preserves their bright colour.

Now, dry fry the cumin and coriander seeds: heat a small heavy pan for a couple of minutes. Add the seeds and roast until their fragrance is released. Do not burn. Set aside. Wash the rice and cook in boiling water until tender (about 25 minutes). Drain, tip into a bowl and stir in the saffron and its water. Keep warm.

While the rice is cooking, put the chopped onion, garlic, poppy seeds, fennel seeds, ginger, chilli powder and garam masala into a blender. Blend until a paste is formed.

For the garnish, preheat the oven to 200°C/400°F/Gas Mark 6. Place the onion slices on a baking sheet and drizzle with 1 tbsp olive oil. Cook for 20-30 minutes, until golden brown and beginning to char. In the same oven, dry roast the cashew nuts – they will only take about 5-8 minutes, so watch them carefully and stir them often. Set aside.

Heat the remaining tablespoon of oil in a large pan over gentle heat. Tip the contents of the blender into the pan and fry for a couple of minutes. Then add the vegetables and fry for about 3 minutes just to heat through. Add the cumin and coriander seeds, yoghurt and salt and stir to mix over gentle heat.

Stir the rice into the vegetable mixture. Serve garnished with the roasted sliced onion, the cashew nuts and chopped fresh coriander. Serves 4.

PER SERVING	
Energy Kcals	472.0
Protein g	13.3
Carbohydrates g	73.3
Dietary Fibre g	9.6
Fat – Total g	17.1
Saturated Fat g	3.1
Polyunsaturated Fat g	3.0
Calcium mg	123.2
Magnesium mg	101.5

As a variation, you could cook this dish on top of the stove, like a ratatouille. Choose a large saucepan, and sweat the vegetables in olive oil with the lid on over a low heat for 30 minutes or so before adding the tomatoes.

Roast West Indian Vegetables

This should be made with West Indian pumpkin, the 'calabaza'; unlike the North American pumpkin, it is more fibrous and less sweet, with quite a different taste.
You should be able to find it in West Indian shops and markets. If not, use the American pumpkin, or any other kind of squash.

2 tbsp	extra virgin olive oil	2 tbsp
6 oz	sweet potato, peeled and cubed	170 g
6 oz	pumpkin, peeled and cubed (weighed after peeling)	170 g
1	aubergine, cubed but not peeled	1
1	red pepper, deseeded and cut into 1 inch/2.5 cm squares	1
1	large onion, peeled and sliced	1
2	garlic cloves, peeled and chopped finely	2
1	small green or red chilli, finely chopped (optional)	1
2 sticks	celery, sliced	2 sticks
4 oz	okra	110 g
1 tsp	fresh thyme leaves	1 tsp
2 tsp	fresh basil, torn	2 tsp
14 oz	can of chopped tomatoes, drained	400 g
	low-sodium salt and freshly ground black pepper	
	fresh basil leaves, to garnish	

PER SERVING	
Energy Kcals	181.7
Protein g	4.3
Carbohydrates g	27.3
Dietary Fibre g	5.5
Fat – Total g	7.1
Saturated Fat g	1.0
Polyunsaturated Fat g	0.7
Calcium mg	61.1
Magnesium mg	42.2

Preheat the oven to 220°C/425°F/Gas Mark 7. Put the olive oil in a large roasting pan and heat in the oven for a few minutes. Then add the sweet potato, pumpkin, aubergine, red pepper, onion and garlic. Toss in the oil until all the vegetables are coated, then bake in the oven for 20 minutes.

Wash and trim the okra, then cut crosswise into $1/2$ inch/ 1 cm slices. (Okra must be washed before slicing rather than afterwards, as otherwise it becomes very sticky.)

Add the chilli (if using), celery, okra and thyme leaves to the pan and continue cooking for another 10 minutes, or until all the vegetables are just tender.

Add the torn basil leaves and tinned, chopped tomatoes and mix well. Season to taste, then return to the oven for another 15 minutes. Serve garnished with fresh basil leaves.
Serves 4-5.

Butternut Squash with Millet Stuffing

I learnt lots of different ways of cooking squash when I was in America, and this was one of them, though at the time I think I used white rice to stuff the squash! Now I appreciate that white rice is a refined grain, I have replaced it with millet, an alkaline grain with a very good protein profile. I think butternut squash are particularly tasty, and a reasonable size, but you could use acorn or small harlequin squashes instead, in which case you would use one per person and slice just the top off to form a lid, not cut them in half.

4 oz	millet	110 g
2	small butternut or other squash (roughly 1½ lb/675 g each in weight)	2
1	medium onion, peeled and finely chopped	1
1 tbsp	extra virgin olive oil	1 tbsp
½ tsp	turmeric	½ tsp
1 tsp	cumin seed	1 tsp
½ tsp	black mustard seed	½ tsp
1 stick	celery, finely sliced	1 stick
	low-sodium salt and freshly ground black pepper to taste	
2 oz	walnuts, chopped	60 g
2 tbsp	fresh parsley, chopped	2 tbsp
2 tbsp	extra virgin olive oil	2 tbsp
	fresh ginger root, peeled and finely grated (2 inch/5 cm piece)	
	a grating of fresh nutmeg	
1 tbsp	maple syrup	1 tbsp

The original American recipe used pecans, but their nutritional profile is nowhere as good as that of walnuts, which have much more protein, calcium, magnesium, and, most important of all, much more Omega-3 fatty acid than pecans. The millet also provides lots of magnesium, so although this is a fairly high calorie dish, it's very nutritious.

Preheat oven to 190°C/375°F/Gas Mark 5.

Cook the millet in a dry frying pan over medium heat for about 10 minutes, until it releases a toasty aroma. Then put it in a pan with 3/4 pt/425 ml cold water. Bring to the boil, then lower the heat, cover and simmer until dry and fluffy – about 25 minutes. Check that the water is not drying out – if so, add another spoonful or so. Set aside when cooked.

Meanwhile, cut each squash in half and scoop out the seeds. Place the cut side down on a lightly oiled baking sheet. Bake in the preheated oven until soft but still firm, about 35-45 minutes, depending on the size.

In a heavy frying pan over medium heat, heat the olive oil and sauté the onion until soft but not browned. Add the turmeric, cumin seed and mustard seed. Cook for a couple of minutes, then add the celery, and continue cooking for a couple more minutes. Remove from the heat, add the cooked millet, half the chopped walnuts and the parsley. Season to taste and set aside.

Next, put the 2 tablespoons of olive oil in a small pan and heat gently. Squeeze the grated ginger in your hands over the pan so that the ginger juice drips into the pan. Then grate in a little fresh nutmeg. Finally, add the maple syrup and warm through.

To assemble the dish, turn the cooked squash the other way up on their baking tray. You might want to scoop out a little more flesh to make room for your filling. Fill the hollows with the millet mixture, tamping it down well and leaving a bit of squash showing, and top with the remainder of the chopped walnuts. Finally, drizzle the ginger/maple syrup mixture over the squash and the filling. Bake until the squash is hot and the top is golden brown. Serve with green vegetables and beans. Serves 4.

PER SERVING	
Energy Kcals	506.5
Protein g	11.2
Carbohydrates g	69.6
Dietary Fibre g	7.2
Fat – Total g	21.9
Saturated Fat g	2.7
Polyunsaturated Fat g	8.7
Calcium mg	83.5
Magnesium mg	158.8

Right: Tempeh with Coconut Milk (page 65)

You could use other toppings on this pizza, such as sliced mushrooms, anchovies or tinned tuna.

Potato Pizza with Walnut Pesto

Trying to create a pizza without a refined flour base or cheese was a challenge. Here is the result of my efforts.

For the base:

1¼ lb	floury potatoes	560 g
2 tbsp	extra virgin olive oil	2 tbsp
1	organic, free-range egg	1
	low-sodium salt and freshly ground black pepper to taste	

For the pesto:

2½ oz	walnuts	75 g
2	garlic cloves, peeled	2
1 bunch	fresh basil, leaves only	1 bunch
1 bunch	flat-leaf parsley, leaves only	1 bunch
1 tbsp	miso	1 tbsp
3 tbsp	extra virgin olive oil	3 tbsp

For the topping:

1	red pepper	1
1	small red onion, sliced finely from root to tip	1
12	cherry tomatoes, cut in half	12
2 tsp	extra virgin olive oil, or use olive oil spray	2 tsp
1 tbsp	pine nuts	1 tbsp
	fresh basil leaves, torn	

Wash and cut the potatoes into smallish pieces but do not peel them. Boil until tender, then mash with the olive oil, beaten egg and seasoning to taste.

Preheat the oven to 200°C/400°F/Gas Mark 6. Roast the red peppers, whole, until charred (about half an hour). Place in a plastic bag to cool, then slip off the skins, remove the seeds and core, and slice into strips.

To make the pesto, whizz the walnuts and garlic in the blender or food processor until chopped. Add the basil, parsley and miso, and whizz again. Then add the olive oil, slowly, as for mayonnaise, until a thick purée is formed.

PER SERVING	
Energy Kcals	313.2
Protein g	6.3
Carbohydrates g	26.9
Dietary Fibre g	4.3
Fat – Total g	21.4
Saturated Fat g	2.8
Polyunsaturated Fat g	7.3
Calcium mg	58.4
Magnesium mg	65.3

Left: Wakame and Lemon Barley Risotto (page 75)

Lightly oil a 9 inch/23 cm flan ring with removable base. Press the potato mixture into the ring and bake for 15 minutes to brown the top slightly and set the egg. Remove from the oven and spread the pesto over the base. Top with the roasted, sliced pepper, the sliced onion and the halved cherry tomatoes. Spray or drizzle with a little more olive oil, then put back in the oven and cook for a further 10 minutes. Sprinkle the pine nuts over the surface and return to the oven for another 5 minutes, or until the tomatoes are collapsing.

Remove the flan ring, and serve the pizza topped with torn basil leaves, and cut into wedges. An unadorned rocket salad would go well with this. Serves 6.

Pumpkin Risotto with Sage

I just had to include this, because I adore risotto, and the pumpkin and sage combination is a winner – a wonderful autumnal taste. Italians would probably throw up their hands in horror at what I've done to risotto, but using brown rice instead of white, and adding the pumpkin seed oil instead of Parmesan cheese, adds to the nutritional value.

1 lb	pumpkin, peeled and cut into $^1/_4$ inch/$^1/_2$ cm dice	500 g
1$^3/_4$ pints	vegetable stock (see page 41)	1 litre
2 tbsp	extra virgin olive oil	2 tbsp
1	onion, peeled and chopped finely	1
1 lb	brown short grain Italian rice	450 g
5 fl oz	white wine	150 ml
2 oz	organic unsalted butter	60 g
6	fresh sage leaves	6
	squeeze of lemon juice	
	low-sodium salt and freshly ground black pepper to taste	
1 tbsp	toasted pumpkin seed oil	1 tbsp

Put the stock in a pot, bring to the boil, and keep at a gentle simmer.

Heat the olive oil in a large pan and sauté the onion gently until soft. Add the rice, and stir to coat all the grains, until

Sage, whose Latin name is *salvia*, meaning good health, has traditionally been associated with longevity and memory. Because it contains phytoestrogens that appear to have a drying effect on body fluids, it is also used to relieve night sweats. Indeed my first acquaintance with herbal remedies was a tincture of sage for reducing hot flushes. You can try making sage tea by pouring some hot water over the leaves and steeping for a few minutes.

PER SERVING	
Energy Kcals	471.3
Protein g	7.4
Carbohydrates g	68.4
Dietary Fibre g	6.2
Fat – Total g	17.0
Saturated Fat g	6.0
Polyunsaturated Fat g	2.6
Calcium mg	61.2
Magnesium mg	122.7

the rice is opaque. Now add the wine. When that has all been absorbed, start adding the hot stock, a ladleful at a time, stirring frequently to prevent the risotto sticking to the bottom of the pan. Because you are using brown rice, this is going to take twice as long as if you were using white rice – about 35 minutes. Halfway through this cooking time, add the pumpkin to the pot and continue stirring and adding the stock until the rice is cooked and all the stock has been used up.

Roll the sage leaves up and slice across the rolls, to give long shreds. Melt the butter over gentle heat in a small pan and stew the sage for a few minutes. Add a squeeze of lemon juice and the seasoning. Remove from the heat and pour into the risotto, which should be slightly sloppy. Serve in hot bowls with a trickle of toasted pumpkin seed oil on top. Serves 6.

Wakame and Lemon Barley Risotto

This is a delicately-flavoured dish – a good introduction to sea vegetables.

1 oz	dried wakame	30 g
2 pints	vegetable stock (see page 41)	1.2 litres
2 tbsp	extra virgin olive oil	2 tbsp
2	leeks, sliced thinly	2
1 lb	pearl barley	450 g
5 fl oz	white wine	150 ml
1	lemon	1
	chopped coriander, to serve	

Soak the wakame in the vegetable stock until reconstituted – about 15 minutes. Remove from the stock and cut into small pieces with scissors. Bring the stock to the boil, and keep at a gentle simmer.

Heat the oil in a pan, add the leeks and fry gently for 1-2 minutes. Add the barley and the wine and bring to a simmer. When all the wine has been absorbed, start adding the hot stock, a ladleful at a time, stirring frequently to prevent the risotto sticking to the bottom of the pan. The risotto should be cooked until it is creamy and the barley is soft to the bite

Wakame is a deep green curly-leafed seaweed, regarded by Japanese women as being good for the complexion. Seaweeds are useful in weight-loss programmes, too, because they can reduce water retention and add bulk while being low in calories and fat. I use Clearspring sea vegetables (see Useful Addresses). Their sea vegetables are harvested in pollution-free water, which is tested frequently to assure quality. Pearl barley, though a refined grain as it has had its husk stripped away, is actually very low on the Glycaemic Index (see Appendix 1), much lower than any other grain, even brown rice. So it releases its sugars slowly and will leave you feeling pleasantly full for a long time.

PER SERVING	
Energy Kcals	383.9
Protein g	7.2
Carbohydrates g	68.7
Dietary Fibre g	6.0
Fat – Total g	7.1
Saturated Fat g	1.0
Polyunsaturated Fat g	1.2
Calcium mg	68.1
Magnesium mg	127.9

– this could take up to 1 hour. Cut the rind from the lemon with a vegetable peeler, and cut the pieces into matchsticks. Squeeze the juice from the lemon and add to the risotto along with the wakame and the lemon peel. Season to taste and serve garnished with chopped coriander leaves and accompanied by green vegetables or a salad. Serves 6.

You could bake the polenta alongside the peppers, but you would not achieve the same crispy texture.

Grilled Polenta with Roasted Pepper Ragoût

This is my favourite way to serve polenta. You can add all sorts of things to the polenta instead of the chopped basil, such as chopped fresh chillies (if you don't suffer from hot flushes), chopped mushrooms or onions. If you ever find buckwheat polenta – difficult to find in the UK – do try it in this dish. It has a very special flavour.

7 oz	polenta	200 g
1 tbsp	chopped basil	1 tbsp
2 tbsp	extra virgin olive oil	2 tbsp
1 lb	mixed sweet peppers	450 g
1	clove garlic, chopped finely	1
3 tbsp	white wine	3 tbsp
4 oz	fresh leaf spinach	110 g
2 tsp	balsamic vinegar	2 tsp
1 tsp	chopped fresh thyme leaves	1 tsp
	low-sodium salt and freshly ground black pepper to taste	

To make the polenta, bring $1^1/4$ pints/725 ml water to the boil in a medium saucepan. Pour in the polenta gradually, stirring all the time. Reduce the heat and cook, stirring frequently, for about 20 minutes, or until the polenta comes away from the sides of the pan. Alternatively you can use instant polenta, which only takes about 5 minutes to cook. Stir the chopped basil into the polenta, season to taste, then pour the polenta out into an oiled 9 x 12 inch/23 x 30 cm baking pan. Leave to cool, then refrigerate until cold and firm. When the polenta is quite cold, cut it into bars or diamonds.

Preheat the oven to 200°C/400°F/Gas Mark 6, and roast the peppers until charred (about 20 minutes). Leave to cool, then skin and cut into strips. Reserve the oily juice from the peppers, pour it into a small pan together with 1 tablespoon of the olive oil, and cook the chopped garlic in it. Add the wine and bring to the boil. Add the spinach, balsamic vinegar, thyme and seasoning, remove from the heat and put the lid on. The spinach will wilt in the residual heat left in the pan.

Brush the polenta on both sides with the remaining tablespoon of olive oil. Heat a ridged pan over medium heat, oil it lightly and grill the polenta on both sides until crispy on the outside and heated through.

Serve the grilled polenta alongside the pepper and spinach mixture. Serves 4.

PER SERVING	
Energy Kcals	239.1
Protein g	5.2
Carbohydrates g	38.8
Dietary Fibre g	6.1
Fat – Total g	7.1
Saturated Fat g	1.0
Polyunsaturated Fat g	0.7
Calcium mg	40.1
Magnesium mg	38.4

Alfalfa sprouts are the only food we consume that contains significant amounts of coumestrol (one of the three sorts of phytoestrogen that may help control menopausal symptoms) – about 4.7 g per 100 g of sprouts. A recent survey by the Food Standards Agency found that out of 51 red clover phytoestrogen supplements tested, only 3 contained any coumestrol at all. It is therefore probably more reliable to eat sprouts than it is to take a red clover supplement.

Wholemeal Tortillas with Beans, Avocados and Alfalfa Sprouts

Flour tortillas are easier to make at home than the more usual corn tortillas, and are best eaten straight from the pan. This is quite a quick recipe provided the beans have been cooked in advance. I don't recommend using tinned beans here because the onion and garlic need to be cooked with the beans, so that the beans will pick up their flavour.

For the tortillas:

4 oz	wholemeal flour	110 g
	pinch of low-sodium salt	
2 tbsp	extra virgin olive oil	2 tbsp
2½ fl oz	warm water	75 ml

For the filling:

4 oz	dried pinto beans or haricot beans	110 g
½	medium onion, peeled and chopped	½
1	garlic clove, peeled and chopped	1
1 tbsp	extra virgin olive oil	1 tbsp
	low-sodium salt to taste	

For the garnish:

1	avocado	1
$1/2$	lime, juiced	$1/2$
	a handful of alfalfa sprouts (see page 126)	

Combine the flour and salt in a bowl. Add the oil, and gradually add enough water to make a soft dough. Divide the dough into 6 pieces. Shape each piece into a small, smooth ball. Flatten the balls with a rolling pin, and roll each one out on a lightly floured surface to a circle about 7 inches/17.5 cm in diameter. Roll out no more than two at a time to prevent their drying out. Cook in an ungreased heavy frying pan or directly on a hot griddle until the top is bubbled and the underside flecked with brown. Turn the tortilla over and cook the other side. Stack the cooked tortillas in a warm place and cover with a cloth.

For the bean filling, which can be prepared in advance, soak the beans overnight. Drain, rinse, cover with fresh water, bring to the boil, add onion and garlic. Cover and simmer for 1-1$1/2$ hours or until tender. Add olive oil and salt to taste. The beans may be mashed or left whole.

Mash the avocado with the lime juice and seasoning to taste.

To serve, place a spoonful of bean filling and a spoonful of mashed avocado on each tortilla. Top with a few alfalfa sprouts, and roll up the tortillas, tucking in the ends. Serve immediately, garnished with more sprouts if desired. Serves 4.

PER SERVING	
Energy Kcals	359.2
Protein g	11.3
Carbohydrates g	44.6
Dietary Fibre g	13.6
Fat – Total g	17.3
Saturated Fat g	2.8
Polyunsaturated Fat g	1.2
Calcium mg	52.2
Magnesium mg	83.1

Nutritionally this is a brilliant dish, in spite of the relatively large number of calories. Quinoa is an exceptionally rich vegetarian source of protein (16-18%), besides having good levels of magnesium and zinc. It also has a good calcium: magnesium balance. Magnesium is needed for bones just as much as calcium, if not more so, so any dish that has more magnesium than calcium helps to redress the balance. Beetroots are very high in folate, which may help you reduce your risk of heart disease by reducing levels of homocysteine. Increased levels of homocysteine have been found in postmenopausal women and may play a role in osteoporosis by interfering with the formation of a strong bone matrix.

Quinoa Pilaff with Roasted Beetroot and Onions

Red onions make good partners for beetroot as the colours are similar. Roasting brings out the sweetness of both.

6	raw beetroot	6
4	red onions	4
	low-sodium salt and freshly ground black pepper to taste	
2 tbsp	extra virgin olive oil	2 tbsp
1 tbsp	balsamic vinegar	1 tbsp
For the pilaff:		
8 oz	quinoa	225 g
1 pint	vegetable stock (see page 41)	570 ml
2 tbsp	extra virgin olive oil	2 tbsp
1	onion, peeled and finely chopped	1
4 sticks	celery, finely chopped	4 sticks
1/2	green pepper	1/2
1 tsp	ground cumin	1 tsp
1 oz	raisins	30 g
1 oz	pine nuts, toasted	30 g
1 oz	sunflower seeds	30 g
2 tbsp	fresh coriander, chopped	2 tbsp

Preheat oven to 180°C/350°F/Gas Mark 4.

Wash the beetroot, place in an ovenproof dish, cover with baking parchment and roast for 45-60 minutes, depending on size. Quarter the onions and add them after about 20 minutes cooking, as they will take less time than the beetroot.

When the beetroot are done, take them out of the oven to cool until you are able to handle them, then slip off the skins (they should come off quite easily), quarter them and return them to the dish of onions together with the salt and pepper, olive oil and balsamic vinegar. Turn up the oven to 200°C/400°F/Gas Mark 6. Cook the beetroot and onions, uncovered, for 15-20 minutes at this higher heat, until the oil and vinegar mixture begins to caramelise.

PER SERVING	
Energy Kcals	558.6
Protein g	13.2
Carbohydrates g	75.1
Dietary Fibre g	9.4
Fat – Total g	24.6
Saturated Fat g	3.0
Polyunsaturated Fat g	3.8
Calcium mg	127.1
Magnesium mg	173.1

Brazil nuts happen to be my favourite nut, so I've done some research on their nutritive value to justify enjoying them so much. The brazil nuts in one serving of this roast will supply you with a good range of minerals – calcium, magnesium, zinc, iron and 500 mcg selenium – more than enough to boost your immune system and protect your heart. Brazil nuts *are* high in fat, but they contain three times as much mono- and polyunsaturated fat (the good sort) as saturated fat (the bad sort) and they are a good protein source too.

Meanwhile, rinse the quinoa in cold water to remove the soapy outer coating, and cook for 20 minutes in the stock. In another pan, sauté the onion in the olive oil over gentle heat for 5 minutes, then add the celery, green pepper and ground cumin and cook for a little longer. Add the raisins and cook for a further minute or two.

When the quinoa is cooked, drain it well and put it back in the pan. Stir in the vegetable and dried fruit mixture, together with the toasted pine nuts, sunflower seeds, seasoning and half the chopped coriander.

Serve the quinoa pilaff on individual hot plates, with the roasted beetroot and onions on top or beside it. Sprinkle over the remaining chopped coriander. Serves 4.

Brazil Nut and Lentil Roast

This is good enough to serve at a celebration meal. In fact you could dress it up for a vegetarian Christmas dinner by substituting a layer of cranberry sauce for the spinach layer. The sauce is the simplest tomato sauce of all. I make huge batches of it, and other tomato sauces, in September and October when our tomatoes are ripening fast, the first frosts are about to arrive, and we cannot eat our tomatoes quickly enough.

2 oz	brown lentils	60 g
1 tbsp	extra virgin olive oil	1 tbsp
1	small onion, finely chopped	1
4 sticks	celery, finely chopped	4 sticks
2	cloves garlic, crushed	2
2	medium carrots, peeled and grated	2
3½ oz	brazil nuts, chopped or grated	100 g
2	organic free-range eggs, beaten	2
1 tbsp	dry sherry	1 tbsp
1 tbsp	tamari sauce	1 tbsp
1 tbsp	chopped parsley	1 tbsp
	low-sodium salt and freshly ground black pepper to taste	

For the filling:

1	small onion, finely chopped	1
1 tbsp	extra virgin olive oil	1 tbsp
14 oz	fresh spinach	400 g
	fresh nutmeg for grating	

For the sauce:

1 tbsp	extra virgin olive oil	1 tbsp
1	small onion, peeled and finely chopped	1
1 lb	fresh ripe plum tomatoes, skinned and coarsely chopped	450 g
	low-sodium salt and freshly ground black pepper to taste	
	small handful of fresh basil leaves (optional)	

Wash the lentils and put them in a pan with cold water to cover. Bring to the boil, reduce the heat to a simmer and cook until tender – about 30 minutes. Drain well and set aside.

While the lentils are cooking, make the sauce: heat the oil in a large heavy saucepan, and sauté the onion gently until starting to colour. Add the tomatoes. Cook uncovered over very low heat for 45 minutes. Stir from time to time, squashing any large pieces of tomato with a wooden spoon. Season to taste, and add fresh torn basil leaves if using. This sauce can be liquidised and sieved if a smoother consistency is desirable.

Heat the olive oil and sauté the onion, celery and garlic until soft. Stir in the lentils, grated carrots and brazil nuts. Add the beaten eggs, sherry, tamari, parsley and seasoning.

Preheat the oven to 170°C/325°F/Gas Mark 3.

To make the filling, fry the chopped onion in the olive oil until soft in a large pan. Wash the spinach and remove any large stems. Add it to the sautéed onion, together with the water clinging to the leaves. Cover tightly and cook for about 5 minutes, until wilted. Drain well, pressing out as much moisture as possible. Grate over some fresh nutmeg.

To assemble the loaf, grease a 2 lb/900 g loaf tin and line with greaseproof paper. I use ready formed paper loaf liners from Lakeland Limited (see Useful Addresses). Spread half the nut and lentil mixture into the tin, pressing down well.

Put the spinach layer on top, and finish with the other half

PER SERVING	
Energy Kcals	297.4
Protein g	11.9
Carbohydrates g	23.0
Dietary Fibre g	8.7
Fat – Total g	19.5
Saturated Fat g	5.4
Polyunsaturated Fat g	1.3
Calcium mg	148.9
Magnesium mg	120.7

of the nut and lentil mixture, pressing down evenly. Cover with baking parchment and bake for 1¹/2 hours, removing the parchment after an hour. Turn out onto a serving plate and serve in thick slices with the tomato sauce. Serves 6.

Sunflower Seed Loaf with Fennel and Red Pepper Sauce

You could experiment with other seeds instead of the sunflower seeds. Pumpkin seeds would be delicious in this loaf. Pine nuts would work well too, or try a mixture of different seeds.

For the loaf:

5 oz	sunflower seeds	140 g
2 tbsp	flax seed	2 tbsp
1 tbsp	extra virgin olive oil	1 tbsp
1	onion, peeled and finely chopped	1
2	garlic cloves, peeled and finely chopped	2
2	courgettes, grated	2
3	medium carrots, grated	3
6 oz	button mushrooms, chopped	170 g
1¹/2 tsp	ground cumin	1¹/2 tsp
2 oz	rolled oats	60 g
1 tbsp	tomato purée	1 tbsp
2 oz	walnuts, chopped	60 g
2	organic free-range eggs, beaten	2
	low-sodium salt and freshly ground black pepper to taste	

For the sauce:

2	red peppers	2
1 tbsp	extra virgin olive oil	1 tbsp
3 oz	fennel, chopped	90 g
¹/2 tsp	fennel seeds	¹/2 tsp
1 tsp	vegetable bouillon powder	1 tsp
5 fl oz	white wine	150 ml
	low-sodium salt and freshly ground black pepper to taste	

Preheat oven to 190°C/375°F/Gas Mark 5.

First, roast the sunflower seeds in the preheated oven for about 8-10 minutes, checking frequently to make sure they don't burn. Leave to cool. Then set aside half the sunflower seeds, and grind the remainder with the flax seeds in an electric grinder.

While the sunflower seeds are roasting, roast the peppers for the sauce for 20-30 minutes or until charred, turning once or twice. Leave to cool.

Next, make the sunflower seed loaf: oil and line a 2 lb/ 900 g loaf tin. Heat the olive oil in a pan over medium heat, and sauté the onion until soft but not browned. Add the garlic, courgettes, carrots and mushrooms and cook for another 5 minutes, stirring occasionally. Stir in the cumin and cook for a couple of minutes longer. Add the rolled oats, tomato purée, ground sunflower and flax seeds, whole sunflower seeds and the chopped walnuts. Lastly, stir in the beaten eggs. Season to taste, then pack into the prepared loaf tin and bake for 30 minutes or until firm.

While the loaf is cooking, finish the sauce. Heat the oil in a small pan and sauté the chopped fennel over a low heat until soft. Peel the cooled roasted peppers, core, deseed and chop roughly, reserving any juice. Put the chopped pepper and juice into the pan with the fennel, then add the vegetable bouillon powder and white wine. Cook for about 10-15 minutes, until the liquid has reduced by about one third. Take off the heat, cool a little, then blend in the blender until smooth. Return to a clean pan to reheat, and season to taste.

When the loaf is done, turn it out, cool for a few moments, and slice with a very sharp knife, as it will be quite crumbly. Serve with the fennel and red pepper sauce. Serves 6.

PER SERVING	
Energy Kcals	424.5
Protein g	13.9
Carbohydrates g	32.8
Dietary Fibre g	10.0
Fat – Total g	27.2
Saturated Fat g	3.3
Polyunsaturated Fat g	14.4
Calcium mg	91.1
Magnesium mg	117.1

Pasta Dishes

Who doesn't like pasta? I've never met anyone who didn't. However, we generally eat refined wheat pasta loaded with extra fat, including cheese. I'm as much an addict of freshly grated Parmesan cheese as anyone, but I have found that nuts and seeds, particularly if roasted to release their flavour, make a tasty substitute. The idea is that they trick your palate into thinking it's had a satisfyingly high fat ingredient when it hasn't. So I have tried here to make Italian style dishes without the dairy products and without the refined wheat – difficult, but, I hope you will agree, not impossible.

As I have mentioned elsewhere, wheat is a difficult food to digest. Additionally, white pasta is made from flour from which most of the fibre and minerals have been removed. Eating lots and lots of pasta is not good for you – presently in Italy, where in many regions wheat pasta is the staple diet, it is reported that one in 186 people has coeliac disease (gluten insensitivity)[25]. It is thought that this may be due to an over-reliance on one grain over many generations or to the high gluten content of modern wheat. So the message, as always, is vary your grains. Eat pasta just once a week or so, and try varieties other than wheat.

There is an extraordinary variety of pastas on the market these days. The menopausal woman, and anyone else who wishes to avoid refined wheat products, has an extensive choice between wholewheat pasta (still wheat, but not so refined), buckwheat pasta (also known as soba noodles), corn pasta, rice pasta, and pasta made of split peas and soya. I have given below a couple of ideas for using these different types of pasta.

---

[25] Braley, J. 'Dangerous Grains – why gluten cereal grains may be hazardous to your health', *Avery*, 2002. pp177-78.

The amounts given for the broad beans and peas are for those vegetables in the pod. If you are using frozen vegetables, use 8 oz/225 g of each.

Pasta Primavera

Make this with the freshest of spring vegetables, though it's hard to find fresh asparagus, fresh broad beans and fresh peas all in the same season. Use frozen peas if you have to. Sadly, the latest research indicates that frozen vegetables are often more nutritious than fresh, as they are picked and frozen while at the peak of freshness, whereas 'fresh' supermarket vegetables have travelled great distances and have often been stored for long periods.

10 oz	garlic, parsley and rice pasta, or other wheat-free pasta	285 g
2 tbsp	extra virgin olive oil	2 tbsp
4	shallots, peeled and chopped	4
1	garlic clove, finely chopped	1
1 tsp	fresh thyme, finely chopped	1 tsp
1 lb	fresh asparagus, cut into 2 inch/5 cm lengths	450 g
	low-sodium salt and freshly ground black pepper to taste	
1 1/2 lbs	fresh broad beans, shelled and peeled unless very small	675 g
1 1/2 lbs	fresh peas, shelled	675 g
1	lemon, juice and grated rind	1
1 tbsp	flat-leaf parsley, chopped	1 tbsp
1 tbsp	chervil, chopped	1 tbsp
1 oz	sesame seeds, toasted	30 g

Heat the olive oil in a large frying pan, add the shallots, garlic and thyme, and sauté gently until transparent. Add the broad beans and asparagus, season to taste and cook for another couple of minutes. Add the peas, lemon rind and juice, and about 150 ml/$1/4$ pint of water. Bring to the boil, cover and cook gently for 3-4 minutes, until the vegetables are tender.

Meanwhile, cook the pasta according to the directions on the packet. Toss with the vegetable mixture, and stir in the fresh herbs. Serve very hot, sprinkled with the toasted sesame seeds, in deep warmed bowls. Serves 4.

PER SERVING	
Energy Kcals	479.1
Protein g	15.2
Carbohydrates g	75.7
Dietary Fibre g	7.0
Fat – Total g	12.5
Saturated Fat g	1.3
Polyunsaturated Fat g	1.4
Calcium mg	80.4
Magnesium mg	76.1

If you can't find Puy lentils, other brown or green lentils will do just as well. Do not use the orange ones for this dish, though, as they disintegrate on cooking.

Soba Noodles with Puy Lentils and Pumpkin Seeds

Soba noodles are made with buckwheat, and have a wonderful, earthy taste. Pumpkin seeds are a great source of zinc.

3 oz	Puy lentils	85 g
10 oz	soba or buckwheat pasta	285 g
1	bay leaf	1
	low-sodium salt and freshly ground black pepper to taste	
2 tbsp	extra virgin olive oil	2 tbsp
2	garlic cloves, finely chopped	2
2	medium carrots, diced	2
1 stick	celery, diced	1 stick
2	leeks, white parts only, chopped	2
8 fl oz	vegetable stock (see page 41)	225 ml
1 tbsp	flat-leaf parsley, chopped	1 tbsp
1$^1/_2$ oz	pumpkin seeds, roasted	45 g

Wash the lentils, then cover with water and bring them to the boil with the bay leaf. Turn the heat down and simmer for 25-30 minutes or until just tender, being careful not to overcook them. They should still keep their shape. Drain and toss with 1 tablespoon of olive oil, salt and black pepper to taste.

Heat the rest of the olive oil in a frying pan, and gently fry the chopped garlic until starting to colour. Add the carrots, celery and leeks. Cook for a minute or two, stirring, then add the vegetable stock. Simmer until the vegetables are tender and there is still a little liquid left in the pan. Just before the vegetables are completely cooked, stir in the lentils to heat through.

Meanwhile, cook the soba according to the directions on the packet. Drain well, and toss the soba with the vegetables. Serve garnished with the chopped parsley and pumpkin seeds. Serves 4.

PER SERVING	
Energy Kcals	489.7
Protein g	23.2
Carbohydrates g	79.6
Dietary Fibre g	8.6
Fat – Total g	12.0
Saturated Fat g	1.9
Polyunsaturated Fat g	2.8
Calcium mg	69.9
Magnesium mg	95.9

Main Dishes – Fish, Poultry and Game

Salmon with Sweet Potato, Courgette and Carrot Rösti
Miso Grilled Salmon
Salmon in Mustard Dressing with Puy Lentils
Lemon Trout with Almond Quinoa
Barley-Stuffed Mackerel with Fresh Coriander Sauce
Mackerel Kedgeree
Fresh Sardines Baked in Tomato Sauce
Sardines and Seaweed
Fresh Tuna Teriyaki
Tuna with Cannellini Beans and Sage
Herring and Oat Fishcakes
Roast Sea Bass with Fennel
Szechuan Chicken with Kale
Chicken with Walnuts, Almonds and Hazelnuts
Grilled Chicken with Tahini Sauce
Braised Rabbit with Herbs and Roasted Shallots
Roast Pheasant with Red Wine and Grapes

Both salmon and flax oil are fantastic sources of Omega-3 fatty acids, which we need for our brains, nerves, eyes and sex organs – not only does this recipe deliver 6.4 g Omega-3 EFAs per portion, but also in a 3:1 proportion to Omega-6, which will help redress the imbalance in our diet.

Salmon with Sweet Potato, Courgette and Carrot Rösti

For this and all salmon dishes, choose wild salmon in season, and farmed organic salmon at other times. Farmed salmon that is not organic is subject to a lot of questionable practices.

4	pieces of wild or organic salmon fillet, about 6 oz/170 g each, with skin	4
1 tbsp	extra virgin olive oil	1 tbsp
	low-sodium salt and freshly ground black pepper to taste	
For the rösti:		
4 oz	sweet potato	110 g
4 oz	carrots, peeled unless organic	110 g
4 oz	courgette	110 g
1	small onion, peeled	1
1-2 tbsp	brown rice flour	1-2 tbsp
	low-sodium salt and freshly ground black pepper to taste	
	olive oil spray	
For the tomato dressing:		
4 tsp	cold pressed flax oil	4 tsp
1 tsp	balsamic vinegar	1 tsp
	low-sodium salt and freshly ground black pepper	
1 tsp	extra virgin olive oil	1 tsp
2	tomatoes, peeled, seeded and finely diced	2
2 tbsp	fresh basil, torn into small pieces	2 tbsp

Preheat the oven to 180°C/350°F/Gas Mark 4.

For the rösti, scrub the sweet potato and steam over boiling water for about 8 minutes, until it feels slightly soft. Cool until it is cold enough to handle, then peel and grate the flesh into a large bowl, using a coarse grater.

Grate the carrots, courgettes and onion into the same bowl

Add the rice flour and seasoning. Generously oil a baking sheet. Squeeze the vegetable mixture with your hands to remove excess moisture, and form it into four flat cakes large enough for the salmon to fit on comfortably. Spray or drizzle with olive oil, and bake in the oven for 30-35 minutes, turning once, until lightly browned. If the rösti fall apart a bit when you turn them, that doesn't matter – just reassemble them.

Place the salmon fillets, skin-side up, on an oiled baking sheet, and bake in the oven for about 20 minutes, until cooked through.

Next, whisk together the flax oil, balsamic vinegar and seasoning for the dressing.

To serve, place a rösti on each plate topped with a salmon fillet. Scatter the diced tomato round the edge of each plate and pour over the oil and vinegar mixture. Garnish with chopped basil. Serves 4.

PER SERVING	
Energy Kcals	450.1
Protein g	45.0
Carbohydrates g	13.4
Dietary Fibre g	2.8
Fat – Total g	23.4
Saturated Fat g	3.3
Polyunsaturated Fat g	9.2
Calcium mg	52.8
Magnesium mg	90.4

Miso is something of a superfood. It's a fermented soybean paste thought to have originated in China some 2,500 years ago, and is made by combining cooked soya beans with a mould and one of a variety of grains, then fermenting for 6 months to two years or more. It's high in protein and B vitamins as well as being a 'living' food because it contains beneficial live bacteria. The sweet white variety contains more bacteria than the darker kind.

Miso Grilled Salmon

If you can find a source of sweet white miso, do use it in this recipe. You can get it online from Clearspring (see Useful Addresses). If you are using Genmai miso, which has a darker colour and stronger taste, use 2-3 tablespoons rather than the 4 suggested here.

1 tbsp	concentrated apple juice	1 tbsp
1 tbsp	sake or dry sherry	1 tbsp
4 tbsp	miso	4 tbsp
4	wild or organic salmon steaks, about 8 oz/225 g each	4
2 tbsp	tamari sauce	2 tbsp
Garnish:		
	fresh ginger root, peeled and shaved with a potato peeler (2 inch/5 cm piece)	
2	spring onions, cut diagonally into $1/2$ inch/1 cm slices	2

Combine the concentrated apple juice, sake or sherry and miso in a small bowl. Mix well. Put the salmon steaks into a shallow dish where they can fit side by side. Spoon over the miso mixture and turn to coat. Cover and refrigerate for a few hours or overnight.

PER SERVING	
Energy Kcals	365.6
Protein g	45.4
Carbohydrates g	8.8
Dietary Fibre g	1.0
Fat – Total g	14.9
Saturated Fat g	2.3
Polyunsaturated Fat g	6.1
Calcium mg	39.3
Magnesium mg	71.3

When ready to cook, remove the fish from the fridge and bring to room temperature. Preheat the grill, drain the fish from the marinade and grill for 5-7 minutes on each side until cooked to your liking.

To serve, sprinkle with tamari and garnish with the pieces of shaved ginger and spring onion. Serves 4.

The lentils provide copper, which is necessary for the formation of collagen, essential for the structure of the skin, and boron, which may help you make the best of your body's own oestrogen. Salmon is high in vitamin D, which increases the absorption of calcium necessary for bone health.

Salmon in Mustard Dressing with Puy Lentils

The combination of fish and lentils here is very high in protein. I serve it with broccoli florets and a few boiled new potatoes to complete what is a highly nutritious meal. Wrapping the salmon up in baking parchment is a low-fat way of cooking and keeps all the moisture in the fish so it doesn't dry out.

4 oz	Puy lentils	110 g
1 tbsp	extra virgin olive oil	1 tbsp
1	large onion, peeled and finely chopped	1
2	garlic cloves, peeled and finely chopped	2
1 tbsp	fresh thyme, chopped	1 tbsp
	low-sodium salt and freshly ground black pepper to taste	
4	pieces of wild or organic salmon fillet, about 5 oz/140 g each, with skin	4
1/2	lemon, juice only	1/2
For the dressing:		
1 tbsp	Dijon mustard	1 tbsp
1 tbsp	lemon juice	1 tbsp
3 tbsp	extra virgin olive oil	3 tbsp
2 tsp	cold pressed flax oil	2 tsp
	low-sodium salt and freshly ground black pepper to taste	
3 tbsp	flat-leaf parsley, chopped	3 tbsp

First, wash the lentils, and place in a pot with cold water to cover. Bring to the boil and cook for 25-30 minutes, or until tender. Drain well.

Heat the 2 tablespoons of olive oil in a large frying pan over medium heat, then add the chopped onion, garlic and thyme and cook until soft but not browned. Add the cooked lentils and seasoning and keep warm while you cook the salmon and broccoli.

Next cook the salmon: lightly oil four pieces of baking parchment (I use my olive oil spray for this) and place a salmon fillet on each one. Sprinkle each with lemon juice and seasoning, then wrap up the parcels, with the seam to the side of each fillet. Put the parcels in a steamer over boiling water and cook, without turning, for 15-20 minutes, depending on the thickness of the salmon. Open up one of the parcels to check that they are done, then keep warm.

For the dressing, whisk together the mustard, salt, pepper and lemon juice, then add the olive oil and flax oil in a thin stream, as for mayonnaise, whisking constantly. Lastly, add half the parsley.

To serve, put a bed of lentils on each plate, open up each salmon parcel and put a salmon fillet on top of the lentils, together with any juices. Drizzle the dressing over the salmon, and sprinkling the remainder of the parsley over everything. Serves 4.

PER SERVING	
Energy Kcals	548.3
Protein g	48.3
Carbohydrates g	26.0
Dietary Fibre g	6.2
Fat – Total g	27.3
Saturated Fat g	4.5
Polyunsaturated Fat g	6.5
Calcium mg	117.6
Magnesium mg	59.8

Both trout and quinoa are excellent sources of easily-digested protein, and trout has the lowest level of fat of any of the oily fish. I've added flax oil to this dish to boost the Omega-3 content.

Lemon Trout with Almond Quinoa

If you're lucky enough to know someone who fishes for trout, you might be able to persuade them to let you have some wild brown trout. If not, the next best thing is to source organic trout, which is very readily available by mail order (see Useful Addresses).

6 oz	quinoa	170 g
1 tbsp	extra virgin olive oil	1 tbsp
1	small onion, peeled and finely chopped	1
9 fl oz	vegetable stock (see page 41)	250 ml
2 oz	unblanched almonds, chopped roughly	60 g

9 fl oz	water	250 ml
4	rainbow trout, filleted (8 fillets)	4
1	lemon, juice only	1
	low-sodium salt and freshly ground black pepper to taste	
2 tbsp	flat-leaf parsley, chopped	2 tbsp
1 tbsp	flax oil	1 tbsp
1	lemon, cut into 4 wedges	1

Rinse the quinoa to remove the saponin coating. Heat the olive oil in a large saucepan over gentle heat and sauté the diced onion until soft. Add the stock and water, turn up the heat and bring to the boil. Stir in the quinoa, cover and simmer until all the liquid is absorbed and the quinoa is cooked – about 15-20 minutes. Stir in the chopped almonds and keep warm.

Meanwhile, preheat the grill, and put the trout fillets on the grill rack flesh side up. Drizzle with olive oil and season. Grill, without turning, until cooked, about 5 minutes.

To serve, put a bed of quinoa on each plate and top with two trout fillets. Sprinkle with the parsley, drizzle over a little flax oil, and garnish with a wedge of lemon. Serves 4.

PER SERVING	
Energy Kcals	564.9
Protein g	43.6
Carbohydrates g	36.6
Dietary Fibre g	4.9
Fat – Total g	26.9
Saturated Fat g	4.6
Polyunsaturated Fat g	8.6
Calcium mg	160.0
Magnesium mg	142.4

Pearl barley has had its outer husk removed, so it is not a whole grain. It does have the advantage, however, of being very low on the Glycaemic Index. You could substitute pot barley, but it takes a very long time to cook, or other whole grains, such as whole wheat berries, quinoa or brown rice, if you prefer.

Barley-Stuffed Mackerel with Fresh Coriander Sauce

There are lots of recipes featuring fresh coriander in this book, because it is such a versatile and tasty addition to so many dishes, and because it contains selenium, a trace mineral which is needed by many enzyme systems in the body, and which also opposes any traces of mercury there may be in ocean fish. This sauce is good with many oriental recipes, and particularly with rice dishes. I like it so much I sometimes make a meal of brown rice with this sauce stirred in and nothing else. This is a very filling dish and needs nothing else except a green salad to go with it.

3 oz	pearl barley	90 g
12 fl oz	vegetable stock or water	330 ml
2	spring onions, chopped	2
1/2	green pepper, diced	1/2
1 tbsp	chopped raw almonds	1 tbsp
	low-sodium salt and freshly ground black pepper to taste	
4	whole fresh mackerel, gutted, with fins removed	4
1 tbsp	extra virgin olive oil	1 tbsp
For the sauce:		
1	large bunch fresh coriander, leaves only	1
4	spring onions, roughly chopped	4
1	garlic clove, roughly chopped	1
	fresh ginger root, peeled and chopped (1/2 inch/1 cm piece)	
1/2	fresh green chilli, deseeded and chopped	1/2
1 tbsp	white wine vinegar	1 tbsp
1 tbsp	fresh lime juice	1 tbsp
1 tbsp	extra virgin olive oil	1 tbsp
2 tsp	flax oil	2 tsp

PER SERVING	
Energy Kcals	575.5
Protein g	44.9
Carbohydrates g	12.7
Dietary Fibre g	3.1
Fat – Total g	36.9
Saturated Fat g	4.4
Polyunsaturated Fat g	2.5
Calcium mg	39.2
Magnesium mg	22.9

Smoked mackerel is a cheap and readily available source of protein, but make sure you choose fillets that have not been artificially coloured. It's easy to spot the difference – the artificially dyed mackerel are a suspiciously orange colour, whereas the naturally smoked ones are a greyish colour.

Wash the barley and put in a small pan with the water. Bring to the boil and simmer until the barley is tender and the liquid absorbed – about 45-60 minutes. Stir in the spring onions, green pepper, almonds and seasoning. Leave to cool. Preheat oven to 200°C/400°F/Gas Mark 6. Stuff the mackerel with the barley mixture, tying them with string if you have difficulty keeping the stuffing in the fish cavity. If there is any barley mixture left over, this can be reheated and served separately with the fish.

Place the fish on a roasting tray, sprinkle with a little olive oil, and bake in the preheated oven for about 15-20 minutes, or until the fish are cooked through and the filling is piping hot.

Meanwhile, make the sauce: put all the ingredients in the blender together with 2 tablespoons of water. Blend until smooth.

Serve the stuffed mackerel on hot plates and pass the coriander sauce separately. Serves 4.

Mackerel Kedgeree

The word kedgeree is a corruption of *khichiri*, an Indian dish of rice and lentils. The English in India substituted smoked haddock for the lentils and ate it for breakfast. Inspired by such a cavalier disregard for tradition, I have substituted smoked mackerel for the smoked haddock, but otherwise this dish is just as my mother used to make, though I use soya cream where she would have used dairy cream.

1 tbsp	extra virgin olive oil	1 tbsp
1	large onion, chopped finely	1
1 tbsp	garam masala	1 tbsp
4 oz	fresh or frozen peas	110 g
2-3	smoked mackerel fillets, skinned and flaked, any bones removed	2-3
8 oz	brown basmati rice	225 g
2	organic, free-range eggs	2
	low-sodium salt and freshly ground black pepper to taste	
2-3 tbsp	soya cream	2-3 tbsp
	a large handful of chopped parsley to serve	

First, cook the rice in $2^1/_2$ times its volume of water until tender, about 30-35 minutes. Drain and reserve. Meanwhile, heat the oil in a large sauté pan, and sauté the onion over gentle heat until soft and transparent. Stir in the garam masala.

Hard boil the eggs for 10 minutes, then peel. Cut one of the eggs into slices or quarters. Scoop out the yolk of the other egg and reserve. Slice or chop the white roughly.

Cook the peas and drain.

When the rice is cooked, add it to the onion and garam masala mixture. Add the peas, flaked mackerel, soya cream and seasoning, and stir over gentle heat for a few minutes before folding in the sliced eggs.

To serve, turn into a hot serving dish or individual plates and sprinkle finely chopped parsley and sieved hard boiled egg yolk over the top. Serves 4.

PER SERVING	
Energy Kcals	520.9
Protein g	22.5
Carbohydrates g	56.7
Dietary Fibre g	7.0
Fat – Total g	23.9
Saturated Fat g	6.2
Polyunsaturated Fat g	5.3
Calcium mg	88.5
Magnesium mg	69.5

This method of cooking fish could be used with other fish such as mackerel.

Fresh Sardines Baked in Tomato Sauce

This is a very superior version of the tinned sardines in tomato sauce you can buy in the supermarket.

12-16	fresh sardines, cleaned and gutted (about 2 lb/900 g in weight)	12-16
1 tbsp	extra virgin olive oil	1 tbsp
1	small onion, peeled and finely chopped	1
1	garlic clove, peeled and finely chopped	1
1	medium carrot, finely diced	1
2	sticks celery, finely diced	2
1 lb	fresh, ripe tomatoes, skinned and chopped	450 g
1 tbsp	tomato purée	1 tbsp
4 fl oz	white wine	120 ml
	low-sodium salt and freshly ground black pepper to taste	
12	green olives stuffed with red pepper	12
2 tbsp	chopped flat-leaf parsley	2 tbsp

PER SERVING	
Energy Kcals	478.0
Protein g	43.7
Carbohydrates g	10.6
Dietary Fibre g	2.6
Fat – Total g	26.4
Saturated Fat g	5.5
Polyunsaturated Fat g	5.6
Calcium mg	178.3
Magnesium mg	109.2

Arame is a particularly good source of minerals, especially selenium which is hard to get in our modern diet, and opposes any mercury there may be in the fish. It contains vitamin B12 too, but some evidence indicates that it is not exactly the form that meets the body's requirements.

PER SERVING	
Energy Kcals	422.8
Protein g	42.8
Carbohydrates g	5.3
Dietary Fibre g	1.0
Fat – Total g	24.7
Saturated Fat g	5.3
Polyunsaturated Fat g	5.3
Calcium mg	166.7
Magnesium mg	99.6

Preheat oven to 180°C/350°F/Gas Mark 4.

Heat the oil in a large saucepan. Sauté the onion, garlic, carrot and celery in the oil for 10 minutes or so over gentle heat until tender. Stir in the tomatoes, tomato purée and wine. Season to taste and cook, covered, for about 30 minutes, stirring from time to time. Stir in the olives at the end. Lightly oil an ovenproof dish, and place the sardines in it. Pour the tomato sauce over the sardines, and bake in the oven until the sardines are cooked and piping hot, about 15 minutes.

Serve with the chopped parsley sprinkled over the top. Serves 4.

Sardines and Seaweed

This is a jokey title for a seriously good way to cook fish which gives it a real taste of the sea.

12-16	fresh sardines, cleaned and gutted (about 2 lb/900 g in weight)	12-16
½ oz	dried arame seaweed (a large handful)	15 g
3	lemons	3
1 tbsp	extra virgin olive oil	1 tbsp
	low-sodium salt and freshly ground black pepper to taste	
1	cucumber	1
4	spring onions	4

Soak the arame in tepid water to cover for about 10 minutes or until it is soft to the bite.

Score the sardines two or three times diagonally on each side if they are large, season and place on a lightly oiled grill rack lined with baking parchment. Squeeze over the juice of one of the lemons, and cut the other two into segments small enough to fit into the belly cavities of the fish. Cook under a hot grill for 3-4 minutes each side, or until cooked in the centre.

Peel the cucumber, cut in half lengthways and scoop out the seeds. Slice as finely as you can into julienne slices. Slice the spring onions into diagonal slices.

When the fish is nearly ready, heat the oil in a wok and stir-fry the arame, cucumber and spring onions until heated through. Serve the fish on a bed of arame, cucumber and spring onions. Serves 4.

Fresh tuna is a very good source of vitamin D and Omega-3 essential fatty acids. However, there is some concern that because it is at the top of the food chain, it may be more contaminated with mercury than are smaller fish. Our bodies can detoxify minute quantities of mercury if we have enough selenium, so I think the answer is to continue to eat fresh tuna occasionally because of its nutritional benefits, and to make sure we get plenty of selenium from seeds and brazil nuts.

Fresh Tuna Teriyaki

Make sure the tuna you buy is really fresh. It should have a good deep red colour, with no brown tinge, and be absolutely firm to the touch.

4 tbsp	shoyu sauce	60 ml
2 tbsp	sake or dry sherry	2 tbsp
1 tbsp	brown rice syrup or honey	1 tbsp
1 tbsp	cold-pressed sesame oil	1 tbsp
	fresh ginger root, peeled and grated (1 inch/2.5 cm piece)	
few drops	rice vinegar	few drops
2	garlic cloves, finely chopped	2
	freshly ground black pepper to taste	
4	fresh tuna steaks, about 8 oz/225 g each	4
2 tsp	extra virgin olive oil, or use olive oil spray	2 tsp
1	lemon, juice only	1
2	spring onions, finely sliced	2

Mix together the shoyu, sake, brown rice syrup or honey, sesame oil, grated ginger, rice vinegar, garlic and pepper. Put the tuna in a dish and pour over the marinade. Turn the fish so that it's coated on all sides, and leave to marinate for a short time – 5-10 minutes at most.

Heat a large heavy frying pan or griddle pan over medium-high heat. Spray with olive oil spray or put a light film of olive oil in the pan, and cook the fish for 3-4 minutes. Sieve the marinade to remove the ginger and reserve.

Turn the fish over to cook the other side, pour in the lemon juice and the sieved marinade. Cook the tuna until lightly browned on the outside but still a little pink in the middle.

Transfer the tuna to hot plates, and turn up the heat under the pan so that the marinade continues to cook and thicken a little. Pour over the fish and garnish with sliced spring onion. Serve hot. Serves 4.

PER SERVING	
Energy Kcals	391.3
Protein g	70.3
Carbohydrates g	7.4
Dietary Fibre g	0.6
Fat – Total g	6.3
Saturated Fat g	1.2
Polyunsaturated Fat g	2.3
Calcium mg	61.6
Magnesium mg	162.0

Rosemary is a good accompaniment for beans because it reduces flatulence and stimulates digestion. Sage contains phytoestrogens that may help to relieve night sweats and hot flushes. It is also associated with long life and is believed to enhance the memory.

Tuna with Cannellini Beans and Sage

This is my version of the well-known Tuscan dish *Tonno e Fagioli*, made even more suitable for the menopausal woman by the addition of rosemary, sage and flax oil.

8 oz	cannellini beans, soaked overnight	225 g
1	sprig of fresh rosemary	1
3	large tomatoes, peeled and roughly chopped	3
3	garlic cloves, peeled and finely chopped	3
6	sage leaves, finely sliced	6
2 tbsp	extra virgin olive oil	2 tbsp
1	onion, peeled and chopped	1
5 fl oz	dry white wine	150 ml
1 lb	fresh tuna, cut into 1 inch/2.5 cm cubes	450 g
	low-sodium salt and freshly ground black pepper to taste	
4	sage leaves for the garnish	4
1 tbsp	flax oil	1 tbsp

Drain the beans, place in a saucepan with the rosemary, cover with fresh cold water and bring to the boil. Boil hard for 10 minutes, then reduce the heat and add one of the chopped tomatoes, the garlic and the 6 sliced sage leaves. Cover and simmer until the beans are tender – 45 minutes to an hour, depending on the age of the beans. Drain and discard what remains of the rosemary.

In a large frying pan, heat the oil and sauté the onion over medium-high heat until soft but not browned. Add the wine and continue to sauté for another couple of minutes.

Reduce the heat and add the tuna, cooked beans, the rest of the tomatoes and seasoning. Cover and cook until the tuna is opaque – 8-10 minutes. Meanwhile, slice the sage leaves for the garnish – roll them up and slice across the rolls with a small sharp knife to make tiny ribbons.

To serve, spoon the beans and tuna into heated wide shallow bowls, drizzle with the flax oil and sprinkle with the sliced sage leaves. Serves 4.

PER SERVING	
Energy Kcals	486.8
Protein g	47.4
Carbohydrates g	39.9
Dietary Fibre g	12.0
Fat – Total g	13.0
Saturated Fat g	1.9
Polyunsaturated Fat g	3.8
Calcium mg	149.7
Magnesium mg	168.8

Herrings are the richest known source of vitamin D. We particularly need to obtain this vitamin from our food in the winter to help our bones absorb calcium. Although vitamin D is made in our bodies by exposure to sunlight, in temperate regions this only happens between March and October.

Herring and Oat Fishcakes

Herrings are fantastic value, and a very rich source of Omega-3 fatty acids. The classic Scottish way to cook herrings is to coat them in oatmeal and fry them in bacon fat. I have adapted the concept and turned it into fishcakes, as some people find the taste of herrings rather strong. Tempered by the mashed potato, these are delicious, and the oats make a wonderfully crispy coating. Fish cakes can be a little dry, so I incorporate a thick parsley sauce into the mixture to counteract this. You could serve them with a tomato sauce if you still find them on the dry side.

1 lb	floury potatoes, peeled and cut into chunks	450 g
3 tbsp	extra virgin olive oil	3 tbsp
	low-sodium salt and freshly ground black pepper to taste	
4	small herrings, cleaned and gutted, or use 1 lb/450 g herring fillets	4
1 pint	soya milk	450 ml
1 tbsp	brown rice flour	1 tbsp
2 tbsp	chopped fresh parsley	2 tbsp
1½ oz	coarse oatmeal	45 g
2 tbsp	extra virgin olive oil for frying	2 tbsp
	lemon wedges, to serve	

Boil the potatoes in water to cover until soft. Drain and mash with seasoning and 2 tbsp olive oil and leave to cool.

Next, put the herrings in a wide shallow pan with the soya milk and enough water to cover, cover with a lid and poach for 10 minutes or so, until the flesh comes away from the bones easily. Leave to cool, then carefully flake the fish, removing all bones and skin. Reserve the cooking liquid.

To make the parsley sauce, heat the other tablespoon of olive oil in a small pan, stir in the flour to form a thick roux, cook for a minute or two, then gradually add 2 fl oz/60 ml of the reserved fish cooking liquid. Bring to the boil and simmer, stirring, for a few minutes (it should be a very thick sauce), then season and add the chopped parsley. Cool.

In a large bowl, mix the flaked fish with the mashed potato and parsley sauce. With floured hands, form the mixture into eight round cakes. Briefly dip them in the remaining fish

PER SERVING	
Energy Kcals	577.5
Protein g	32.5
Carbohydrates g	36.8
Dietary Fibre g	4.1
Fat – Total g	33.0
Saturated Fat g	5.8
Polyunsaturated Fat g	5.7
Calcium mg	100.0
Magnesium mg	111.1

cooking liquid just to moisten the surface, then dip them into the oats so they are quite covered. If you have time, refrigerate the fish cakes to allow them to firm up.

Finally, heat the remaining 2 tbsp olive oil in a heavy frying pan, and sauté the fish cakes over medium heat until golden brown and crispy on both sides.

Serve with wedges of lemon. Serves 4.

There's quite a lot of fennel in this book not only because it's one of my favourite vegetables, but, more importantly, because it contains good levels of phytoestrogens. You will notice that there are two shapes of fennel – some bulbs are quite round and some are longer and thinner. Italians consider the latter to be more tender and less fibrous, so I always pick them out if I have a choice. I was once told that the long ones are male, while the round ones are female. Whether this is just an Italian fancy, I'm not sure.

Roast Sea Bass with Fennel

Sea bass is an expensive fish, and, if you do get hold of some, I think it is best to do as little with it as possible. So here is a simple method of roasting it just with a touch of lemon and fennel, so that you can enjoy the exquisite flavour of the fish without too many distractions.

3-4 lb	whole sea bass, (this may be one or two fish, depending on size), cleaned, scaled, and with fins removed	1.35-2 kg
2	onions, peeled and thinly sliced	2
2	lemons, sliced	2
2	bulbs fennel, sliced thinly, any leaves reserved	2
	low-sodium salt and freshly ground black pepper to taste	
4 fl oz	dry white wine	120 ml
2 tbsp	extra virgin olive oil	2 tbsp

Preheat the oven to 200°C/400°F/Gas Mark 6.

Rinse and dry the fish. Put the onions, lemon and sliced fennel into a large roasting tin, and place the sea bass on top. Pour over the white wine and olive oil. Roast in the hot oven for about 30 minutes, testing it at the fattest part to make sure the flesh is cooked all the way through.

Transfer the fish to a serving dish together with the fennel mixture and garnish with the reserved fennel leaves. I think this is delicious just as it is, but if you would prefer to serve a sauce with it, you could liquidise the fennel mixture, having first removed the lemon slices, and pass it through a sieve, to give an instant fennel sauce. Serves 4.

PER SERVING	
Energy Kcals	382.9
Protein g	46.5
Carbohydrates g	17.5
Dietary Fibre g	5.5
Fat – Total g	12.2
Saturated Fat g	2.2
Polyunsaturated Fat g	2.5
Calcium mg	105.5
Magnesium mg	134.0

There is a place for chicken in the menopausal woman's diet, provided you discard the (high fat) skin. Chicken is an excellent source of low-fat protein, and contains useful amounts of zinc and selenium, both of which are needed to help build up the immune system and to help the thyroid gland function as it should. You could substitute any other leafy green vegetable for the kale in this recipe, such as spring greens, purple sprouting broccoli or savoy cabbage.

Szechuan Chicken with Kale

Szechuan peppercorns have a pungent smell but only a faintly hot taste. They should be roasted before use in a small dry pan on top of the stove.

4	organic or free-range boneless chicken breasts, skinned	4
1 tbsp	extra virgin olive oil	1 tbsp
1 tbsp	shoyu sauce	1 tbsp
1 lb	kale, sliced with thick ribs removed	450 g
For the marinade:		
1 tbsp	szechuan peppercorns, roasted	1 tbsp
1 tsp	coriander seeds	1 tsp
	fresh ginger root, peeled and grated (1 inch/2.5 cm piece)	
2	garlic cloves, peeled and chopped	2
1 tsp	cold-pressed sesame oil	1 tsp
1	orange, juice and grated rind	1
2 tbsp	sake or dry sherry	2 tbsp
1 tbsp	brown rice syrup	1 tbsp

For the marinade, crush the szechuan peppercorns and the coriander seeds together in a pestle and mortar, then pound in the grated ginger and garlic. Lastly add the sesame oil, orange juice and rind, sake and brown rice syrup.

Score the chicken breasts diagonally 2 or 3 times with a sharp knife to allow the marinade to penetrate. Put them into a dish and spoon over the marinade, turning so that the chicken is coated on all sides. Cover and refrigerate overnight or for at least 3 hours.

Preheat the oven to 200°C/400°F/Gas Mark 6.

Heat a large frying pan over high heat, add the olive oil and sauté the chicken breasts a couple of minutes on each side to seal. Then transfer to a baking dish, baste with any remaining marinade, and bake in the hot oven for 15 minutes or so, or until the chicken is cooked through.

Meanwhile, cook the kale in a wok or large pan with the shoyu sauce and a little boiling water until tender but still bright green – about 5-6 minutes.

Serve the chicken sliced on a bed of kale. Serves 4.

PER SERVING	
Energy Kcals	304.8
Protein g	32.3
Carbohydrates g	15.8
Dietary Fibre g	3.6
Fat – Total g	11.8
Saturated Fat g	2.7
Polyunsaturated Fat g	2.2
Calcium mg	120.4
Magnesium mg	57.4

Although the fat content of this dish is high, only one-eighth of the total is saturated fat. Most of the rest is mono- and polyunsaturated fats provided by the nuts, which are a good source of essential fatty acids. I call these 'essential thinny acids', as they can help with weight loss, and are called essential because we really need them, so don't worry about the high fat content.

Chicken with Walnuts, Almonds and Hazelnuts

When I was cooking on charter yachts in the West Indies, I wrote a cookery book for other charter cooks that was never published. This recipe, and the one that follows, come from that old, tattered manuscript, which is still in my possession. I was delighted to find that I had written recipes back then that fit the criteria for menopause-friendly cooking. This chicken recipe is an amalgamation of Middle Eastern and Caribbean cooking styles.

4	organic or free-range chicken joints, skin removed	4
2 tbsp	wholemeal flour or Doves Farm gluten-free flour	2 tbsp
	low-sodium salt and freshly ground black pepper to taste	
1 tbsp	extra virgin olive oil	1 tbsp
1	small onion, peeled and finely chopped	1
4	garlic cloves, peeled and crushed	4
5½ fl oz	chicken stock	160 ml
2 oz	walnuts	60 g
2 oz	almonds	60 g
2 oz	hazelnuts	60 g
	paprika, hot sauce and low-sodium salt to taste	

Garnish:

1 oz	raisins, plumped in boiling water	30 g

Coat the chicken in seasoned flour by putting the flour and seasoning into a plastic bag, adding the chicken pieces, and shaking them until the chicken is well coated.

Heat the oil over gentle heat in a large frying pan and sauté the chicken pieces until browned all over. Transfer the chicken pieces to a large pot or casserole. Sauté the onion in the frying pan until soft but not browned, and add that to the casserole. Add the stock, cover and simmer over a low heat for half an hour or until chicken is tender.

Meanwhile, pulverise all the nuts in a blender.

PER SERVING	
Energy Kcals	572.4
Protein g	41.0
Carbohydrates g	18.8
Dietary Fibre g	5.4
Fat – Total g	38.1
Saturated Fat g	5.1
Polyunsaturated Fat g	11.9
Calcium mg	62.7
Magnesium mg	88.5

When the chicken is cooked, place it on a serving dish and keep warm. Add the pulverised nuts to the sauce remaining in the casserole and cook for a few minutes. Add paprika, salt and a few drops of hot sauce to taste and pour over the chicken. Garnish with raisins which have been plumped in boiling water.

Serve on a bed of brown rice. Serves 4.

Choose dark tahini in preference to light tahini, as it is made with the whole seed. Most of the calcium is in the outer covering of the seed, so the light tahini has considerably less calcium.

Grilled Chicken with Tahini Sauce

This is a rich sauce with a Middle Eastern flavour. It can be used equally well with fish or vegetables, and goes particularly well with grilled vegetables such as aubergines and courgettes.

4	organic or free-range chicken leg joints, skinned	4
For the marinade:		
3	garlic cloves, peeled	3
1 tsp	low-sodium salt	1 tsp
1½ tsp	paprika	1½ tsp
1 tsp	ground cumin	1 tsp
1	lemon, juice only	1
4 tbsp	extra virgin olive oil	4 tbsp
For the sauce:		
2	garlic cloves, peeled and crushed	2
½ tsp	low-sodium salt	½ tsp
2	lemons, juice only	2
3½ fl oz	tahini	100 ml
½ tsp	ground cumin	½ tsp
2 tbsp	chopped flat-leaf parsley	2 tbsp

For the marinade, crush the garlic in a pestle and mortar with the salt, then transfer to a dish and add the paprika, cumin, lemon juice and olive oil. Whisk to mix, then add the chicken pieces, turning them in the marinade until thoroughly coated. Cover and refrigerate for at least 3 hours or overnight.

Even if I'm going to barbecue chicken, I always like to cook it in the oven first to make sure that it's cooked all the way through. So in this case, preheat the oven to 190°C/375°F/Gas Mark 5, take the chicken out of the marinade, discarding the marinade, place on a baking tray and cook in the preheated oven for about 15 minutes. Then transfer either to the barbecue or to a preheated grill to finish off the cooking.

Make the sauce while the chicken is cooking. Put the garlic, most of the lemon juice and tahini into a blender and blend until smooth. Season to taste with cumin and salt. Add a little water if the sauce is too thick, and only add the rest of the lemon juice if you think it needs it.

Serve the grilled chicken with a little of the tahini sauce drizzled over, and garnish with chopped parsley. Put the rest of the tahini sauce in a dish and pass separately. Serves 4.

PER SERVING	
Energy Kcals	430.8
Protein g	33.0
Carbohydrates g	9.5
Dietary Fibre g	1.9
Fat – Total g	29.8
Saturated Fat g	5.8
Polyunsaturated Fat g	9.2
Calcium mg	62.4
Magnesium mg	57.6

In this Italian dish, the rabbit is cooked with two herbs helpful to the menopausal woman – rosemary and sage. Not only that, but rabbit is one of the few animal sources of Omega-3 fatty acids – about 1 g per 100 g rabbit.

Braised Rabbit with Herbs and Roasted Shallots

It is surprising how rarely rabbit is available, considering that it is relatively inexpensive, and a low-fat meat somewhat akin to chicken. You can order it from your butchers, in which case ask them to cut the legs and loin from the rabbit, and bone the loin. Otherwise, use a pack of jointed rabbit from the supermarket. Try to ensure it is wild rabbit. This dish would adapt equally well to chicken.

1	whole wild rabbit (about 2¼ lb/ 1 kg), jointed	1
2 tbsp	extra virgin olive oil	2 tbsp
1	small onion, peeled and finely chopped	1
1	sprig of fresh rosemary	1
1	sprig of fresh sage	1
	low-sodium salt and freshly ground black pepper to taste	
5 fl oz	dry white wine	150 ml
1 pint	chicken stock	570 ml

Right: Salmon with Sweet Potato, Courgette and Carrot Rösti (page 88)

For the shallots:

9 oz	whole shallots	250 g
1 tbsp	extra virgin olive oil	1 tbsp
1 tsp	balsamic vinegar	1 tsp

For the garnish:

1 tbsp	chopped fresh rosemary	1 tbsp
1 tbsp	chopped fresh sage	1 tbsp

Preheat the oven to 180°C/350°F/Gas Mark 4.

Heat the olive oil in an ovenproof casserole over medium heat and brown the rabbit joints. Remove to a plate. Then sauté the onion gently in the casserole, adding a touch more oil if necessary. Return the rabbit legs to the casserole, together with the rosemary and sage, the wine and the stock. Cover and cook in the oven for half an hour. After this time, remove the casserole from the oven, add the rabbit loins (they cook more quickly than the legs) and return to the oven for a further half hour or until the rabbit is tender. Take it out when cooked and keep warm while you reduce the sauce over high heat, until it is thick. Season to taste.

To cook the shallots, which can be roasted at the same time as the rabbit, peel them (this is most easily done by plunging them into boiling water, leaving for a few minutes, then cooling and peeling with a sharp knife. The skins should come off quite easily. If the shallots fall into segments, that doesn't matter.) Put the shallots, whole or in segments, into a small roasting tin with the olive oil, and cook for 40-45 minutes, stirring from time to time, until deeply browned and caramelised. Take out of the oven, and sprinkle over the balsamic vinegar.

Serve the rabbit with the thickened sauce poured over, garnished with caramelised shallots and with chopped rosemary and sage sprinkled over the top. Serves 4.

Roast Pheasant with Red Wine and Grapes

This way of cooking pheasant is actually a combination of braising and roasting. The legs are braised first in a slow oven so that they are really tender, and the breasts added at the end and roasted at a higher temperature. The addition of red wine and grapes makes this a luxurious dish to serve on a festive occasion.

PER SERVING	
Energy Kcals	412.8
Protein g	46.5
Carbohydrates g	12.9
Dietary Fibre g	1.4
Fat – Total g	15.7
Saturated Fat g	2.9
Polyunsaturated Fat g	1.9
Calcium mg	73.4
Magnesium mg	65.1

I had always thought of pheasant as a healthy meat. Although the birds are grown to be shot, they seem to be bred in relative freedom. However, I recently read about a drug called Emtryl which is used in this country to prevent disease in pheasants. The drug is banned in the rest of Europe, and soon will be here. In the meantime, it is wise to ascertain from your supplier that the pheasant you wish to buy has been reared without the use of Emtryl.

Left: Szechuan Chicken with Kale (page 101)

2	medium sized hen pheasant	2
2	bay leaves	2
2-3	sprigs of fresh thyme	2-3
2-3	sprigs of fresh parsley	2-3
6	black peppercorns	6
1	onion, peeled and chopped	1
½ oz	organic unsalted butter	15 g
2	dessert apples, peeled, cored and sliced	2
1	onion, chopped	1
5 fl oz	red wine	150 ml
4 oz	seedless black or red grapes	125 g
1 bunch	watercress, for garnish	1 bunch

Preheat the oven to 160°C/325°F/Gas Mark 3.

Joint the pheasants by first removing the legs, then by cutting away the breast section intact with its bones. Then cut the breasts in two and set aside.

Put the leftover pheasant carcases, the neck and the giblets (if there are any) into a pan, together with the bay leaves, thyme, parsley and black peppercorns. Cover with cold water, bring to the boil, lower the heat, cover and simmer for about half an hour, then strain the stock into a jug.

Wipe the pheasant legs clean and remove any stray feathers. Put the chopped onion in a roasting tin, and fill the tin to a depth of ¼ inch/0.5cm with the pheasant stock. Place the pheasant legs in the tin and cook for about an hour, basting frequently. Pour more pheasant stock in the pan if it is drying out. Raise the oven temperature to 180°C/350°F/Gas Mark 4. Smear the pheasant breasts with butter, then add them to the roasting tin and cover with apple slices, adding more stock if necessary. Cook for a further 20-25 minutes, or until the breasts are cooked through.

Take the pheasant joints out of the pan and keep warm. Add the red wine to the roasting pan, place it over high heat on top of the stove and boil vigorously, stirring, to reduce the liquid and turn the apple pieces to pulp. Push through a sieve into a clean saucepan. Bring to the boil, season to taste and add the grapes, just to warm them through.

Serve the pheasant with the wine and grape sauce, and garnish with watercress. Serves 6.

PER SERVING	
Energy Kcals	503.2
Protein g	75.6
Carbohydrates g	13.4
Dietary Fibre g	2.2
Fat – Total g	13.0
Saturated Fat g	4.9
Polyunsaturated Fat g	2.0
Calcium mg	45.3
Magnesium mg	73.4

Vegetable Accompaniments

Green Greens
Moroccan-Style Spring Greens
Cabbage with Dried Cranberries
Stir-Fried Brussels Sprouts
Sesame Broccoli and Carrots
Purple Sprouting Broccoli with Raisins
Cauliflower with Tahini Sauce
Wilted Watercress with Olive Oil and Garlic
Spicy Spinach
Sweet Potato Chips
Beetroot with Beet Greens
Dhal
Stir-Fried Green Beans and Cashew Nuts
Runner Beans with Fresh Tomatoes
Vegetables with Lime and Coconut Cream
Roast Fennel with Lemon
Braised Celery with Thyme
Grilled Asparagus with Sun-Dried Tomatoes

Green leafy vegetables ought to be top of our list of fresh ingredients. They contain everything we need to keep our bones healthy – vitamin C, vitamin K, calcium, magnesium and boron. All we need as well is a bit of sunlight to provide the vitamin D. Drinking the water that the greens have been cooked in enables you to absorb all the minerals and water-soluble vitamins from the greens that have been dissolved in the water.
It's also a natural appetite-suppressant if you drink it just before a meal.

Green Greens

The latest research suggests that lightly cooked vegetables may be better for you than raw vegetables. To vary these greens, you could add a sprinkling of seeds, such as toasted sesame seeds or sunflower seeds, which would boost the mineral content. Or you could serve them simply steamed, without stir-frying them afterwards. Use a mixture of greens, such as curly kale, spring greens, dark green cabbage, carrot tops, turnip tops or Brussels sprout tops (not spinach as it cooks too quickly).

1 lb	fresh greens	450 g
1 tbsp	extra virgin olive oil	1 tbsp
1	onion, peeled and sliced	1
2	garlic cloves, peeled and sliced	2
	low-sodium salt and freshly ground black pepper to taste	
1	lemon, juice only	1
1 tbsp	flax oil	1 tbsp

Bring $2^1/_2$ pints/$1^1/_2$ litres of water to the boil in a large pot.
Wash all the greens really well in several changes of water. Put them in the boiling water and cook, uncovered, until tender – 5-8 minutes, depending on the type of greens – but the less time the better, as more nutrients will be preserved. Have a large bowl of very cold water ready, and as soon as the greens are cooked, drain them, reserving the cooking water (see margin note), and plunge them into the cold water. This stops the cooking and preserves their green colour.
Drain the greens from their cold water bath and dry them well. Chop coarsely.
In a large wok or sauté pan, heat the olive oil. Add the onion and garlic and sauté over medium heat for 5 minutes or so, until soft.
Add the chopped greens to the onions and garlic in the wok. Mix and stir-fry for 3 more minutes, until the greens are warmed through. Season to taste.
Transfer the greens to a serving bowl and add the lemon juice and flax oil. Toss to mix and serve warm. Serves 4.

PER SERVING	
Energy Kcals	107.2
Protein g	2.2
Carbohydrates g	10.2
Dietary Fibre g	3.2
Fat – Total g	7.4
Saturated Fat g	0.9
Polyunsaturated Fat g	2.9
Calcium mg	90.8
Magnesium mg	22.1

The short cooking time means that there is minimal loss of water-soluble vitamins such as vitamin C and the B vitamins. To further prevent vitamin loss, buy your greens as fresh as possible and prepare them just before cooking. Don't be tempted by those bags of ready-cut greens in the supermarket – they probably have few nutrients left by the time you get to eat them.

Moroccan-Style Spring Greens

This is a delicious way to eat your greens. The addition of apricots and spices makes it quite exotic.

1 tbsp	extra virgin olive oil	1 tbsp
1	large onion, sliced	1
2	garlic cloves, crushed	2
	fresh root ginger, peeled and grated (1 inch/2.5 cm piece)	
1 tsp	ground coriander	1 tsp
	low-sodium salt and freshly ground black pepper to taste	
1 tsp	paprika	1 tsp
1 tsp	turmeric	1 tsp
2 oz	dried unsulphured apricots	60 g
1/2 pint	vegetable stock (see page 41)	275 ml
12 oz	spring greens, shredded, with tough ribs removed	340 g
2 tbsp	flaked almonds	2 tbsp

Heat the oil in a large sauté pan over medium heat, and cook onion and garlic until soft but not browned. Add the ginger, spices, apricots, seasoning and stock. Bring to the boil, and simmer until reduced by half. Add spring greens and simmer for 3-5 minutes until tender but still bright green. Keeping the pot uncovered helps to preserve the colour. Drain and serve garnished with flaked almonds.

Variation
Try this with kale or spinach. With kale you would have to cook for a bit longer, and with spinach possibly less. Serves 4.

PER SERVING	
Energy Kcals	110.5
Protein g	3.1
Carbohydrates g	16.5
Dietary Fibre g	3.4
Fat – Total g	4.1
Saturated Fat g	0.5
Polyunsaturated Fat g	0.4
Calcium mg	80.7
Magnesium mg	20.1

Cabbage has long been used in traditional medicine, and is especially helpful to the menopausal woman. It has been known to help with fluid retention and bloating.

It contains phytonutrients called indoles which work on enzymes that break down the hormones involved in causing breast cancer, so it has a protective role. Cranberries are used to relieve cystitis, but the small amount in this recipe would not contribute much – they are there for flavour and colour as much as anything else.

Cabbage with Dried Cranberries

This is cabbage with a difference. The addition of cranberries not only gives extra flavour but can make it a festive side dish for Christmas. But do be careful not to overcook the cabbage. I am convinced that there is some sort of chemical reaction that takes place after 7-8 minutes of cooking cabbage, when it starts to take on that old, boiled smell redolent of school dinners. Not only that, but the water-soluble vitamins will mostly have turned up their toes and died if you cook it for too long.

1 lb	green cabbage, quartered and cored	450 g
1 tbsp	extra virgin olive oil	1 tbsp
1	small onion, peeled and thinly sliced	1
1	medium carrot, grated	1
1	green apple, cored and grated but not peeled	1
3/4 oz	dried cranberries	20 g
4 tbsp	cider vinegar	4 tbsp
1 tbsp	maple syrup	1 tbsp
1 tbsp	fresh flat-leaf parsley, chopped	1 tbsp

Shred the cabbage finely, using a sharp knife.

Heat the olive oil in a large saucepan over medium heat. Add the onion and carrot and sauté until soft, about 10 minutes.

Add the apple, cranberries, seasoning, vinegar, maple syrup and 5 tablespoons of water. Stir to mix well, then bring to the boil. Reduce heat, cover and simmer for 10 minutes, until the liquid has reduced by half. Then add the cabbage and continue cooking until the cabbage is tender but still has some bite to it and most of the liquid has evaporated – about another 5-7 minutes.

Serve sprinkled with chopped parsley. Serves 4.

PER SERVING	
Energy Kcals	113.2
Protein g	1.6
Carbohydrates g	19.3
Dietary Fibre g	4.8
Fat – Total g	4.0
Saturated Fat g	0.6
Polyunsaturated Fat g	0.6
Calcium mg	47.5
Magnesium mg	15.2

Brussels sprouts contain more folate than any of the other members of the cabbage family. Folate can protect us from homocysteine, raised levels of which can be a predictor of heart disease and osteoporosis. Folate works by turning the homocysteine into a harmless amino acid. Eating sprouts can protect your heart and bones.

PER SERVING	
Energy Kcals	114.9
Protein g	3.2
Carbohydrates g	11.0
Dietary Fibre g	3.2
Fat – Total g	7.6
Saturated Fat g	1.1
Polyunsaturated Fat g	0.9
Calcium mg	47.4
Magnesium mg	24.9

Broccoli should be on your menu at least twice a week. It contains phytonutrients which have weak oestrogenic activity and these may help reduce hot flushes and vaginal dryness. Broccoli is rich in potential anticancer substances such as indoles, glucosinolates, beta carotene and vitamin C. In particular it contains sulforaphane that stimulates enzymes which help the liver remove toxins from the body. However if you have a thyroid deficiency avoid broccolis. See note on page 112.

PER SERVING	
Energy Kcals	100.2
Protein g	4.6
Carbohydrates g	11.8
Dietary Fibre g	5.2
Fat – Total g	5.1
Saturated Fat g	0.8
Polyunsaturated Fat g	2.1
Calcium mg	90.1
Magnesium mg	43.1

Stir-Fried Brussels Sprouts

Even though Brussels sprouts are rich in nutrients, I was not a fan until I came across Sophie Grigson's way of cooking sprouts, which is to shred and stir-fry them. Eaten like this they are a revelation. Here is Sophie's recipe, with a little extra twist.

1 lb	Brussels sprouts	450 g
2 tbsp	extra virgin olive oil	2 tbsp
2	garlic cloves, peeled and finely chopped	2
	low-sodium salt and freshly ground black pepper to taste	
1 tbsp	fresh parsley, finely chopped	1 tbsp
1 tbsp	Super Seed Mix, ground (see page 13)	1 tbsp

Shred the Brussels sprouts finely. Heat the olive oil in a large frying pan over medium heat and add the garlic and sprouts. Saute until the sprouts are lightly browned. Season with salt and pepper. Sprinkle with parsley and Super Seed Mix, and serve hot. Serves 4.

Sesame Broccoli and Carrots

If you want to jazz this up a bit, add a crushed clove of garlic and/or a few dried chilli flakes when you're tossing the vegetables with the sesame oil.

1 lb	broccoli	450 g
1/2 lb	carrots	225 g
1 tbsp	cold-pressed sesame oil	1 tbsp
1 tbsp	tamari sauce	1 tbsp
1 tbsp	unhulled sesame seeds, toasted	1 tbsp

Cut the broccoli into florets. Peel and slice the stalk diagonally. Peel the carrots and cut diagonal slices the same size as the slices of broccoli stem. Steam both vegetables together for 7-8 minutes. When the vegetables are cooked, drain and return to the hot pan, toss with the sesame oil and tamari, and serve sprinkled with the toasted sesame seeds. Serves 4.

Along with the more familiar green broccoli (calabrese), purple sprouting broccoli contains lots of iron and beta-carotene. Recent research has shown that the beta-carotene in iron-rich vegetables may make the iron more available. Since many women have iron stores below the recommended 500 mg, eating dark green leafy vegetables can often help prevent anaemia. A note of caution, however: if you have a thyroid deficiency you should avoid broccoli as it contains chemicals which disrupt the body's ability to use iodine, needed to make thyroid hormones.

Purple Sprouting Broccoli with Raisins

Purple sprouting broccoli grows very well in our allotment. It's quite delicious absolutely fresh and steamed for just 3 minutes. When we've eaten it like that for a week, we're looking for something a bit different, and here is one alternative suggestion.

1 tbsp	extra virgin olive oil	1 tbsp
1	large red onion, peeled and sliced into rings	1
4 fl oz	vegetable stock or water	120 ml
1 lb	purple sprouting broccoli, trimmed	450 g
3 tbsp	raisins	3 tbsp
4 fl oz	apple juice	120 ml
1 tsp	cornflour	1 tsp
1 tbsp	fresh oregano, chopped	1 tbsp
1 tbsp	flax oil	1 tbsp

Heat the olive oil in a large sauté pan over medium heat, and cook the onion rings until soft but not browned. Add the stock or water and bring to the boil. Add the broccoli and raisins. Cover and cook for 3 minutes.

Mix the apple juice with the cornflour and pour over the broccoli. Cover and cook for another 3-4 minutes until the broccoli is tender but still bright green.

Turn out into a serving bowl, scatter with chopped fresh oregano and drizzle over the flax oil. Serves 4.

PER SERVING	
Energy Kcals	173.9
Protein g	4.5
Carbohydrates g	25.2
Dietary Fibre g	4.6
Fat – Total g	7.5
Saturated Fat g	0.9
Polyunsaturated Fat g	2.9
Calcium mg	75.5
Magnesium mg	37.2

Cauliflower is one of the few vegetables to contain a measurable amount of boron, a trace mineral that appears to reduce the urinary excretion of calcium and magnesium. In one study[26] it was also found to raise oestrogen levels to the same concentration as that found in women taking oestrogen replacement therapy. Although it would be unwise to draw too many conclusions from one study, eating boron-rich foods such as cauliflower would be a sensible move.

Cauliflower with Tahini Sauce

I grew up in a world where the only thing you ever did with a cauliflower was smother it in cheese sauce. It was a delight to find that other cultures treat it with more imagination. Try this Middle-Eastern inspired dish, which would go well with chicken or a bean dish.

1	large cauliflower	1
2	garlic cloves, crushed	2
4 tbsp	tahini	4 tbsp
1	lemon, juice only	1
1/2 tsp	ground cumin	1/2 tsp
	low-sodium salt to taste	
1 tbsp	sunflower seeds, toasted	1 tbsp

Break the cauliflower into bite-sized florets and steam over boiling water for 8-10 minutes, just until tender but still with some 'bite'.

Meanwhile, to make the sauce, put the garlic, most of the lemon juice and tahini into a blender and blend until smooth. Season to taste with cumin and salt. Add just enough water to make a creamy pouring sauce, and only add the rest of the lemon juice if you think it needs it.

When the cauliflower is cooked, arrange in a serving dish, and pour the sauce over it. Garnish with toasted sunflower seeds. Serves 4-6.

PER SERVING	
Energy Kcals	127.4
Protein g	5.9
Carbohydrates g	13.0
Dietary Fibre g	5.1
Fat – Total g	7.6
Saturated Fat g	1.0
Polyunsaturated Fat g	3.5
Calcium mg	59.5
Magnesium mg	42.7

26 Beattie JH, Peace HS. The influence of a low-boron diet and boron supplementation on bone, major mineral and sex steroid metabolism in postmenopausal women. *Br J Nutr* 1993 May;69(3):871-84

Watercress is so nutritious, we should be eating it as often as we can, usually raw. Include it in salads, sandwiches and fresh vegetable juices, or just eat it on its own. Choose organic watercress if possible, but certainly not wild watercress which may carry liver flukes (parasites). Why eat it? There are lots of reasons, but for the menopausal woman its main advantage is that it is a very rich source of calcium and vitamin C.

Wilted Watercress with Olive Oil and Garlic

I'm a great fan of watercress in salads, but am a bit concerned when cooking it that it's going to lose its lovely bright green colour. That doesn't happen in this delicious watercress dish, which comes courtesy of Richard Cawley. It's from his book *Green Feasts*.

2 tbsp	extra virgin olive oil	2 tbsp
2 bunches	watercress, washed and drained thoroughly	2 bunches
2	garlic cloves, crushed	2
1	squeeze of lemon juice	1
1 oz	toasted flaked almonds	30 g
	low-sodium salt and freshly ground black pepper to taste	

Heat the oil in a heavy based pan over a moderate heat. Put in the watercress, garlic and seasoning. Cover and cook for 1 minute. Stir well, replace the lid and cook for 2 more minutes.

Take off the heat, stir again, replace the lid and leave to cook in its own steam for 2 more minutes.

Tip the watercress into a serving dish and sprinkle with lemon juice and toasted flaked almonds. Serve warm. Serves 4.

PER SERVING	
Energy Kcals	117.6
Protein g	3.6
Carbohydrates g	3.2
Dietary Fibre g	1.9
Fat – Total g	10.9
Saturated Fat g	1.3
Polyunsaturated Fat g	1.3
Calcium mg	128.0
Magnesium mg	22.4

While the spinach contains an excellent 3 mg of iron per serving, it also contains phytates that to a certain extent block the absorption of the iron. However, the good news is that, in mixtures of vegetables such as this, the vitamin C and beta-carotene in the red peppers and carrots help to make the iron more absorbable.

PER SERVING	
Energy Kcals	115.7
Protein g	4.6
Carbohydrates g	11.1
Dietary Fibre g	4.0
Fat – Total g	7.2
Saturated Fat g	1.2
Polyunsaturated Fat g	1.0
Calcium mg	99.3
Magnesium mg	91.4

Sweet potatoes are a very good source of the three antioxidants beta-carotene, vitamin C and vitamin E. They are also very low on the Glycaemic Index (see Appendix 1), which means that they help to keep the blood sugar level even. As a nutritional therapist I find people seem to have trouble balancing their blood sugar levels, and I always advise them to include low Glycaemic Index foods such as sweet potatoes in their diet.

PER SERVING	
Energy Kcals	203.1
Protein g	2.2
Carbohydrates g	32.4
Dietary Fibre g	2.4
Fat – Total g	7.4
Saturated Fat g	1.1
Polyunsaturated Fat g	0.8
Calcium mg	28.8
Magnesium mg	13.8

Spicy Spinach

This is another brightly coloured mixed vegetable dish. Eating colourful vegetables is a way of making sure you get a good mix of antioxidants.

1 tbsp	extra virgin olive oil	1 tbsp
2	small carrots, halved then sliced on the diagonal	2
1	red pepper, deseeded and cut into fine matchsticks	1
4	spring onions, sliced	4
1	lime, juice only	1
12 oz	baby spinach leaves	340 g
1 oz	cashew nuts, toasted, roughly chopped	30 g
1 tbsp	tamari sauce, or to taste	1 tbsp

Heat the oil in a wok and stir-fry the carrots and red pepper for 2-3 minutes. Add the spring onions and continue to stir-fry for another minute. Remove from the heat and stir in the rest of the ingredients. Toss together until the spinach is warmed through and starting to wilt. Serve immediately. Serves 4.

Sweet Potato Chips

I learnt to cook these at The Vegetarian Society some years ago, and find them very 'more-ish'. I cook them in my ridged pan, but they can equally well be grilled. This is one dish that I think demands sea salt rather than low-sodium salt – just go easy on it, you don't need much.

1$^1/_2$ lbs	sweet potatoes, washed	675 g
2 tbsp	extra virgin olive oil	2 tbsp
	coarse sea salt to taste	
$^1/_2$ tsp	paprika	$^1/_2$ tsp

Parboil the sweet potatoes, whole, for 10 minutes until just beginning to soften. Cool, peel, then cut into slices or chip shapes (2 inches x $^1/_2$ inch/5 cm x 1cm). Brush with olive oil and sprinkle with paprika. Either cook under a hot grill or in a ridged pan, turning once. Serve sprinkled with sea salt. Serves 4.

Beetroot is very rich in folate which helps to neutralise homocysteine, a dangerous metabolite of protein, so beetroot is heart-protective. Together the beetroot and beet greens in this recipe supply over 100 mg of folate, making it one of the richest sources of this vitamin. Beetroot leaves contain oxalic acid which can block the absorption of calcium if you eat too many of them, but they contain other nutrients too, such as magnesium, vitamin C and lots of potassium, so it's good to eat them once in a while.

Beetroot with Beet Greens

I discovered this revelatory way of cooking beetroot when I lived in Washington DC, where it was easy to buy beetroot with the tops on. It's not so easy in the UK, unless you go to a farmers market, or get an organic vegetable box or, best of all, grow your own.

1	large bunch beetroot with tops	1
2 tbsp	cold pressed walnut oil	2 tbsp
1 tbsp	balsamic vinegar	1 tbsp
	low-sodium salt and freshly ground black pepper to taste	

Cut the beetroots from their stalks, and the stalks from the leaves, discarding the stalks. Rinse the beetroot carefully. Do not scrub as you don't want to break the skin. Put the beetroot in a large pot and cover with plenty of cold water. Bring to the boil, turn down the heat to a simmer and cover. Cook for 1-1$\frac{1}{2}$ hours, depending on the size of the beetroot, checking the water level from time to time. Drain and leave until cool enough to handle, then rub off the skins. Keep warm while you cook the leaves.

Wash the leaves well, then boil or steam them until wilted. Drain well.

Make a dressing by whisking together the walnut oil, balsamic vinegar and seasoning. Slice the beetroot and arrange in a serving dish surrounded by the wilted greens. Dress with the walnut oil and vinegar mixture and serve warm or at room temperature. Serves 4.

PER SERVING	
Energy Kcals	110.5
Protein g	2.5
Carbohydrates g	11.1
Dietary Fibre g	2.9
Fat – Total g	7.0
Saturated Fat g	0.7
Polyunsaturated Fat g	4.4
Calcium mg	64.7
Magnesium mg	48.9

Eating lentils is an excellent way to help even out your blood sugar levels, because they are digested slowly, and because they contain both protein and carbohydrate. They are also a good source of iron, calcium and potassium.

Dhal

There are hundreds of recipes for dhal, probably thousands. This is a very simple, slightly Anglicized version of this nutritious staple. Personally, I could eat it every single day, and sometimes I do, if I have greedily made rather too big a pot of it.

6 oz	red lentils, washed and drained	170 g
2 tbsp	extra virgin olive oil	2 tbsp
1	medium onion, sliced into thin rings	1
1	garlic clove, crushed	1
	root ginger, peeled and grated (1 inch/2.5 cm piece)	
1 tsp	ground turmeric	1 tsp
1 tsp	ground cumin	1 tsp
1/2 tsp	low-sodium salt	1/2 tsp

Cover the lentils with cold water and bring to the boil, partially cover the pan and simmer for 20-25 minutes or until soft and thick, adding more water if necessary. Heat 1 tablespoon of olive oil in a small pan, and fry the onion until browned. Add the garlic, ginger, turmeric and cumin and cook for another 3 minutes, stirring. Stir the onion mixture into the lentils together with another tablespoon of olive oil and low-sodium salt to taste. Serves 4.

PER SERVING	
Energy Kcals	197.5
Protein g	9.2
Carbohydrates g	24.6
Dietary Fibre g	6.2
Fat – Total g	7.2
Saturated Fat g	1.0
Polyunsaturated Fat g	0.7
Calcium mg	46.0
Magnesium mg	13.6

Stir-Fried Green Beans and Cashew Nuts

2 tbsp	extra virgin olive oil	2 tbsp
2	garlic cloves, finely chopped	2
	fresh ginger root, peeled and grated (1 inch/2.5 cm piece)	
1 lb	French beans, cut into 1 inch/2.5 cm lengths	450 g
3½ oz	cashew nuts, sliced	100 g
1 tbsp	miso	1 tbsp
1 tbsp	tamari	1 tbsp
2 tsp	cornflour	2 tsp

Heat the oil in a wok over medium-high heat. Stir-fry the garlic and ginger for a couple of minutes, then add the beans, and stir-fry for another 3-4 minutes. Add the cashew nuts at the end of this time.

Mix the cornflour with a little water until smooth, then add the miso and tamari. Add this mixture to the wok, stir to combine, then reduce the heat, cover the pan and simmer for another minute or two, until the beans are tender. Serves 4.

PER SERVING	
Energy Kcals	292.5
Protein g	6.8
Carbohydrates g	14.8
Dietary Fibre g	5.7
Fat – Total g	24.5
Saturated Fat g	7.9
Polyunsaturated Fat g	0.9
Calcium mg	57.8
Magnesium mg	32.3

All green beans, including runner beans, are relatively good sources of beta-carotene. We tend to think that this nutrient is only available from carrots and other orange vegetables and fruits, but actually it is present in green vegetables, only its colour is masked by chlorophyll – the green colouring. Beans also contain lots of potassium, which helps to control blood pressure.

Runner Beans with Fresh Tomatoes

I've always grown runner beans up a wigwam in the summer whenever I've had a bit of spare ground. Gardeners will tell you that they need lots of feeding and deep trenches full of organic material, but you can get fairly decent beans without going to all that trouble, though not perhaps competition-winners. Runner beans need to be as fresh and firm as possible, and not too large. The only way to get them like that is to grow your own, in which case simply steam them and eat them as they are, fresh off the vine. However, if you are faced with 'green giants' that you've bought in the market, or if you just want a change, cook them like this.

1 lb	runner beans	450 g
1 lb	fresh tomatoes	450 g
2 tbsp	extra virgin olive oil	2 tbsp
	low-sodium salt and freshly ground black pepper to taste	
2 tbsp	chopped flat-leaf parsley	2 tbsp

If the runner beans are young enough, just slice them diagonally into 1 inch/2.5 cm lengths. If they are larger, it is worth taking the time to peel the strings off and cut them lengthwise. I push mine through a little square bean cutter with 4 blades, but if you haven't got one of these invaluable little gadgets, just cut with a very sharp knife down the length of each bean into 3 or 4 long strips. This is tedious, but worth it.

Peel the tomatoes by nicking the skins at the stalk end, then plunging them into boiling water for a minute or two. The skins should peel off easily after that. Cut into quarters and gently squeeze out the seeds. Chop the remaining flesh into neat dice.

Cook the beans in plenty of water for 10 minutes, or until tender. Drain well. Heat the oil gently in a large pan over low heat and add the diced tomatoes to warm through without really cooking. Add the cooked beans and seasoning and stir to mix. Serve hot sprinkled with chopped parsley. Serves 4.

PER SERVING	
Energy Kcals	126.4
Protein g	3.1
Carbohydrates g	14.2
Dietary Fibre g	4.9
Fat – Total g	7.7
Saturated Fat g	1.1
Polyunsaturated Fat g	0.9
Calcium mg	59.5
Magnesium mg	45.2

It is good to include fresh broad beans in your diet when they are in season. Their long taproots, going down five feet or more into the soil, enable them to absorb minerals that other plants cannot reach, such as selenium and zinc.

Vegetables with Lime and Coconut Cream

This is a lovely way to give young vegetables a slightly Far Eastern flavour. Serve with any oriental meal. They are particularly good with fish, and should be served warm or at room temperature rather than hot.

4 oz	French beans	110 g
4 oz	courgettes	110 g
4 oz	shelled young broad beans	110 g
4 oz	young asparagus, trimmed	110 g
1 tbsp	rice vinegar	1 tbsp
1	lime, grated rind and juice	1
1 tsp	concentrated apple juice	1 tsp
2 tbsp	extra virgin olive oil	2 tbsp
3 tbsp	coconut cream	3 tbsp
1 tbsp	chopped mint	1 tbsp
	mint leaves, for garnish	

Trim the beans and cut in half. Cut the courgettes and asparagus into sticks about 1 inch/2.5 cm long. Bring a pan of water to the boil and cook the broad beans and French beans for 2 minutes. Then add the asparagus and courgettes and continue cooking for 3 more minutes. Drain and refresh in cold water.

For the dressing, whisk together the rice vinegar, lime rind and juice, seasoning and apple juice concentrate. Then whisk in the oil and coconut cream.

When you are ready to serve, plunge all the vegetables back into boiling water for 30 seconds, then drain and pour over the lime and coconut dressing. Add the chopped mint and garnish with fresh mint leaves. Serves 4.

PER SERVING	
Energy Kcals	151.1
Protein g	4.1
Carbohydrates g	13.3
Dietary Fibre g	4.1
Fat – Total g	9.8
Saturated Fat g	3.2
Polyunsaturated Fat g	0.8
Calcium mg	31.7
Magnesium mg	35.7

Fennel is a good diuretic, and valued in Italy for its digestive properties. It is beneficial during the menopause as it contains phytoestrogens.

Roast Fennel with Lemon

Fennel has a naturally sweet taste, enhanced here by the combination of honey and lemon.

1¼ lb	fennel (3 bulbs)	650 g
2 tbsp	extra virgin olive oil	2 tbsp
1	lemon	1
1 tsp	honey	1 tsp
	low-sodium salt and freshly ground black pepper to taste	
1	sprig fresh rosemary	1

Preheat the oven to 200°C/400°F/Gas Mark 6.

Trim the fennel and cut downwards into quarters. Put in a roasting tin and spoon over the olive oil, honey, and juice from the lemon. Cut the lemon shell into quarters and add to the tin. Season to taste and tuck in the sprig of rosemary.

Cover the dish with a lid or baking parchment and cook in the oven for half an hour. Remove the lid or parchment and cook for another 20-25 minutes until the fennel is tender and browned at the edges, but don't let it get too charred.
Serves 4.

PER SERVING	
Energy Kcals	118.0
Protein g	2.1
Carbohydrates g	14.7
Dietary Fibre g	5.7
Fat – Total g	7.4
Saturated Fat g	1.0
Polyunsaturated Fat g	0.7
Calcium mg	86.7
Magnesium mg	31.6

As well as being a source of phytoestrogens, celery can help control your appetite if eaten between meals, and it also has the ability to bring down blood pressure. Furthermore, it is very high in silicon, which makes it helpful in renewing joints, bones, arteries and all connective tissue. Because of this it is useful for people with arthritis.

Braised Celery with Thyme

I was keen to include a celery recipe as it is a source of phytoestrogens. I usually eat it raw, but it is very good braised like this as well – it has quite a different taste when cooked.

1	head of celery (about 1 lb/450 g)	1
¹/₂ oz	organic unsalted butter	15 g
2	onions, peeled and finely chopped	2
¹/₂ pint	vegetable stock	275 ml
1	bay leaf	1
2-3	sprigs of thyme	2-3
	low-sodium salt and freshly ground black pepper to taste	
¹/₂ oz	organic unsalted butter	15 g
¹/₂ oz	wholemeal or gluten-free flour	15 g
1 tsp	fresh thyme leaves	1 tsp

Preheat the oven to 180°C/350°F/Gas Mark 4.

Trim the celery, and cut the stalks into batons. Retain the leaves for another use – they're good in salads, for example. Wash the celery really well.

Melt the butter in an ovenproof casserole over a low heat, and sauté the onions until soft but not browned. Add the celery, stock, bay leaf, thyme sprigs and seasoning and bring to the boil.

Cover the casserole with a lid and transfer to the oven. Cook for 30 minutes or until the celery is tender.

Meanwhile, with your fingers, rub the flour into the other ¹/₂ oz/15 g butter until amalgamated. This is *beurre manié* – a mixture used to thicken sauces.

When the celery is cooked, transfer the casserole to the top of the stove over a medium heat. When it is boiling, add the *beurre manié* in little pieces, stirring all the time. Simmer until thickened – about 3 minutes.

To serve, remove the bay leaf and thyme branches, transfer to a serving dish and sprinkle over the fresh thyme leaves. Serves 4.

PER SERVING	
Energy Kcals	98.8
Protein g	1.6
Carbohydrates g	11.2
Dietary Fibre g	2.3
Fat – Total g	6.0
Saturated Fat g	3.6
Polyunsaturated Fat g	0.3
Calcium mg	49.5
Magnesium mg	20.1

If you cannot get sun-dried tomatoes in oil, use the dried ones, but soak them in boiling water for 10 minutes first to soften. On the market now are sunblush tomatoes, which are only partly dried. They would also be delicious in this dish.

Grilled Asparagus with Sun-Dried Tomatoes

In general I think asparagus shouldn't be messed with, nor should it be eaten out of season. I deplore the food-miles involved in stocking our supermarket shelves with Peruvian asparagus all year round. English asparagus is the best in the world, and my husband and I are lucky enough to live just up the road from an asparagus farm. So when it is in season we eat it at every meal, usually just plainly steamed. However, once in a while it is good to ring the changes, and grilling it retains all the flavour.

1½ lb	asparagus, not too thin	675 g
1-2 tbsp	extra virgin olive oil	1-2 tbsp
1 oz	sun-dried tomatoes packed in oil, chopped	1 oz
2 tsp	balsamic vinegar	2 tsp
	freshly ground black pepper	

Trim the asparagus at the root end, and peel the stalk ends with a potato peeler up to about 1 inch/2.5 cm if they are very tough. Arrange on a grill pan, brush with olive oil and grind some black pepper over them. Grill under a hot grill for 5 minutes, turning once or twice to brown evenly.

Serve the asparagus hot or at room temperature. Sprinkle with a few drops of balsamic vinegar and scatter over the chopped sun-dried tomatoes. Serves 4.

PER SERVING	
Energy Kcals	117.8
Protein g	4.5
Carbohydrates g	8.7
Dietary Fibre g	2.9
Fat – Total g	8.5
Saturated Fat g	1.2
Polyunsaturated Fat g	1.0
Calcium mg	35.8
Magnesium mg	21.6

Salads and Salad Dressings

Bean and Seed Sprouts
Flageolet Bean Salad with Herbs and Tomatoes
June's Wholewheat Salad
Millet Tabbouleh
Arame and Rice Salad with Nuts and Raisins
Coriander, Tofu and Cashew Salad
Soba Noodle Salad
Dark Red Salad
Apple, Celery and Carrot Salad with Walnuts
Kale and Orange Salad with Tahini Mustard Dressing
Fennel and Baby Spinach Salad with Almond Romesco Dressing
Watercress and Kiwi Fruit Salad
Coreen's Roasted Sweet Potato Salad
Winter Root Salad
Pear, Walnut and Rocket Salad
Dijon Chicken Salad
Black Bean and Pepper Salad with Fresh Tuna
Basic Vinaigrette
Walnut Oil Vinaigrette
Hazelnut Vinaigrette
Pumpkin Seed Vinaigrette
Citrus Vinaigrette
Sweet Vinaigrette
Tomato Vinaigrette
Nut Butter Dressing
Ginger Dressing
Sesame Oil Dressing
Tahini, Garlic and Tamari Dressing
Honey Mustard Dressing
Yoghurt Dressing

Eating salads is a wonderful opportunity to add nutrients to your diet in the form of nuts, seeds and sprouts. They also, along with fruit, provide the raw element thought to be so essential.

A salad, of course, can be made from any food, raw or cooked, warm or cold, and you will find some salads here which can constitute a whole meal in themselves.

A salad consists of two main elements – the actual ingredients and the dressing. I have kept the two separate, and you can mix and match them at will. The suggestions I have given are based on nutritional balance and the marriage of appropriate tastes, but all are interchangeable. The ingredients are obviously the most important element in a salad, and must not be swamped by the dressing, but enhanced by it. At the Vegetarian Society we were encouraged to follow the principle of including roots, fruits and shoots in every salad – that is, something which grows below the surface of the soil, such as a carrot, a fruit such as a tomato, and a leaf or stem, such as lettuce. I can't say I always abide by this principle, but it is worth bearing in mind that variety, while being the key, must not be allowed to run wild. Keep your main ingredients down to three, and try to have one of each category.

I serve a salad for every main meal, whether it is lunch or dinner. This is partly because I find salads more digestible than cooked vegetables (although many people find the opposite to be true), but mostly because I crave raw foods and love the variety that salads offer. No two salads ever have to be the same, and it is fun to look in the fridge and make up a salad from what you find there. So I urge you to experiment, but here are a few ideas to be going along with.

Bean and Seed Sprouts

We were all eating bean sprouts in the sixties and seventies, then they went out of fashion as more sophisticated foods elbowed them off the menu. But sprouts are a wonder food – when a seed sprouts it increases its nutritional content about six times over. The sprouting process induces a frenzy of biochemical activity in which enzymes convert to carbohydrates, and proteins are broken down into amino acids which makes them more digestible. Vitamin C concentrations also increase. Alfalfa contains that elusive and little understood mineral, boron (needed for bone health). The fibre found in sprouts is good for the gut flora, and all sprouts are alkaline, which is good for the blood pH balance. Best of all for the menopausal woman, sprouts contain the isoflavones, genistein and daidzein, also found in soya beans. These isoflavones act as mild oestrogens in the body, which can help relieve menopausal symptoms and may even be able to help prevent breast cancer. It is so easy to add sprouts to your diet either in salads or in sandwiches.

To sprout seeds or beans, cover 2-3 tablespoons of seeds with tepid water overnight (their volume will increase by about sixfold). In the morning, rinse with fresh tepid water and leave to drain, not in the sun – for the first day or two you should keep them in a dark place. You can purchase sprouters specially made for the purpose, or use a glass jar with muslin over the top so the water can drain through it. Continue doing this twice a day until the sprouts are big enough to eat. The time varies according to the type of sprout. My favourites are alfalfa sprouts, which make great sandwich additions as well as a crunchy salad ingredient, particularly in winter when organic salad stuffs may be in short supply. Alfalfa seeds take about four days to sprout. I usually start them off on a Monday night and they are ready by the weekend. When they are ready, rinse them one last time, drain well and store in the fridge. Any seeds that have not sprouted should be discarded. The sprouts will keep for up to a week, but are really best used as soon as possible after sprouting to get the full nutritional benefit, and to avoid the possibility of moulds developing.

Another way to grow sprouts is in a tray of soil or compost, just as you would grow seedlings. This is a particularly good method of sprouting sunflower seeds, whole wheat and buckwheat. Sprinkle the seeds on top of the soil, water well, and keep in a dark place for 2-3 days, then bring out into the light and water or spray regularly until ready to eat.

Other sprouts to try are: lentils, chickpeas, mung beans, barley, oats and maize.

Only a handful of the salads that follow specify beansprouts, but please feel free to add them into practically any salad.

All beans contain isoflavones, which act as weak oestrogens and help to dampen down menopausal symptoms, so you should try to include them in your diet on a regular basis. Not all beans taste the same, so it is worth experimenting to find the ones you like best. You could make this salad with other beans of course – chickpeas or cannellini beans would be good here.

Flageolet Bean Salad with Herbs and Tomatoes

Flageolet beans are the aristocrat of the dried beans, having a delicate flavour and pretty pale green colour. They are a good bean to begin with if you are not used to eating pulses.

1	small head of radicchio	1
1	head of chicory	1
3½ oz	dried flageolet beans, soaked overnight, or one 14 oz/400 g can of flageolet beans, rinsed and drained	100 g
	low-sodium salt and freshly ground black pepper to taste	
2 tbsp	chopped chives	2 tbsp
6	spring onions, thinly sliced	6
	fresh basil leaves, a handful	
3	tomatoes, peeled, deseeded and chopped	3
	parsley, a small bunch	
	tomato vinaigrette (see page 141)	

If you are using soaked, dried flageolet beans, throw away the soaking water, cover with fresh water, bring to the boil and cook until tender – 1-1½ hours depending on the age of the beans. Drain and proceed with the recipe.

Rinse the radicchio and chicory leaves. (You may not need all the radicchio for this recipe.) Reserve a few leaves of radicchio for serving, and tear the rest into small pieces. Slice the chicory quite thinly. Mix the cooked beans with seasoning, chopped chives, sliced spring onions, and basil. Mix the bean mixture, torn radicchio, sliced chicory and tomatoes together, and stir in the vinaigrette. Leave for a little while for the flavours to blend. Serve in a mound on a bed of the reserved radicchio leaves, and sprinkle the top with the chopped parsley. Serves 4.

PER SERVING	
Energy Kcals	294.4
Protein g	7.7
Carbohydrates g	27.2
Dietary Fibre g	6.9
Fat – Total g	18.6
Saturated Fat g	2.5
Polyunsaturated Fat g	4.0
Calcium mg	80.6
Magnesium mg	68.7

The wheat in this recipe is truly a 'whole grain', just as it comes off the stalk of wheat in the field. Try to find organic wholewheat, or blé (its French name) as it is sometimes known in health food shops. You can also try sprouting wheat berries (see page 126). Sprouting increases the nutritional value. Note that this recipe also has a good magnesium:calcium ratio, which is good for your bones.

June's Wholewheat Salad

My sister-in-law, June, makes a delicious curry-flavoured wholewheat salad. This is the recipe I managed to pry from her.

6 oz	wholewheat berries (blé)	170 g
1	onion, studded with whole cloves	1
1 tsp	extra virgin olive oil	1 tsp
	vegetable stock (see page 41)	
1	large onion, peeled and finely chopped	1
2	sticks celery, sliced	2
1/4	fresh pineapple, peeled and cut into small chunks	1/4
1/2	green pepper, diced	1/2
1	apple, cored and diced	1
2 tbsp	raisins	2 tbsp

For the dressing:

2 tsp	curry powder	2 tsp
1 tbsp	shoyu	1 tbsp
2 tbsp	cider vinegar	2 tbsp
2 tbsp	extra virgin olive oil	2 tbsp
	low-sodium salt and freshly ground black pepper to taste	

First, soak the wheat in warm water for a few hours or overnight.

Drain from the soaking water, rinse and cover with vegetable stock. Add the onion studded with cloves and the teaspoon of olive oil, bring to the boil, reduce the heat and simmer for 3-4 hours, until the wheat is tender to the bite, adding more water as necessary. Drain well, and place in a large bowl. Add all the other ingredients and mix well. Whisk together all the dressing ingredients and toss with the salad to combine. Serves 4-6.

PER SERVING	
Energy Kcals	311.1
Protein g	7.3
Carbohydrates g	54.6
Dietary Fibre g	9.5
Fat – Total g	9.3
Saturated Fat g	1.3
Polyunsaturated Fat g	1.1
Calcium mg	54.7
Magnesium mg	77.2

Millet contains no gluten, unlike wheat, and is considered to be the most alkaline of grains (along with buckwheat which, strictly speaking, isn't a grain at all). It is wise to eat more alkaline foods than acid foods, to help our bodies maintain a balance that is slightly on the alkaline side. This is beneficial because the right pH level helps the body to absorb and utilise food and helps enzymes and hormones to function better. Other alkaline foods are all vegetables and most fruits.

Millet Tabbouleh

I learnt to make tabbouleh the Middle Eastern way from my Syrian-Lebanese sister-in-law, Ros. It was a revelation to me to discover that the principal ingredient should be the parsley, not the cracked wheat. I have substituted cooked, toasted millet for the bulgur wheat and added a discreet amount of flax seed for extra nutrition. This is also very good using brown rice or quinoa instead of the millet.

2 oz	millet	60 g
6	chopped spring onions or 1 large mild onion, chopped	6
	low-sodium salt and freshly ground black pepper	
10 oz	flat-leaf parsley, finely chopped	285 g
3 oz	finely chopped fresh mint	85 g
4 tbsp	extra virgin olive oil	4 tbsp
4 tbsp	fresh lemon juice	4 tbsp
2 tbsp	flax seed, ground very briefly	2 tbsp

For the garnish:

	black olives, cherry tomatoes, sliced cucumber	

Toast the millet in a dry frying pan for 10 minutes or so over medium heat, until it releases its aroma. Put the millet into a pan with plenty of cold water, bring to the boil and cook until tender (about 30 minutes). Leave to stand, covered, for 5 minutes, then drain off any surplus water. Put into a large bowl and mix in the onions, seasoning, parsley, mint, olive oil and lemon juice while the millet is still warm. Mix well and taste for seasoning. Serve in a mound, decorated with the olives, tomatoes and cucumber slices. Serves 4-6.

PER SERVING	
Energy Kcals	277.2
Protein g	6.7
Carbohydrates g	31.5
Dietary Fibre g	6.1
Fat – Total g	15.2
Saturated Fat g	2.4
Polyunsaturated Fat g	2.1
Calcium mg	137.6
Magnesium mg	100.8

Arame, like other seaweeds, contains more iodine than fish. Since very many menopausal women have slightly underactive thyroid glands, and iodine is a key nutrient for the production of the thyroid hormones, it is important to get some iodine into our diet.

PER SERVING	
Energy Kcals	357.0
Protein g	7.3
Carbohydrates g	52.1
Dietary Fibre g	4.1
Fat – Total g	15.3
Saturated Fat g	2.4
Polyunsaturated Fat g	1.9
Calcium mg	36.2
Magnesium mg	48.3

Arame and Rice Salad with Nuts and Raisins

	arame (a small handful)	
6 oz	cooked brown basmati rice	170 g
2 oz	whole roasted cashews	60 g
2 oz	raisins, plumped in water or apple juice for 10 minutes and drained	60 g
1	cucumber, unpeeled but seeded and cut into 1 inch/2.5 cm batons	1
	ginger dressing (see page 141)	

Soak the arame in tepid water to cover for about 10 minutes. Drain, chop and mix with the other ingredients. Toss with the dressing and serve. Serves 4.

Tofu provides an excellent source of calcium, particularly if it is coagulated with calcium sulphate, as is Cauldron Foods tofu, which I used for testing the recipes because it is widely available. Cashew nuts are rich in magnesium, needed for healthy bones.

PER SERVING	
Energy Kcals	321.9
Protein g	19.9
Carbohydrates g	9.3
Dietary Fibre g	1.7
Fat – Total g	27.1
Saturated Fat g	4.4
Polyunsaturated Fat g	9.8
Calcium mg	155.3
Magnesium mg	56.4

Coriander, Tofu and Cashew Salad

Coriander takes centre stage in this recipe instead of being just a flavouring. This idea comes from David Scott, author of *The Demiveg Cookbook.*

8¹⁄₂ oz	firm tofu, drained and pressed (1 packet)	250 g
1 tbsp	cold-pressed sesame oil	1 tbsp
1¹⁄₂ oz	whole cashews, roasted	45 g
2	large bunches of fresh coriander leaves	2
	sesame oil dressing (see page 141)	
To serve:		
1	soft lettuce	1

Cut the tofu into cubes, brush with the sesame oil and grill under a hot grill or cook in a ridged pan until golden. Leave to cool. Wash the coriander well, removing the stems. Throw into a large pan of boiling water, then drain immediately. Plunge into ice-cold water and leave until cool.

Drain, squeezing out any excess moisture, and chop roughly. Mix gently with the tofu cubes and roasted cashews, and dress with the sesame dressing.

To serve, separate the lettuce leaves and wash and dry them carefully. Arrange on 4 serving plates and divide the salad between them. Serves 4.

Shiitake mushrooms, which are a rich source of selenium, are used in Japan to prevent heart disease, treat fatigue and build up the immune system. Additionally, it is now thought that they may contain anti-cancer properties.

Soba Noodle Salad

If you can find fresh shiitake mushrooms, increasingly available in supermarkets, substitute them for the dried mushrooms in this recipe. They will not require soaking.

4 oz	dried shiitake mushrooms	110 g
16 fl oz	water	450 ml
3	carrots	3
8 oz	sugar snap peas or mangetout	225 g
1	red pepper	1
6	spring onions	6
	ginger dressing (see page 141)	
8 oz	soba (buckwheat) noodles	225 g

Pour boiling water over the shiitake mushrooms and leave to soak for half an hour to rehydrate. Drain, remove and discard the stems, and slice thinly. Meanwhile, cut the carrots into julienne matchsticks, trim and slice the sugar snaps or mangetout into 1 inch/2.5 cm diagonal slices, and cut the red pepper and spring onions into 2 inch/5 cm strips. Blanch the carrots, peas and red pepper separately in boiling water for a minute or two each. Drain and refresh.

Cook the noodles until just tender, about 5-7 minutes. Drain and plunge into cold water. Drain again. Toss with 1 tablespoon of dressing, and cool completely.

To serve, layer the noodles, vegetables and shiitake mushrooms in a serving bowl and pour the remaining dressing over. Serves 6.

PER SERVING	
Energy Kcals	253.1
Protein g	9.1
Carbohydrates g	40.0
Dietary Fibre g	4.2
Fat – Total g	7.3
Saturated Fat g	0.7
Polyunsaturated Fat g	0.4
Calcium mg	42.4
Magnesium mg	23.8

The hazelnuts and, particularly, the hazelnut oil here provide a rich source of vitamin E, an antioxidant that protects the skin against loss of elasticity, as well as protecting the cells of the body from oxidative damage, protecting against heart disease and helping to control hot flushes.

Dark Red Salad

I made this up for fun, trying to use all the red-coloured vegetables and fruits whose tastes went together and whose colours didn't actually clash. Try it for yourself with orange (carrots, orange peppers, oranges, cooked sweet potato), or the lighter reds (tomatoes, red peppers, red apples). The more colourful the vegetable or fruit, the more antioxidants it contains. In Oriental tradition, red foods are associated with stimulation of the blood and circulation.

1	large orange, juice and finely grated rind	1
1 tbsp	concentrated apple juice	1 tbsp
1 tbsp	cider vinegar	1 tbsp
4 oz	red cabbage, finely shredded	110 g
1	small red onion, sliced into rings	1
6	radishes, sliced	6
1	red-skinned apple, diced but not peeled	1
1	head radicchio	1
2	small cooked beetroot, diced	2
	hazelnut vinaigrette (see page 140)	
2 tbsp	hazelnuts, toasted and roughly chopped	2 tbsp

First, cook the cabbage. Put the orange juice and rind in a saucepan together with the maple syrup and cider vinegar. Heat the mixture, then add the red cabbage, and cook for 5 minutes until the cabbage turns from red to pink, and most of the liquid has evaporated. Drain and leave to cool.

When cool, mix with the red onion rings, sliced radishes and diced apple. Pour over the the hazelnut vinaigrette and toss well.

Arrange radicchio leaves on four plates and pile the salad on top. Scatter the diced beetroot around the edges of each plate, and sprinkle chopped hazelnuts on top of the salad. Serves 4.

PER SERVING	
Energy Kcals	2512.5
Protein g	2.6
Carbohydrates g	27.0
Dietary Fibre g	4.6
Fat – Total g	16.4
Saturated Fat g	1.3
Polyunsaturated Fat g	1.9
Calcium mg	56.0
Magnesium mg	31.3

For a variation, try adding seeds to this salad. Especially good here would be crunchy hemp seeds, though it is a good idea to crush them a little first before adding them to the salad, so that the essential fatty acids they contain are more available. Essential fatty acids are needed for hormonal balance.

PER SERVING	
Energy Kcals	263.3
Protein g	1.9
Carbohydrates g	17.6
Dietary Fibre g	4.3
Fat – Total g	21.9
Saturated Fat g	2.0
Polyunsaturated Fat g	14.2
Calcium mg	33.7
Magnesium mg	25.3

This salad looks very pretty with pink grapefruit instead of oranges, or try blood oranges in season (January-February). You can sometimes find purple kale, too, and a mixture of purple and green looks fantastic.

Apple, Celery and Carrot Salad with Walnuts

This is one of my favourite everyday salads, and takes only minutes to assemble. Make it just before eating so that the apple doesn't turn brown.

2	apples, any variety, such as Cox's or Russets	2
2	medium carrots	2
4	celery sticks, chopped	4
1 oz	walnuts, roughly chopped	30 g
	walnut oil vinaigrette (see page 140)	
2 tbsp	live natural yoghurt or soya yoghurt	2 tbsp

Wash the apples and scrub the carrots. Grate the apples, together with their skins, and the carrots. Mix with the chopped celery and walnuts. Mix the walnut oil vinaigrette with the yoghurt and toss the salad with it. Serves 4.

Kale and Orange Salad with Tahini Mustard Dressing

Kale is far too nutritious a vegetable to be consigned to being a side dish. This salad is a very palatable way to eat kale, pretty enough to serve at a dinner party, and remarkably filling.

3¹/₂ oz	kale, sliced or torn into bite-sized pieces	100 g
2	large oranges	2
1	large carrot	1
4	sticks celery	4
For the dressing:		
1 tbsp	flax oil or extra virgin olive oil	1 tbsp
¹/₂ tsp	English mustard powder	¹/₂ tsp
1 tbsp	natural yoghurt or plain soya yoghurt	1 tbsp

| 2 tsp | clear honey or maple syrup | 2 tsp |
| | salt and freshly ground black pepper to taste | |

Blanch the kale in boiling water, covered with a lid, for exactly one minute. Drain and immediately plunge into very cold water. Leave until cold, pour off the water and then drain well on kitchen paper to dry thoroughly. Arrange on four plates.

Peel the oranges, and cut into segments over a bowl to catch the juice. Set aside.

Add all the dressing ingredients to the orange juice in the bowl and whisk to mix.

Wash the carrots and celery, and slice into fine julienne strips no longer than 2 inches/5 cm. Toss in the dressing and pile up in the centre of the plates of kale. Arrange the orange segments on top and serve. Serves 4.

PER SERVING	
Energy Kcals	111.1
Protein g	2.2
Carbohydrates g	19.6
Dietary Fibre g	4.2
Fat – Total g	3.8
Saturated Fat g	0.4
Polyunsaturated Fat g	2.4
Calcium mg	82.4
Magnesium mg	16.8

Try this dressing with any robust green leaf, such as frisée. Alternatively, it goes well with grilled or roasted vegetables, particularly onions. This salad is very bone-protective, as it is rich in vitamin K, calcium and magnesium. One of the functions of vitamin K is to convert inactive osteocalcin to its active form. Osteocalcin is a bone protein that anchors calcium molecules and holds them in place within the bone, so vitamin K helps calcium form new bone.

Fennel and Baby Spinach Salad with Almond Romesco Dressing

This is a very simple salad, the point of which is the delicious and nutritious dressing.

Romesco dressing can be used as a sauce with pasta as well as a salad dressing. It is originally a Spanish sauce from Tarragona – 'romesco' is the word for dried sweet red peppers. Here, I have substituted tomatoes and paprika for the dried peppers.

1 oz	whole blanched almonds	30 g
2	ripe tomatoes	2
1	garlic clove	1
5 tbsp	extra virgin olive oil	5 tbsp
1¹/₂ tbsp	red wine vinegar	1¹/₂ tbsp
	small bunch flat-leaf parsley	
1 tsp	paprika	1 tsp
2	fennel bulbs	2
12 oz	baby spinach leaves, well washed	340 g
	sea salt and freshly ground black pepper	

For the garnish:

1/2	red pepper, finely diced	1/2

Preheat the oven to 180°C/350°F/Gas Mark 4.

For the dressing, roast the almonds on a dry baking tray until golden, about 10 minutes, checking frequently. Meanwhile peel the tomatoes by nicking the skin, then plunging them into boiling water for a minute or two, after which the skins will come off easily. Deseed the tomatoes and chop the flesh. Cook the garlic in a little of the oil until golden, then transfer to a food processor together with the toasted nuts. Pulse briefly, then add the chopped tomatoes, vinegar, parsley, paprika, remaining oil and seasoning. Blend until smooth.

Halve or quarter the fennel bulbs, take out the triangular core, and slice the rest into 1/4 inch/0.5 cm slices. Mix with the spinach leaves.

Toss the salad with the dressing (you may not need to use it all), and divide between four plates. Garnish with the diced red pepper. Serves 4.

PER SERVING	
Energy Kcals	276.3
Protein g	6.3
Carbohydrates g	17.9
Dietary Fibre g	7.9
Fat – Total g	21.9
Saturated Fat g	2.8
Polyunsaturated Fat g	2.7
Calcium mg	166.8
Magnesium mg	120.0

There are nearly 100 mg of vitamin C in each serving of this salad, kiwi fruit being a particularly rich source. Our adrenal glands need vitamin C to help us handle stress. Since menopause symptoms are worse if you are adrenally stressed, it makes sense to take in more vitamin C. Kiwi fruit also contain an enzyme that helps reduce cholesterol and improve circulation.

Watercress and Kiwi Fruit Salad

This is a pretty salad that could be served as a starter. Rocket could equally well be used in place of watercress, but watercress wins in the nutrition stakes, being an excellent source of calcium, iron and vitamin C.

The box of organic vegetables and fruit I receive every week is often heavy on the kiwi fruit, and I sometimes find myself with a kilo of them to dispose of. They are wonderful in juice and fruit salads, or try them in a savoury salad like this one:

2 bunches	watercress	2 bunches
4	kiwi fruit	4
2 tsp	balsamic vinegar	2 tsp
	walnut oil vinaigrette (see page 140)	

Wash the watercress well and tear into bite sized sprigs. Put it in a bowl, toss with the walnut oil vinaigrette and divide between 4 plates. Peel and slice the kiwi fruit, sprinkle with balsamic vinegar (be careful not to overdo it, as the flavour is very powerful) and place on top of the watercress. Serves 4.

PER SERVING	
Energy Kcals	214.8
Protein g	2.2
Carbohydrates g	12.9
Dietary Fibre g	3.4
Fat – Total g	18.0
Saturated Fat g	2.5
Polyunsaturated Fat g	1.8
Calcium mg	89.8
Magnesium mg	39.0

Sweet potatoes are an excellent source of beta-carotene. They are also lower on the Glycaemic Index than ordinary potatoes, so they make a good choice if you are watching your weight.

Coreen's Roasted Sweet Potato Salad

Coreen Tucker helped me test the salad recipes, and this was one of her suggestions. She uses feta cheese, but since we are looking to increase the isoflavone content of our diet, I have substituted baked tofu.

2	sweet potatoes (about 12 oz/340 g)	2
4	small raw beetroot (about 12 oz/340 g)	4
2 tbsp	extra virgin olive oil	2 tbsp
4½ oz	tofu (½ packet)	125 g
	rocket, a handful	
	pumpkin seed vinaigrette (see page 141)	

Preheat the oven to 200°C/400°F/Gas Mark 6.

Peel the sweet potatoes and cut into chunks. Place in a roasting pan, drizzle with 1 tablespoon of olive oil and roast for about 40 minutes, or until golden but not charred. Roast the beetroot separately without peeling – this prevents the colour bleeding into the sweet potatoes.

When the beetroot are done, cool until you can handle them, then slip off the skins and cut into chunks.

Rinse, drain and press the tofu, cut into bite-size chunks, drizzle with 1 tablespoon of olive oil and bake in the oven for about 15 minutes or until golden.

To assemble the salad, arrange the washed rocket leaves on four salad plates, then divide the sweet potato, beetroot and tofu between them. Drizzle with pumpkin seed vinaigrette. Serves 4.

PER SERVING	
Energy Kcals	345.4
Protein g	7.5
Carbohydrates g	18.0
Dietary Fibre g	3.8
Fat – Total g	27.8
Saturated Fat g	3.9
Polyunsaturated Fat g	4.8
Calcium mg	174.1
Magnesium mg	84.9

Right: Roast Fennel with Lemon (page 121) and (back) Sweet Potato Chips (page 115)

The combination of pumpkin seeds, celery and beetroot contributes to the relatively high magnesium content of this salad.

Winter Root Salad

This salad features beetroot in its raw state – in my opinion a much underrated way to eat this delicious and nutritious vegetable (rich in minerals, vitamin C and folic acid).

4	carrots	4
$1/2$	celeriac	$1/2$
2	medium raw beetroot	2
$1/2$	red onion	$1/2$
	pumpkin seed vinaigrette (see page 141)	
1	head chicory	1
1 oz	toasted pumpkin seeds	30 g
	flat-leaf parsley	

Peel and grate the carrots, celeriac, beetroot and onion. Only combine just before serving, or the beetroot will bleed into the other vegetables. Toss with the dressing. Separate the chicory spears and arrange like the spokes of a wheel on a flat dish. Pile the grated vegetables in a mound in the middle and sprinkle with the toasted pumpkin seeds and chopped flat-leaf parsley. Serves 4.

PER SERVING	
Energy Kcals	79.9
Protein g	5.2
Carbohydrates g	18.3
Dietary Fibre g	4.9
Fat – Total g	21.8
Saturated Fat g	3.1
Polyunsaturated Fat g	4.9
Calcium mg	55.8
Magnesium mg	84.9

I love the peppery taste of rocket. It's very easy to grow, though you have to cut it quickly before it runs to seed. It's a good source of magnesium, iron and calcium, though not quite as rich in minerals as watercress, which you could substitute here.

Pear, Walnut and Rocket Salad

2	ripe Williams pears, peeled if desired, and sliced	2
7 oz	rocket	200 g
$1/2$	red pepper, diced	$1/2$
For the walnut dressing:		
1 oz	walnuts	30 g
1	garlic clove	1
	rocket, a handful	
4 tbsp	extra virgin olive oil	4 tbsp
	low-sodium salt and freshly ground black pepper to taste	

Left: Dark Red Salad (page 132) and (back) June's Wholewheat Salad (page 128)

PER SERVING	
Energy Kcals	247.3
Protein g	2.5
Carbohydrates g	19.2
Dietary Fibre g	3.8
Fat – Total g	19.3
Saturated Fat g	2.4
Polyunsaturated Fat g	4.8
Calcium mg	72.9
Magnesium mg	38.4

Preheat the oven to 200°C/400°F/Gas Mark 6.

For the dressing, roast the walnuts on a dry baking tray for 8-10 minutes, or until lightly toasted. Cool, then put in food processor with rest of the dressing ingredients. Add the oil slowly. Season to taste.

Wash the rocket and mix with the chopped red pepper. Arrange on individual serving plates. Fan out the pear slices either on top or beside the rocket, and drizzle over the dressing. Serves 4.

Dijon Chicken Salad

This is a good main course salad for a summer lunch.

4	small organic chicken breasts, skinless and boneless	4
1 tbsp	extra virgin olive oil	1 tbsp
1/2	lemon, juice only	1/2
	low-sodium salt and freshly ground black pepper	
4 oz	sugar snap or mangetout peas	110 g
7 oz	rocket leaves	200 g
4	radicchio leaves	4
1/2	cucumber, peeled, seeded, and cut into julienne strips	1/2
2 tbsp	pine nuts, toasted	2 tbsp

For the dressing:

	honey mustard dressing (see page 141)	
1 tbsp	Dijon mustard	1 tbsp
2 tbsp	soya yoghurt	2 tbsp

PER SERVING	
Energy Kcals	393.7
Protein g	32.1
Carbohydrates g	9.5
Dietary Fibre g	1.7
Fat – Total g	24.5
Saturated Fat g	4.0
Polyunsaturated Fat g	3.7
Calcium mg	98.6
Magnesium mg	63.5

Whisk together the olive oil, lemon juice and seasoning, and marinate the chicken in this mixture for 2 hours or overnight. Then grill the chicken under a preheated grill until cooked, turning from time to time. Leave to cool, then cut into diagonal slices.

Steam the sugar snap peas or mangetout over boiling water until lightly cooked but still firm to the bite. Plunge into cold water to refresh and set the colour, then drain and reserve.

For the dressing, whisk together the honey mustard dressing, the extra spoonful of Dijon mustard and the soya yoghurt.

To assemble the salad, put one radicchio leaf on each plate and top with the rocket. Mix together the chicken, sugar snap or mangetout peas, and cucumber. Arrange on the bed of rocket and drizzle over the dressing. Garnish with toasted pine nuts. Serves 4.

The coriander here is more than a garnish. Coriander contains selenium (0.9 g per 100 g), which, besides being an essential part of many enzyme systems, is antagonistic to any mercury in tuna. So pile on the coriander leaves – they serve a useful purpose.

Black Bean and Pepper Salad with Fresh Tuna

This salad reminds me of the Caribbean – not just the taste, but the bright colours too. You could make it without the tuna, of course, for a vegetarian salad.

5 oz	dried black turtle beans, soaked overnight	140 g
1	bay leaf	1
1	sprig thyme	1
1	sprig rosemary	1
1	onion, peeled and finely chopped	1
2 tsp	ground cumin	2 tsp
1/2	red pepper, cut into small dice	1/2
1/2	yellow pepper, cut into small dice	1/2
4	spring onions, sliced diagonally	4
	citrus vinaigrette (see page 141)	
	low-sodium salt and freshly ground black pepper to taste	
2	tuna steaks, about 4-5 oz/125 g each	2
2 tsp	extra virgin olive oil, or use olive oil spray	2 tsp
1	lime, juice only	1

For the garnish:

1	lime, sliced into quarters	1
	coriander leaves	

Drain the beans, cover with fresh cold water and add the bay leaf, thyme, rosemary and chopped onion. Bring to the boil and cook for about an hour, until the beans are tender. Drain, remove the bay leaf and what remains of the herbs, then place in a bowl with the vinaigrette and stir to mix.

Dry fry the cumin in a small pan until starting to colour, then tip into the beans.

Mix the spring onions into the beans, and half the peppers, reserving the rest for garnish. Season the bean salad to taste.

Slice the tuna steaks in half horizontally, so you have four thin steaks. Heat a ridged pan or other frying pan, oil lightly or use olive oil spray, and briefly sear the steaks so they're still a little pink in the middle. Remove from the pan, season lightly, sprinkle with lime juice and cool to room temperature.

To serve, put a tuna steak on each plate, pile the bean salad on top in a neat mound, and garnish with the reserved diced peppers, a lime wedge and coriander leaves. Serves 4.

PER SERVING	
Energy Kcals	367.1
Protein g	26.2
Carbohydrates g	27.9
Dietary Fibre g	7.0
Fat – Total g	17.3
Saturated Fat g	2.6
Polyunsaturated Fat g	1.8
Calcium mg	93.8
Magnesium mg	92.9

SALAD DRESSINGS

If you make your dressings in large quantities, keep them in the fridge, as cold-pressed oils are prone to oxidation and need to be protected from light and heat. I always seem to be making a dressing at the last minute before a meal, so I keep one or two screw top jars for the purpose, then throw in all the ingredients and shake vigorously. So where I've said 'whisk' in the guidelines below, substituting 'shake hard' achieves the desired effect.

Basic Vinaigrette
Whisk together 4 tablespoons cold pressed extra virgin olive oil, 1 tablespoon flax oil and 1 tablespoon cider vinegar, wine vinegar or lemon juice. Season with low-sodium salt, freshly ground black pepper and a little dry mustard powder to taste.

Walnut Oil Vinaigrette
As above, but substitute cold-pressed walnut oil for the olive oil, and use sherry vinegar.

Hazelnut Vinaigrette
Whisk together 4 tablespoons cold-pressed hazelnut oil, $1/2$ teaspoon Dijon mustard, 1 teaspoon red wine vinegar, the juice of 1 orange, 1 teaspoon of the finely grated rind, low-sodium salt and freshly ground black pepper to taste.

Pumpkin Seed Vinaigrette
Whisk together 4 tablespoons extra virgin olive oil, 1 tablespoon toasted pumpkin seed oil and 1 tablespoon balsamic vinegar with 1 tablespoon ground pumpkin seeds, low-sodium salt and freshly ground black pepper to taste.

Citrus Vinaigrette
As for basic vinaigrette, but use orange juice instead of vinegar or lemon juice, and add 1 teaspoon finely grated orange rind.

Sweet Vinaigrette
To one quantity vinaigrette made with cider vinegar, add 1 tablespoon concentrated apple juice. For an even sweeter vinaigrette, substitute 1 tablespoon honey or maple syrup.

Tomato Vinaigrette
Peel, deseed and finely chop two ripe tomatoes, and whisk into 1 quantity basic vinaigrette for a chunky tomato dressing. If a smoother dressing is required, blend the ingredients together.

Nut Butter Dressing
Mix together 2 tablespoons coconut milk, 1 tablespoon any nut butter (smooth or crunchy), 1 tablespoon tamari sauce and 1 tablespoon lime or lemon juice. This is very tasty with grated raw vegetables or chopped lightly steamed vegetables.

Ginger Dressing
Mix together 3 tablespoons cold-pressed sunflower oil, 1 tablespoon cider vinegar and 1 teaspoon tamari. Grate a 1 inch/2.5 cm piece of peeled fresh root ginger, and squeeze the grated ginger with your hands into the bowl containing the other ingredients, so that ginger juice drips into the mixture. Stir together and add seasoning to taste.

Sesame Oil Dressing
2 tablespoons rice vinegar or cider vinegar, 1 tablespoon tamari, 4 tablespoons cold-pressed sesame oil, 1 clove garlic, crushed, $1/4$ teaspoon dried red pepper flakes and 1 teaspoon runny honey. Whisk all ingredients well together.

Tahini, Garlic and Tamari Dressing
Mix together 1 tablespoon tahini, 2 tablespoons rice wine vinegar or cider vinegar, 1 tablespoon cold-pressed sesame oil, 2 tablespoons sherry, 1 tablespoon tamari and 1 clove crushed garlic.

Honey Mustard Dressing
Whisk together 5 tablespoons extra virgin olive oil, 2 teaspoons balsamic vinegar, 1 teaspoon honey, 1 teaspoon Dijon mustard and seasoning to taste.

Yoghurt Dressing
Mix together 4 tablespoons yoghurt, 1 tablespoon extra virgin olive oil, 1 tablespoon lemon juice, low-sodium salt and freshly ground black pepper to taste.

Desserts

Baked Apples with Tofu Almond Cream
Pear, Date and Walnut Cake
Apricot and Almond Tart
Menopause Muesli Plum Crumble
Berry Jelly with Cashew Cream
Almond Rice Custard with Berries
Brown Rice Pudding with Poached Apricots
Strawberry Tofu Cheesecake
Poached Rhubarb with Molasses Sugar Meringue
Mangopause Mousse
Tropical Fruit with Ginger and Lemon Syrup
Buckwheat Pancakes with Grilled Pineapple and Dates
Iced Banana and Walnut Cream
Raspberry and Coconut Cream Mousse
Coconut Parfait with Mango and Passion Fruit Sauce
Walnut-Stuffed Prunes with Yoghurt
Gratin of Dried Fruit
Peruvian Fruit Compôte

To my mind, the best possible dessert is fresh fruit and/or freshly shelled nuts, and nine times out of ten that is how I will finish a meal. Variations are fresh fruit salads, using whatever combinations of fruit comes to hand, or dried fruit compôtes. Check out pages 6-8 in the breakfast chapter for some ideas. However, those with a sweeter tooth than I are catered for here, as I have come up with a handful of healthful, nutrient-rich puddings using, for the most part, alternative sweeteners to sugar.

This recipe is a very rich source of calcium and magnesium, thanks to the blackstrap molasses and the almonds.
If you don't like cooking with molasses, try to think of it as a liquid mineral supplement, and just eat a spoonful on its own. It really has such a good nutritional profile.

Baked Apples with Tofu Almond Cream

Baked apples really don't need a recipe, so this is just a reminder of how good they can be.

4	large cooking apples	4
4 tbsp	dried fruit such as raisins, sultanas, chopped dates, chopped figs, chopped prunes	4 tbsp
2 tbsp	blackstrap molasses	2 tbsp
For the tofu almond cream:		
3 oz	ground almonds	85 g
1/4 pint	soya milk	150 ml
1/2 tsp	almond essence	1/2 tsp
1 oz	silken tofu	30 g
1 tbsp	concentrated apple juice	1 tbsp

Preheat the oven to 180°C/350°F/Gas Mark 4.
Hollow out the apple cores, and lightly score round the equator of each apple with a very sharp knife. Fill with the dried fruit and drizzle with molasses. If you find the taste of molasses too strong, substitute honey, maple syrup or date syrup. Place the apples in an ovenproof dish with a spoonful or two of water, and cook in the preheated oven for about 40 minutes, checking after half an hour to make sure the apples aren't burning or bursting.
For the sauce, simply blend all the ingredients together in the blender. Serves 4.

PER SERVING	
Energy Kcals	343.0
Protein g	6.6
Carbohydrates g	54.9
Dietary Fibre g	8.7
Fat – Total g	12.6
Saturated Fat g	1.0
Polyunsaturated Fat g	3.0
Calcium mg	165.2
Magnesium mg	109.9

Pears are a very good source of soluble fibre which helps to reduce cholesterol levels. They are also one of the lowest fruits on the Glycaemic Index (See Appendix 1). This means that the sugars in pears are released very slowly, and this helps to maintain your blood sugar levels on an even keel. They are also one of the least allergenic of foods, so even if you are on an exclusion diet to try to identify possible food allergens, you need never give pears a miss.

Pear, Date and Walnut Cake

This is a very quick pudding to put together – good, solid fare ideal for a winter evening, but nutritious as well.
As a variation, you could make it with apples or plums instead of pears.

1¹/₂ lb	Conference pears, peeled, cored and roughly chopped	675 g
1	lemon, juice only	1
2 oz	walnuts, quite finely chopped	60 g
2 oz	stoned dates, chopped	60 g
4 tbsp	date syrup	4 tbsp
2	organic, free-range eggs, beaten	2
¹/₂ tsp	vanilla extract	¹/₂ tsp
5 oz	wholemeal flour or Doves Farm gluten-free flour	150 g
1 tsp	salt-free baking powder	1 tsp
2 tbsp	ground flax seed	2 tbsp

Preheat the oven to 180°C/350°F/Gas Mark 4.
Lightly oil a 20 cm/8 inch loose-bottomed cake tin (I use my olive oil spray for this). Place the chopped pears in a large bowl and sprinkle with lemon juice to stop them oxidising. Combine the walnuts, dates, date syrup, beaten eggs and vanilla extract. In another bowl, sift together the flour and baking powder, then add the ground flax seed. Add the date mixture and the flour mixture to the chopped pears, and stir well to combine. Turn into the prepared cake tin, then bake in the preheated oven for 35-40 minutes, or until lightly browned on top. Turn out and serve either warm or at room temperature with soya yoghurt or tofu whizz (see page 20). It's also delicious cold the next day for breakfast.
Serves 6.

PER SERVING	
Energy Kcals	304.5
Protein g	8.1
Carbohydrates g	51.4
Dietary Fibre g	7.7
Fat – Total g	9.7
Saturated Fat g	1.3
Polyunsaturated Fat g	5.6
Calcium mg	92.1
Magnesium mg	72.6

This tart is an extremely rich source of magnesium due to the almonds in both the pastry and the filling. The balance between calcium and magnesium in the diet is very important to the menopausal woman, and is a constant subject of debate amongst nutritionists. Some experts believe that the ratio should be 1:1, but our diet tends to lean more towards calcium, so any food that favours magnesium should be frequently on the menu.

Apricot and Almond Tart

I think the combination of apricots and almonds is a marriage made in heaven. However, if you can't get fresh apricots, try this with plums, but cook the plums in water for a few minutes first to draw off some of the juice. This tart is also delicious with greengages in season, though these do not need the precooking treatment.

I unashamedly use butter in pastry – liquid oils just don't work as well – but have used prune purée instead of fat in the filling.

For the pastry case:

4 oz	wholewheat flour or Dove's Farm gluten-free flour	110 g
3/4 tsp	ground cinnamon	3/4 tsp
2 1/2 oz	ground almonds	75 g
2 oz	organic unsalted butter	60 g
1 tbsp	brown rice syrup	1 tbsp

For the filling:

2 oz	prunes	60 g
3 1/2 oz	ground almonds	100 g
4 tbsp	brown rice syrup	4 tbsp
2	organic free-range eggs	2
1 lb	fresh apricots, halved and stoned	450 g

Preheat the oven to 200°C/400°F/Gas Mark 6.

For the pastry, whizz all the ingredients in the food processor until lightly combined. Wrap and refrigerate for at least half an hour before proceeding with the recipe.

To prepare the filling, first, make the prune purée. Simmer the prunes in water to cover in a small pan for 25-30 minutes, until soft. Cool, then purée in a food processor or liquidiser with a little of the cooking liquid until smooth.

Add the ground almonds and rice syrup to the prune purée in the food processor and process for a few seconds. Then add the eggs and process briefly.

Roll out the pastry on a lightly floured surface, then transfer to an oiled 9 inch/23 cm tart tin with removable base. Press into the sides of the tin and trim off the excess. Prick the base several times with a fork, and part-bake blind (For this I use baking parchment and very old dried beans). Cook for 10 minutes or so just until starting to colour,

PER SERVING	
Energy Kcals	424.5
Protein g	12.0
Carbohydrates g	42.6
Dietary Fibre g	7.1
Fat – Total g	24.5
Saturated Fat g	6.4
Polyunsaturated Fat g	3.8
Calcium mg	104.7
Magnesium mg	120.0

removing the parchment and beans for the last few minutes. Cool.

Reduce the oven temperature to 180°C/350°F/Gas Mark 4.

Spoon the filling into the tart case. Place the apricots cut side up on the filling. Bake for 30 minutes until the filling has puffed up and the apricots are starting to char. You may need to cover the pastry with a strip of baking parchment to protect it if it is getting too brown. Serve the tart warm or at room temperature. Serves 6.

Plums are a good source of beta carotene and potassium. They are one of the few purple foods that we eat, and we know that the greater the variety of colourful foods we eat, the more nutrients we will be ingesting. Plums may well contain some phytonutrients that haven't been discovered yet, so think of them as dietary insurance.

Menopause Muesli Plum Crumble

This is another quick, easy pudding. Try it with apples, pears, apricots or rhubarb. If you don't have Muesli for the Menopause, substitute any other sugar-free muesli.

2½ lbs	eating plums, halved and stones removed	1.25 kg
6 oz	Muesli for the Menopause (see page 12)	170 g
3 tbsp	honey	3 tbsp
2 oz	organic unsalted butter, softened	60 g

Preheat the oven to 180°C/375°F/Gas Mark 4.

Put the stoned plums in an ovenproof dish. Using eating plums should mean that you don't need to add any sweetener.

Put the muesli in a bowl and rub in the butter using your fingers. Then add the honey and mix well. Spread this mixture on top of the plums. Cover with baking parchment and bake in the oven for 30-35 minutes, removing the parchment about half way through to allow the topping to crisp up without getting too brown. Serve hot with plain yoghurt. Serves 4.

PER SERVING	
Energy Kcals	362.9
Protein g	5.7
Carbohydrates g	58.4
Dietary Fibre g	6.9
Fat – Total g	15.2
Saturated Fat g	6.5
Polyunsaturated Fat g	1.9
Calcium mg	44.0
Magnesium mg	51.1

All berries are packed with useful nutrients such as vitamin C, potassium and beta-carotene. Their bright and dark colours indicate that they are bursting with bioflavonoid activity which gives them a wide range of health-giving properties.

Berry Jelly with Cashew Cream

Having once been a vegetarian, I still do not eat beef or pork products, so I use agar agar for jellies instead of gelatine. Agar agar is a kind of seaweed, which produces a rather softer set than gelatine. Unlike gelatine, it has to be dissolved by cooking in hot liquid, and sets at room temperature. I find it easier to use than gelatine and much more predictable. You could use Gelozone instead, which is a commercially produced vegetarian version of gelatine.

1¹/₂ lbs	fresh raspberries, blackberries, blueberries or a mixture	675 g
1 pint	fresh, unfiltered apple juice	570 ml
1¹/₂ tbsp	agar agar flakes (or 2 tsp agar agar powder)	1¹/₂ tbsp
2 tbsp	runny honey	2 tbsp
For the cashew cream:		
4 oz	cashew nuts	110 g
4 fl oz	water	120 ml
few drops	vanilla extract	few drops

Arrange three quarters of the berries in the bottoms of 6 dessert glasses or dishes. In a small pan, bring the apple juice, agar agar and the rest of the berries to the boil. Reduce the heat and simmer until the agar agar has dissolved, about 10 minutes. (If you're using the powder, it's much quicker.) Remove the pan from the heat. Strain the juice through a fine sieve, add the honey and leave to cool for 10 minutes or so. Pour the juice over the berries, making sure that all the fruit is covered. It will set almost immediately. Chill before serving.

For the cashew cream, put the cashew nuts in the blender. Blend until pulverised, then pour in the water slowly with the machine running, until the mixture forms a thick cream. Finally, stir in the vanilla. The mixture will thicken on standing. Serves 6.

PER SERVING	
Energy Kcals	189.0
Protein g	4.3
Carbohydrates g	25.7
Dietary Fibre g	6.3
Fat – Total g	9.4
Saturated Fat g	1.6
Polyunsaturated Fat g	1.9
Calcium mg	32.0
Magnesium mg	73.6

The nutritional combination of almonds, soya and berries is a winner here. The almonds supply protein, essential fatty acids and minerals, the soya provides isoflavones – weak oestrogens that help balance your hormones – and the berries provide vitamin C and all sorts of bioflavonoids that may protect you against cancer and heart disease. In addition, giving women vitamin C with bioflavonoids was shown in one study to reduce hot flushes.

Almond Rice Custard with Berries

This recipe uses ground rice, which is a refined product, so I have added a tablespoon of rice bran to increase the fibre and mineral content, which is a bit like putting back what the refining process has taken out. Unfortunately I have not been able to find a source of ground brown rice.

¹/₂ pint	soya milk	275 ml
3¹/₂ oz	ground almonds	100 g
2 oz	ground rice	60 g
1 tbsp	rice bran	1 tbsp
5 fl oz	soya cream or silken tofu	150 ml
5 tbsp	rice syrup	5 tbsp
¹/₄ tsp	almond essence	¹/₄ tsp
6 oz	berries, such as blackberries, raspberries or red currants or a mixture	170 g
2 tbsp	chopped blanched almonds	2 tbsp
1 tbsp	icing sugar for dusting (optional)	1 tbsp

Bring half the soya milk to the boil in a saucepan. Pour onto the ground almonds in a bowl, stir to mix and set aside.

In another bowl, whisk together the ground rice, rice bran and the soya cream or silken tofu. Heat the remaining milk, pour onto the ground rice mixture, then whisk. Return to the pan, bring to the boil, then simmer, stirring, for 2-3 minutes or until thickened. Add the ground almond mixture and the rice syrup. Continue to cook over a very low heat, stirring continuously, for another couple of minutes, taking care not to let the mixture at the bottom of the pan get too thick, then take off the heat and stir in the almond essence. Cool to room temperature covered, then pour into individual serving glasses, cover and chill. (The pudding needs to be kept covered to prevent it forming a skin on the top.) To serve, put a pile of berries and chopped almonds on top of each glassful and dust with icing sugar, if using, just before serving. Serves 6.

PER SERVING	
Energy Kcals	265.3
Protein g	7.1
Carbohydrates g	28.5
Dietary Fibre g	5.1
Fat – Total g	13.9
Saturated Fat g	1.0
Polyunsaturated Fat g	2.9
Calcium mg	67.3
Magnesium mg	91.5

Brown rice is a complex carbohydrate although its Glycaemic Index is quite high (see Appendix 1). Even if it releases its sugars fairly quickly, it contains lots of minerals and B vitamins, and a good amount of fibre. This pudding also makes a very good nutritious breakfast heated up the next morning with some fresh fruit and yoghurt or soya milk.

Brown Rice Pudding with Poached Apricots

I know brown rice pudding might sound unappealing, but in fact it is delicious. All rice pudding recipes seem to be made with white rice, whereas we all know that brown rice is much better for us as it is the whole, unrefined grain. So I thought I'd give it a go, and it's actually just as appetizing as old-fashioned rice pudding – though it is not such a good colour.

	butter for greasing the dish	
2^1/$_2$ oz	brown rice	75 g
1 tbsp	maple syrup	1 tbsp
1^3/$_4$ pint	rice milk	1 litre
1	vanilla pod	1
For the sauce:		
4 tbsp	pure maple syrup	4 tbsp
4 tbsp	water	4 tbsp
1 lb	fresh apricots	450 g

Preheat the oven to 170°C/325°F/Gas Mark 3. Butter an ovenproof dish.

Wash the rice and put it with the maple syrup, rice milk and vanilla pod into the prepared dish. Bake uncovered in the preheated oven for 3 hours. Remove the vanilla pod. Brown rice pudding made in this way does not form a crust like a rice pudding made with dairy milk. If you would like a crust, put the dish under a hot grill for a few minutes.

Wash the apricots, then halve and stone them. Place in an ovenproof dish together with the maple syrup and water. Cover and cook in the oven for about half an hour, until the apricots are tender. Serve hot or cold with the rice pudding and a spoonful of yoghurt. Serves 6.

PER SERVING	
Energy Kcals	227.7
Protein g	4.2
Carbohydrates g	48.8
Dietary Fibre g	4.0
Fat – Total g	2.1
Saturated Fat g	0.3
Polyunsaturated Fat g	1.0
Calcium mg	35.9
Magnesium mg	64.6

The tofu here is an excellent source of calcium. There is also a good range of other minerals because there is quite a variety of foods in the one recipe. For example, iron is provided by the oats, the tofu, and the almonds. Each item only provides a small amount, but taken together they provide a total of 2.8 grams – one third of the reference nutrient intake for an adult woman.

Strawberry Tofu Cheesecake

Strawberries are a rich source of Vitamin C, and the cheesecake is made with tofu and ground almonds for extra nutrition. It is, however, quite high in calories, so reserve it for a special treat. If you prefer, you could blend the strawberries in with the tofu mixture and omit the strawberry jam, or serve the cheesecake without a topping, using the strawberries and jam to make a coulis to serve beside it.

8 oz	Muesli for the Menopause (see page 12)	225 g
4 oz	organic unsalted butter	125 g
12 oz	tofu (1½ packets)	340 g
2 tbsp	extra virgin olive oil	2 tbsp
4 tbsp	honey	4 tbsp
1	lemon, juice and grated rind	1
1 tsp	pure vanilla extract	1 tsp
1½ oz	ground almonds	45 g
8 oz	fresh strawberries, halved	225 g
2 tbsp	all fruit strawberry jam	2 tbsp

Preheat oven to 180°C/350°F/Gas Mark 4.
    Process the muesli in a food processor until it forms fine crumbs (you might have to remove the raisins from the muesli to achieve this). Melt the butter over gentle heat and mix it with the ground muesli. Spread it in an oiled 8 inch/ 20 cm flan tin with a removable base, and bake for 5 minutes.
    Meanwhile, put the tofu, olive oil, honey, lemon juice and rind and vanilla extract into the food processor and blend well. Stir in the ground almonds.
    Remove the muesli base from the oven and put the filling on top, smoothing the surface evenly. Return to the oven and cook for a further 30 minutes or until firm. Cool, then place the strawberries on top in concentric circles. Warm the jam in a small pan with a little water, sieve if necessary, then glaze the strawberries by brushing with the warmed strawberry jam. Chill thoroughly before serving. Serves 6.

PER SERVING	
Energy Kcals	467.2
Protein g	14.6
Carbohydrates g	38.9
Dietary Fibre g	5.1
Fat – Total g	29.8
Saturated Fat g	11.3
Polyunsaturated Fat g	3.6
Calcium mg	209.1
Magnesium mg	85.7

Instead of the vanilla, try substituting $1/2$ inch/1 cm piece of fresh ginger root, peeled and grated, or the juice and grated rind of an orange.

If you cannot find molasses sugar, use raw cane sugar instead.

Rhubarb is a good source of calcium for our bones, potassium to help regulate water balance in the body and phytoestrogens for our hormone balance. It also contains a trace of boron, a trace mineral that appears to reduce the urinary excretion of calcium and magnesium.

Poached Rhubarb with Molasses Sugar Meringue

Rhubarb contains phytoestrogens and calcium, so we should try to eat it frequently. As it is bitter, the temptation is to add sugar, but try to resist this and use an alternative sweetener. I have suggested concentrated apple juice here, but maple syrup also works well. For the meringue I have used molasses sugar which has a little of the mineral content of molasses itself, being a biproduct of the final extraction of sugar refining.

1 lb	young, pink rhubarb	450 g
4 tbsp	concentrated apple juice	4 tbsp
$1/2$	vanilla pod	$1/2$
2	organic free-range eggs, whites only	2
$11/2$ oz	molasses sugar	45 g

Preheat the oven to 180°C/350°F/Gas Mark 4.

Cut the rhubarb into 1 inch/2.5cm lengths. Place in an ovenproof dish with the apple juice concentrate. Scrape the seeds out of the vanilla pod and add them to the rhubarb. Bake, covered, for 20 minutes.

Reduce the oven temperature to 150°C/300°F/Gas Mark 2.

For the meringue, whisk the egg whites until they are stiff, then gradually whisk in the sugar until the meringue is stiff and glossy. Pile onto the rhubarb and bake at the lower temperature for 20 minutes or until the top is lightly coloured. Serves 4.

PER SERVING	
Energy Kcals	109.9
Protein g	2.6
Carbohydrates g	24.5
Dietary Fibre g	1.5
Fat – Total g	0.3
Saturated Fat g	0.1
Polyunsaturated Fat g	0.1
Calcium mg	80.2
Magnesium mg	14.2

Tropical fruits tend to have better levels of minerals than fruits grown in temperate climates, because the soil in tropical parts of the world has been less depleted of its essential minerals. This isn't always true, of course, but they do contain good levels of potassium which should help regulate blood pressure. They also provide antioxidants such as vitamin C, beta-carotene and beta cryptoxanthin, high levels of which have been shown to protect against cervical cancer.

Mangopause Mousse

I used to make mango mousse when I was a charter boat cook. The recipe I used in those days was replete with whipping cream, and used gelatine. This is lighter and more healthy, but equally delicious, and, with the addition of tofu, beneficial for the menopausal woman – hence the name.

3 or 4	large mangoes	3 or 4
1	lime, juice only	1
13 oz	silken tofu (1 packet)	350 g
2 tbsp	pure maple syrup	2 tbsp

Peel the mangoes. Chop the flesh of half a mango into neat dice and reserve for the garnish. Cut the rest into rough chunks and purée with the lime juice in a blender or food processor until smooth, then sieve into a bowl to remove any strings. The sieving may not be necessary if you are using grafted mangoes as they are not as stringy as the mangoes we used to get in the Caribbean. Put a spoonful of the purée into the bottom of each of 4 tall serving glasses. Whip together the silken tofu and maple syrup, then fold into the remaining mango purée. Ladle into the glasses and chill before serving. Garnish with the reserved diced mango. Serves 4.

PER SERVING	
Energy Kcals	214.0
Protein g	5.5
Carbohydrates g	45.4
Dietary Fibre g	3.9
Fat – Total g	3.1
Saturated Fat g	0.5
Polyunsaturated Fat g	1.5
Calcium mg	56.8
Magnesium mg	47.3

The combination of all these different fruits provides plenty of nutrients, particularly minerals. Papayas and mangoes are good sources of carotenes and potassium and they provide a huge amount of vitamin C – more than 200% of our daily requirement. In addition, pineapple contains an enzyme called bromelain which has been shown to dissolve blood clots. It has a similar effect on food in the stomach, and is helpful for people whose digestion is poor. This often happens as we age and our stomachs produce less stomach acid, so a case could be made for eating more pineapple as we get older.

Tropical Fruit with Ginger and Lemon Syrup

This is really just a glorified fruit salad. The combination of ginger and lemon is very refreshing.

2 oz	fresh ginger root	60 g
1	lemon	1
16 fl oz	water	450 ml
5 tbsp	honey	5 tbsp
1	mango	1
1	papaya	1
2	kiwi fruit	2
1/4	fresh pineapple	1/4

Peel the ginger root and slice about half of it into thin slices. Pare off the peel from the lemon with a potato peeler. Combine the water and honey, and add the ginger slices and half the lemon peel. Bring to the boil, then simmer for 7 minutes. Remove and discard the ginger and lemon.

Slice the rest of the ginger and lemon peel into tiny slivers and add to the syrup. Continue simmering for a further 10 minutes. Leave to cool.

Prepare the fruit by peeling and cutting into bite-sized pieces. Put into a serving bowl. Flavour the lemon syrup with the juice of the lemon to taste and pour over the fruit. Serve chilled. Serves 4.

PER SERVING	
Energy Kcals	186.6
Protein g	1.8
Carbohydrates g	48.1
Dietary Fibre g	5.5
Fat – Total g	0.7
Saturated Fat g	0.1
Polyunsaturated Fat g	0.2
Calcium mg	61.8
Magnesium mg	38.3

I first came across buckwheat pancakes about 15 years ago in the Pyrenees, where buckwheat is called *sarrazin*. Was this because it was brought to that part of the world by the Saracens, I wonder? Anyway, I tracked some down, brought it home and learned to make these delicious pancakes. It was only later that I discovered buckwheat to be such a useful ally for the menopausal woman, as it is the only grain source of phytoestrogens.

Buckwheat Pancakes with Grilled Pineapple and Dates

This is a substantial pudding, to be served after a light main course. Feel free to vary the fruit – pineapple and dates just happen to be a favourite combination of mine, but they are only a suggestion. Peeled and chopped apples or pears with raisins would work well, or baked bananas and dried apricots.

3 oz	buckwheat flour	90 g
1 oz	unbleached white flour or gluten-free flour	30 g
1	large, organic free-range egg	1
1 tbsp	flax seeds, ground	1 tbsp
½ pint	soya, nut or rice milk	275 ml
1	orange	1
1	lemon	1
1	cinnamon stick	1
1	vanilla pod	1
2 tbsp	date syrup	2 tbsp
8	dates, stoned and chopped	8
2	thick slices of fresh pineapple	2
1 tbsp	raw cane sugar	1 tbsp
1 tsp	ground ginger	1 tsp

To serve:

| | live natural yoghurt or soya yoghurt | |

For the pancakes, put the flour, egg, milk and ground flax seeds in the blender, and blend until well mixed. Leave the batter to rest while you make the syrup.

For the syrup, peel off the rind of the orange and lemon as thinly as possible, and put in a small saucepan. Squeeze the juice out of the orange and lemon and add that. Add the cinnamon stick and vanilla pod, date syrup and 4 tablespoons of water. Bring to the boil and then simmer for 15 minutes or so until reduced by about half. Strain, and add the chopped dates. Set aside.

For the pineapple, preheat the grill. Peel and core the pineapple and cut into chunks. Sprinkle with raw cane sugar

PER SERVING	
Energy Kcals	373.4
Protein g	11.6
Carbohydrates g	70.5
Dietary Fibre g	10.8
Fat – Total g	7.8
Saturated Fat g	1.2
Polyunsaturated Fat g	3.6
Calcium mg	83.2
Magnesium mg	157.4

Bananas are the most heavily sprayed major food crop in the world – fungicides and pesticides are applied up to 40 times during the 9 month cultivation cycle[27]. So it is well worth paying a little extra for organic, or at least fairly-traded, bananas. They are a fantastic source of potassium and also provide magnesium and iron. The walnuts here provide 2.5 g of Omega-3 essential fatty acids, which are anti-inflammatory and may help control hot flushes.

PER SERVING	
Energy Kcals	373.4
Protein g	11.6
Carbohydrates g	70.5
Dietary Fibre g	10.8
Fat – Total g	7.8
Saturated Fat g	1.2
Polyunsaturated Fat g	3.6
Calcium mg	83.2
Magnesium mg	157.4

and ground ginger and grill in a foil-lined grill pan for 6-8 minutes or until golden brown and caramelised.

To cook the pancakes, lightly oil a non-stick frying pan (or use olive oil spray) and ladle in enough batter just to cover the base of the pan. Cook over medium-high heat until the surface bubbles and starts to dry. Turn and cook the other side until lightly browned. Repeat with the remaining mixture. This should make 8 large pancakes.

To serve, add the pineapple to the dates and syrup. Spoon some of the mixture on each pancake and fold into quarters. Serve with a dollop of yoghurt. Serves 4.

Iced Banana and Walnut Cream

Although it is possible to make healthy ice creams, not many people have ice cream machines, and I do think they are necessary to achieve the right consistency. However, when you crave a frozen dessert, this fits the bill satisfactorily, and is very easy to make.

4	ripe bananas	4
4 oz	walnuts	110 g
2 tbsp	honey	2 tbsp
1 tsp	pure vanilla extract	1 tsp
4 tbsp	apple juice	4 tbsp
1	orange, finely grated rind and juice	1
Garnish:		
4	walnut halves	4

First, peel the bananas and freeze them for at least 12 hours.

For the walnut cream, grind the walnuts as finely as you can in the food processor or blender, then gradually add the honey, vanilla extract, apple juice, orange juice and finely grated orange rind. Cover and chill until needed – the mixture will thicken up on standing.

When you are ready to serve, take the frozen bananas from the freezer, cut them into chunks and put in the food processor. Add the walnut cream and process until smooth.

Spoon into individual glasses and decorate with a walnut half on each serving. Serve immediately. Serves 4.

27 Pearce F, 'Going Bananas', *New Scientist* 18 January 2003 pp.26-29.

Although coconut cream contains saturated fat, it is cholesterol-free, and contains some minerals, such as potassium, magnesium, manganese, copper and iron. Coconut also contains a fatty acid called caprylic acid which is a natural antibiotic.

Raspberry and Coconut Cream Mousse

This is a very easy and pretty dessert. Any berries could be used here instead of the raspberries, such as blueberries, strawberries, cherries, blackcurrants or redcurrants, or you could even use frozen fruit if fresh fruit is unavailable.

8 oz	raspberries	225 g
4 tbsp	concentrated apple juice	4 tbsp
1/2	lemon, juice only	1/2
2 tsp	agar agar powder (or 1 1/2 tbsp agar agar flakes)	2 tsp
7 fl oz	coconut cream	200 ml
1	organic free-range egg white	1
1 tbsp	desiccated coconut, to garnish	1 tbsp

Reserving a few of the raspberries for the garnish, gently cook the rest with the concentrated apple juice, lemon juice and agar agar, for 5 mins or until the juice starts to run from the raspberries and the agar agar has dissolved. (If you are using the agar agar flakes, you will need to cook a bit longer). Put through a wire sieve into a bowl and leave to cool. Just as the mixture is starting to set, stir in the coconut cream. Whisk the egg white until stiff and fold in. Spoon into individual glasses or bowls and garnish with the reserved raspberries and desiccated coconut. Serves 4.

PER SERVING	
Energy Kcals	181.6
Protein g	3.4
Carbohydrates g	13.6
Dietary Fibre g	5.9
Fat – Total g	14.1
Saturated Fat g	12.2
Polyunsaturated Fat g	0.3
Calcium mg	15.9
Magnesium mg	26.9

Coconut milk or cream is one of the few vegetable sources of saturated fat. Although a topic of some controversy in the nutrition world, it is currently thought that natural saturated fats are much less harmful than the artificially saturated (hydrogenated) fats in processed foods. You can make both coconut milk and coconut cream from the blocks of creamed coconut available in supermarkets.

Passion fruit is rich in vitamin C and beta-carotene, and also contains useful amounts of iron and zinc.

Coconut Parfait with Mango and Passion Fruit Sauce

Here is another frozen pudding, this time a parfait, which is a sort of ice-cream that has not been churned. It is a good idea to transfer the parfait from the freezer to the refrigerator for half an hour before you turn it out, just to make it a little less hard to slice.

4	organic free-range eggs, yolks only	4
2 tsp	cornflour	2 tsp
2 tbsp	brown rice syrup	2 tbsp
12 fl oz	coconut milk	340 ml
2$^{1}/_{2}$ oz	desiccated coconut	75 g
10 fl oz	coconut cream	275 ml
For the sauce:		
4	passion fruit	4
1	large, ripe mango	1
2 tbsp	apple juice	2 tbsp

Mix together the egg yolks, cornflour and rice syrup in a bowl. Add the coconut milk, beating to mix, then stir in the desiccated coconut. Put the mixture into a saucepan and cook over a low heat, stirring constantly, until thick. Do not cook too fast or the egg yolks will curdle. Remove the pan from the heat, cool a little, then stir in the coconut cream.

Line a 1 lb/450 g loaf tin with clingfilm. When the parfait mixture is quite cold, pour into the loaf tin, cover, and place in the freezer. It will take at least 4 hours to freeze.

To make the sauce, halve the passion fruit and scoop out the pulp. Peel the mango, slice the flesh off the stone and purée in the liquidizer. Mix this purée with the apple juice and passion fruit pulp. Pass through a sieve, adding a little more apple juice if it seems too thick.

To serve the parfait, dip the base of the terrine in warm water, then turn it out onto a chopping board. Cut into 1 inch/2$^{1}/_{2}$ cm slices. Pour a little sauce round the outside of each of 6 serving plates and place a slice of parfait in the middle of each. Serves 6.

PER SERVING	
Energy Kcals	401.2
Protein g	6.0
Carbohydrates g	23.6
Dietary Fibre g	5.8
Fat – Total g	34.2
Saturated Fat g	28.2
Polyunsaturated Fat g	0.9
Calcium mg	34.5
Magnesium mg	55.2

This recipe provides lots of calcium, thanks to the combination of prunes, walnuts and yoghurt, so it is naturally bone-protective.

PER SERVING	
Energy Kcals	289.5
Protein g	8.3
Carbohydrates g	25.4
Dietary Fibre g	5.6
Fat – Total g	19.6
Saturated Fat g	2.4
Polyunsaturated Fat g	13.4
Calcium mg	141.4
Magnesium mg	56.7

There is a huge amount of potassium in dried fruit – 973 mg in each serving of this gratin. Potassium is often deficient in the modern diet, as it is opposed by sodium, of which we generally eat far too much. As potassium is essential for proper water balance in the body, it is important to get as much of it as we can. It is freely available in all fruits and vegetables, and seems to be even more concentrated by the drying process.

Walnut-Stuffed Prunes with Yoghurt

Serve these with the yoghurt as a pudding, or without the sauce as little sweet bites to have with herbal tea at the end of a meal, where you might otherwise have been tempted to indulge in chocolates.

8 oz	stoned prunes, soaked overnight in cold water	225 g
4 oz	walnut halves	110 g
8 fl oz	live natural yoghurt or soya yoghurt	225 fl oz

Stoned prunes each have a hole where the stone was removed. Enlarge the hole in each prune with the point of a knife and insert a walnut half in each one. Put the stuffed prunes in a pan and cover with about half a pint of water. Simmer gently for 20 minutes or until the prunes are soft and most of the liquid is absorbed. Leave to cool. Transfer the prunes to a serving bowl. Mix any remaining liquid with the yoghurt and pour over the prunes. Serve chilled. Serves 4.

Gratin of Dried Fruit

This is a good standby to have for when the fruit bowl is empty. I use a dried fruit salad mixture which contains dried apple, prunes, apricots, pears and peaches, but you could use a mixture of any dried fruit.

12 oz	mixed dried fruit	340 g
10 fl oz	orange juice	275 ml
2 tbsp	maple syrup	2 tbsp
1/2	lemon, grated rind and juice	1/2
4	organic free-range eggs, whites only	4

Wash the fruit, then put it in a bowl with the orange juice, grated lemon rind and 1/2 pint/275 ml water. Leave to soak overnight.

PER SERVING	
Energy Kcals	309.4
Protein g	6.5
Carbohydrates g	76.7
Dietary Fibre g	7.8
Fat – Total g	0.7
Saturated Fat g	0.1
Polyunsaturated Fat g	0.1
Calcium mg	64.4
Magnesium mg	50.9

There is a very high potassium content in this dish, so it would be helpful in lowering blood pressure and in regulating the body's water balance.

Next day, place the fruit, orange juice and maple syrup in a saucepan, bring to the boil and simmer over a gentle heat for 10 minutes. Leave to cool, then drain, reserving 1 tablespoon of the liquid.

Chop the fruit into bite-size pieces, then add the lemon juice and the reserved tablespoon of marinade.

Preheat the oven to 200°C/400°F/Gas Mark 6. Lightly oil a shallow 10 inch/25 cm ovenproof gratin dish.

Whisk the egg whites until they are stiff, then fold gently into the fruit with a metal spoon. Put into the prepared gratin dish and bake in the hot oven for 15-20 minutes. Serve immediately. Serves 4.

Peruvian Fruit Compôte

This dish can be made with fresh or frozen fruit. It's very flexible – if you don't have the fruit listed below, feel free to substitute whatever fresh and dried fruit you have to hand.

6 oz	dried peaches	170 g
3	thick slices of fresh pineapple, peeled, cored and chopped	3
2	pears, peeled, cored and chopped	2
2	fresh nectarines, peeled, stoned and chopped	2
5 oz	blackberries	150 g
4 tbsp	concentrated apple juice	4 tbsp
3	whole cloves	3
1	cinnamon stick	1
$1/2$	lemon, juice only	$1/2$
1 oz	cornflour	30 g

Soak the dried peaches in cold water for 2-3 hours or overnight, then chop roughly. Combine with all the other fruit in a large saucepan. Add 1$1/4$ pints/730 ml water, the concentrated apple juice and spices, bring to the boil over a gentle heat, and simmer, covered, until the fruit is tender – about 10 minutes.

Mix the cornflour with the lemon juice, then add a spoonful of the cooking liquor. Return to the pan and stir gently for 5 minutes, until the sauce has thickened slightly. Turn the mixture into a serving bowl, cool, then chill before serving. Serves 4.

PER SERVING	
Energy Kcals	244.8
Protein g	1.9
Carbohydrates g	60.4
Dietary Fibre g	6.5
Fat – Total g	1.2
Saturated Fat g	0.1
Polyunsaturated Fat g	0.3
Calcium mg	28.2
Magnesium mg	25.0

Breads and Baking

Sourdough Starter
Sourdough Rye with Seeds
Pumpernickel (Wheat-Free)
Calcium Bread
Poppy Seed and Molasses Bread
Millet Bread
Spelt Rolls with Walnuts
Corn Bread (Gluten-Free)
Quinoa, Rice and Potato Bread (Gluten-Free)
Banana Bread
Apple and Brazil Nut Loaf
Spelt, Apple and Oat Muffins
Seeded Oatcakes
Date, Oat and Walnut Cookies
Apricot, Apple and Oat Bars
Dried Fruit and Seed Squares
Carrot Cake
Buckwheat, Quinoa and Apricot Cake (Gluten-Free)
Carob, Raisin and Walnut Cake
Lemon and Almond Polenta Cake (Gluten-Free)

BREADS

Unsatisfied with what was on offer in the supermarkets, I have done a lot of research to find the perfect loaf to meet the nutritional needs of the menopausal woman. Inspired by attending a breadmaking course at the Village Bakery in Cumbria, I set about designing a loaf that contained as much extra calcium and phytoestrogens as I could cram in. From Andrew Whitley at the Village Bakery, I learned about leavens or sourdoughs, and became fascinated by the age-old tradition of making bread without yeast. There is a good reason for menopausal women to eat sourdough bread: I learned that wheat bran (present in all wholemeal breads) contains phytic acid which can make calcium and other minerals unavailable to the body. The process of fermentation in an acid environment, such as that provided by the sourdough, encourages the action of the enzyme phytase, which has the effect of releasing the minerals locked up by the phytic acid. Sourdough has traditionally been used to leaven rye breads – this is because rye flour has quite a bland taste, and the acid sourdough improves the flavour. So, although I do not eschew yeast breads, most of my research has been with sourdough.

Since I have been studying nutrition, I have come to believe that over-reliance on one grain – wheat – is not good for our bodies. In terms of the history of mankind, wheat is a relatively new grain, and it could be that our bodies have not completely adapted to digesting it. The protein in wheat is resistant to the digestive process, and can be irritating to the digestive system of some people. Coeliacs are a separate issue – they cannot metabolise wheat or any other gluten-containing grain at all. But there are also a lot of people who, without actually having coeliac disease, find that wheat makes them feel bloated and uncomfortable. Added to that, there are some researchers who believe that a large proportion of us are actually latent coeliacs. I firmly believe that the answer lies, as so often, in moderation. Wheat is fine for the large majority of people, as long as you don't eat it for every meal. When you think about it, it is quite possible to have a wheat cereal and toast for breakfast, a sandwich for lunch and pasta for dinner. In my opinion, that is overloading the body with too much wheat. So, as a nutritionist, my mantra is: vary your grains, and that means varying your breads, as well as ringing the changes with different kinds of pastas and wholegrains, as already discussed.

Having said that, it remains an incontrovertible fact that to make good bread, you need gluten. The grain highest in gluten is wheat, so most of the breads that follow do contain some wheat flour, but you will find that a lot of them contain other flours as well. The only other grain apart from wheat (and spelt, which is a form of wheat) that makes successful bread is rye, which, although also a gluten grain, contains a little less gluten than wheat. For this reason some people find that they can tolerate rye where they can't tolerate wheat. So I have included a recipe for pumpernickel that contains only rye. The other gluten grains, although possessing much less gluten than wheat or rye, are barley and oats, and you will find a couple of recipes that use barley flour in these pages. I have also created one gluten-free bread based on a mixture of flours, including quinoa flour, which gives the bread an interesting, slightly sweet, taste. For a more in-depth discussion of gluten-free baking, and some wonderful recipes, read *The Everyday Wheat-Free and Gluten-Free Cookbook* by Michelle Berriedale-Johnson in this series.

For recipes that use baking powder and/or bicarbonate of soda as a raising agent, you can choose whether or not to use wheat flour. I have specified wholewheat flour in the muffins and cakes, but you can use Dove's Farm gluten-free flour instead. It is a mixture of rice flour, potato flour, buckwheat flour and maize flour, and makes an excellent substitute for white or wholemeal flour in most recipes that don't specifically need gluten. Though be aware that it does not have the same rising qualities as wheat flour, with the result that your cakes and muffins will be a bit heavier.

Where a recipe requires yeast, I have specified fresh yeast because personally I prefer working with a living entity. Fresh yeast is available from the bakery section of supermarkets, often free of charge. It can be frozen, but its behaviour may be a little unpredictable after thawing so that it is difficult to be precise about quantities. If you cannot obtain fresh yeast, substitute half the amount of active dried yeast (eg 1 tablespoon of dried yeast for 1 oz fresh yeast), and follow the manufacturer's instructions for rehydrating the yeast.

FLOURS USED IN BAKING

Listed below are all the flours that I use in baking. This is not necessarily a comprehensive list.

Flour	Properties	Interchangeable with	Notes
Strong white wheat flour	Milled from hard wheat, high proportion of gluten	Spelt flour Wholemeal (extra liquid will be needed)	English wheat is softer and contains less protein (10-14%) than Canadian (10-18%). Refined, so many nutrients have been removed
Wholemeal	Made from complete grain, more nutritious than white flour. Contains gluten	Strong white flour (less liquid will be needed) Spelt flour	13% protein. Rich in niacin. Canadian wheat rich in selenium
Spelt flour	An ancient form of wheat, contains less gluten than wheat	Strong white flour, wholemeal flour	13% protein, high fibre
Rye flour, dark or light	Contains gluten, but much less than wheat. Strong flavour (the dark rye is tangier than light rye)	Spelt flour. Can be mixed with wheat flour for breads	14% protein, high fibre Rich in niacin, biotin, vitamin E, calcium, magnesium, manganese, iron, potassium, zinc
Barley flour	Ground from pearl barley, so not a whole grain. Has a sweet taste Contains some gluten	Oat flour. Can be mixed with wheat flour for yeasted breads	12% protein, rich in iron
Oat flour	Ground from cleaned, hulled oats. Contains some gluten	Barley flour. Can be mixed with wheat flour for yeasted breads	16% protein. Rich in thiamine and calcium
Buckwheat flour	Gluten-free, nutty flavour. Very good in pancakes	Brown rice flour	10% protein. Rich in magnesium, potassium and folate
Brown rice flour	Made from brown rice, so it is whole-grain. Sweet flavour. Gluten-free	Doves Farm gluten-free flour	6% protein. Rich in niacin and vitamin B6
Quinoa flour	High protein, high mineral content. Sweet taste. Gluten-free	Millet flour	15% protein. Rich in vitamin E, iron
Millet flour	High protein, high mineral content. Sweet taste. Gluten-free	Quinoa flour	11% protein. Rich in riboflavin, iron and boron
Cornmeal	Cornmeal can be coarse, medium (polenta) or fine. Gluten-free. Sweet flavour, crunchy texture	No suitable substitute	8% protein. Rich in biotin, boron and chromium
Gram flour (chick pea flour or besan) Potato flour	Gluten-free, rich flavour. Good in pancakes and falafel. A very fine starchy flour, mostly used as a thickener. Keeps breads moist. Gluten-free	Quinoa flour, millet flour. No suitable substitute	20% protein. Rich in calcium and magnesium 7% protein. Rich in vitamin B6, calcium, potassium
Dove's Farm Gluten-free flour	A mixture of flours, including brown rice and buckwheat	Any gluten-free flour. Use in recipes that do not require gluten	5% protein

SOURDOUGH BREADS

Sourdough Starter

If you don't want to go to the trouble of making your own starter, you can buy it freeze-dried in packets from some health-food shops. I have not tried this myself so I can't comment on its flavour or performance. Follow the instructions on the packet for bringing the starter to life.

You can't afford to be in a hurry to make sourdough bread, because it takes 4-5 days to produce your first batch. From then on, things do speed up somewhat, as you only have to make the starter once. After that, the starter can be frozen and then brought back to life as and when you need it.

In a large non-metallic bowl, mix together 1 cupful of flour (wholemeal, rye, strong white or spelt flour) and 1 cupful of water – the size of the cup is not critical. Crumble over it 1 tsp fresh yeast and stir well. The yeast is not strictly necessary – you can make sourdough without any yeast at all – but it does help start the process off. Cover loosely (this allows the natural yeasts in the air to feed on the flour) and leave at room temperature for 3-4 days, stirring twice a day. After this time the starter will be bubbly and smell a little sweet/sour, rather like cider. At this point it is ready to use, although it will not yet have achieved much depth of flavour, which only comes with time. From now on you should continue adding flour and water (a little more flour than water) daily for a week or so, and then every 2 or 3 days – a starter needs to be nurtured. When you use some starter in a recipe, replace with an equal volume of flour and water. If you do not use it for a week or so, discard half of it and replace with fresh flour and water. If cared for, a starter can be kept indefinitely – The Village Bakery in Cumbria is still using a starter Andrew Whitley brought back from Russia in 1990. The starter can be frozen for up to two months. To use, defrost at room temperature overnight. When it begins to bubble again, it is ready to use.

When your sourdough starter is ready, draw off the amount you need for any of the recipes below.

Sourdough Rye with Seeds

This loaf is my staple and I make it often. It's packed with the nutrients the menopausal woman needs – phytoestrogens, calcium, magnesium and Omega-3 fatty acids. You will find it heavier than conventional bread because of the addition of the seeds, and therefore I have introduced a small amount of yeast to help with the rising process. The proving and baking times are longer than for normal yeasted bread, and the sour taste takes some getting used to at first but you will get used to it and quickly come to prefer it to 'regular' bread. Eat and enjoy!

¹⁄₂ oz	flax seeds	15 g
¹⁄₂ oz	sunflower seeds	15 g
¹⁄₂ oz	pumpkin seeds	15 g
¹⁄₂ oz	fresh yeast	15 g
3-4 fl oz	warm water	90-120 ml
1 lb	rye sourdough starter (see page 164)	450 g
6 oz	strong white flour	170 g
5¹⁄₂ oz	rye flour	160 g
¹⁄₂ oz	low-sodium salt	15 g
1 tbsp	soya milk, to glaze	1 tbsp

Grind half the seeds in an electric grinder. Set aside.

Dissolve the yeast in a little of the water. Pour the sourdough starter into a large bowl, and gradually add the two flours and the salt, then the water and the dissolved yeast. You may need a little more or less water depending on the age and quality of the flour. Mix to a soft dough, then turn out onto a floured surface and knead in all the ground seeds and all but 1 tablespoon of the whole seeds, setting the remainder aside for the topping. Turn into an oiled bowl and leave to rise in a warm place, covered with a damp teatowel, until doubled in bulk (2-4 hours). Punch down and form either into a loaf to fit an oiled 2 lb/1 kg loaf tin, or into a round loaf and place on an oiled baking tray. Leave for a second rising of about one hour.

Preheat the oven to 190°C/375°F/Gas Mark 5. Brush the top of the loaf with the soya milk, and scatter over the reserved seed mixture, pressing the seeds into the surface a little. Bake for 45-50 mins, or until the bottom of the loaf sounds hollow when tapped. Makes one 2 lb/900 g loaf – about 18 thickish slices.

You can usually find fresh yeast at the bakery counter of your supermarket, and, what's more, some supermarkets don't even charge for it. If you can't find it, substitute half the quantity of active dry yeast. You would have to prove the dried yeast first, by sprinkling it on to a little warm water with a pinch of sugar added, and leaving it for 10 minutes or so, until it froths up. This loaf can be successfully made with spelt flour instead of rye flour.

PER SERVING	
Energy Kcals	111.9
Protein g	5.2
Carbohydrates g	20.5
Dietary Fibre g	3.4
Fat – Total g	1.9
Saturated Fat g	0.1
Polyunsaturated Fat g	0.5
Calcium mg	18.2
Magnesium mg	10.9

Nutritionists are increasingly recommending that we eat rye bread instead of wheat, so I have included this for you to try. It's delicious used for open sandwiches, and has a particular affinity with smoked or pickled fish, such as rollmop herrings or smoked mackerel. It's also very tasty toasted with (sugar-free) jam for breakfast.

Pumpernickel (Wheat-Free)

This is a traditional German bread recipe adapted from one I learnt to make at The Village Bakery in Cumbria some years ago and have been making ever since. The method of making the bread is quite interesting. Because it contains no yeast and not much flour, it doesn't rise much, and when you come to bake it, you weigh it down with a heavy weight to give it that characteristic flat top and square shape.
The bread takes some time to mature, but requires absolutely no skill from the baker – just patience! You can get cracked rye from suppliers such as The Watermill at Little Salkeld (see Useful Addresses).

For the starter:

3 oz	rye sourdough starter (see page 164)	90 g
11½ oz	whole cracked rye	330 g
8 fl oz	warm water	225 ml

For the dough:

4 fl oz	warm water	120 ml
6 oz	whole cracked rye	170 g
¼ oz	low-sodium salt	10 g

Mix together the ingredients for the starter in a bowl, cover loosely and leave in a warm place overnight. It will ferment, but you probably won't see any activity because the rye is quite dense. If you put your ear to it you should be able to hear it bubbling gently.

Next day (you can leave the starter up to 24 hours if you want to), mix the starter with all the other ingredients – you might have to use your hands for this. Place the dough in an oiled 2 lb/900 g loaf tin or two 1 lb/450 g loaf tins. Smooth the top, cover loosely and leave to rise in a warm place for about two hours. It will not rise very much, but you should see a bit of movement to show that it's still alive.

Next, preheat the oven to 150°C/300°F/Gas Mark 2. Put the loaf tin into a bain-marie (a roasting pan with about an inch of water in it), put a baking sheet on top and a heavy heatproof weight on top of that (I use a brick). Bake for about 4 hours, adding more water to the roasting pan if it looks as though it's drying out. (This would be ideal left overnight in the cool oven of an Aga.) Leave to cool, then wrap and refrigerate. It should be allowed to mature for a day before eating, then consumed within a week.
Makes about 18 servings.

PER SERVING	
Energy Kcals	101.5
Protein g	4.5
Carbohydrates g	21.1
Dietary Fibre g	4.4
Fat – Total g	0.8
Saturated Fat g	0.1
Polyunsaturated Fat g	0.3
Calcium mg	11.1
Magnesium mg	34.6

For oiling the bowl in which the dough is going to rise, I use a pump-action olive oil spray to spray a light film over the bowl and the dough. This uses less oil and is very effective.

YEASTED BREADS

Calcium Bread

There's not much wheat bran in this loaf – therefore the calcium in the seeds is more available than if the flour used was 100% wholewheat. The soya flour contains magnesium to help your body absorb the calcium. To add even more calcium you could knead in 1¾ oz/50 g chopped brazil nuts or almonds before baking.

½ oz	fresh yeast	15 g
12 fl oz	soya milk	340 ml
7 oz	strong white flour	200 g
7 oz	wholemeal flour	200 g
2 tbsp	sesame seeds, ground	2 tbsp
3 oz	soya flour	90 g
1 tsp	low-sodium salt	1 tsp
2 tbsp	poppy seeds	2 tbsp
1 tbsp	sesame or poppy seeds, for sprinkling	1 tbsp
1 tbsp	soya milk, to glaze	1 tbsp

Heat the soya milk to blood heat (110°F/38°C) and dissolve the yeast in it – leave for about 10 minutes. Stir to make sure it is all dissolved. Mix together the white flour, wholemeal flour, ground sesame seed, soya flour, salt and poppy seeds. Gradually add the dry ingredients to the milk/yeast mixture, one handful at a time, stirring at first with a wooden spoon, and latterly mixing by hand. This process should take about 10 minutes. When the mixture forms a ball, turn out onto a surface dusted with white flour and continue kneading until glossy and smooth. Turn into an oiled bowl, cover with a damp teatowel and leave in a warm place to prove until doubled in size – this should take 1-2 hours.

Punch down and form into a tight round loaf. Place on an oiled baking tray and leave in a warm place for the second rising – about 40 minutes. Meanwhile preheat the oven to 200°C/400°F/Gas Mark 6. Brush the loaf with soya milk and sprinkle with poppy or sesame seeds. Bake for 35-40 minutes, until golden brown and crusty.

Makes one 2 lb/900 g loaf – about 18 thick slices.

PER SERVING	
Energy Kcals	137.3
Protein g	6.4
Carbohydrates g	21.0
Dietary Fibre g	3.0
Fat – Total g	3.6
Saturated Fat g	0.4
Polyunsaturated Fat g	1.5
Calcium mg	50.5
Magnesium mg	51.9

Poppy seeds are the unsung allies of the menopausal woman. They don't get the same press as flax seed, yet they are an incredibly rich source of calcium and magnesium. Barley is thought to reduce circulating cholesterol and is an antioxidant and antiviral. It also improves bowel function and helps with constipation.

Poppy Seed and Molasses Bread

This is a sweet, flavourful bread, packed with calcium and B vitamins, and with a lovely crumbly texture from the barley flour. It's also rather pretty when you cut into it, as the molasses/poppy seed mixture forms a dark swirl in each slice.

¹/₂ oz	fresh yeast	15 g
¹/₂ pint	mixed water and soya milk, blood temperature	275 ml
2 tbsp	blackstrap molasses	2 tbsp
2 tbsp	honey	2 tbsp
3 tbsp	poppy seeds	3 tbsp
3¹/₂ oz	wholemeal flour	100 g
3¹/₂ oz	cornmeal or polenta	100 g
2 oz	barley flour	60 g
5¹/₂ oz	strong white flour	160 g
2 oz	soya flour	60 g
1 tsp	low-sodium salt	1 tsp
2 tbsp	soya flour/water mixture to glaze	2 tbsp

Dissolve the yeast in the water and soya milk. Mix together the molasses, honey and poppy seeds. Mix the different kinds of flour and the salt. Pour the yeast mixture into the flour and knead until silky – the dough will be quite sticky at first, but persevere, adding a little more wholemeal flour if necessary. Leave to rise until doubled in bulk (about 1¹/₂ hours).

Knock back the dough, then roll out into an oblong approx 9 x 12 inch/22 x 30 cm. Spread the molasses/honey/poppy seed mixture over the dough with a palette knife, leaving a ³/₄ inch/2 cm margin all round and roll up from one of the long edges like a Swiss roll. Tuck in the ends and make sure all seams are sealed, then place in an oiled 2 lb/900 g loaf tin seam side down. Leave to prove until doubled in bulk. Meanwhile, preheat the oven to 180°C/350°F/Gas Mark 4. Glaze the loaf with 1 tablespoon of soya flour mixed with 1 tablespoon water. Bake for 50-60 minutes. Makes one 2 lb/900 g loaf – approximately 18 thick slices.

PER SERVING	
Energy Kcals	117.8
Protein g	4.6
Carbohydrates g	21.3
Dietary Fibre g	2.4
Fat – Total g	2.3
Saturated Fat g	0.3
Polyunsaturated Fat g	1.3
Calcium mg	65.2
Magnesium mg	39.4

Right: Strawberry Tofu Cheesecake (page 150)